WESTERN PHILOSOPHERS AND THEIR PHILOSOPHIES

VOLUME 1

THRINADH SAI

TO

MY MOTHER

SUJATHA

Contents

Preface

People have been asking questions about the world and their position in it since the dawn of time. Religion gave solutions to early cultures‘ most fundamental questions: the activities of the gods explained the workings of the cosmos and provided a framework for human civilizations. However, other individuals considered conventional religious explanations unsatisfactory, and they began to seek solutions based on logic rather than convention or religion. The start of philosophy was characterised by this transition, and the first famous thinker we know of was Thales of Miletus—Miletus was a Greek colony in modern-day Turkey. Thales utilised logic to investigate the nature of the cosmos and urged others to do the same. He passed on not just his solutions, but also the process of rational thought, as well as a sense of what kinds of explanations may be regarded adequate. As a result, Thales is often considered as the first philosopher.

The early philosophers were preoccupied with Thales' fundamental question: "What is the universe comprised of?" Their responses formed the basis of scientific thought and established a link between science and philosophy that continues to this day. Pythagoras‘ work was a watershed moment, since he tried to explain the world via mathematics rather than primordial stuff. He and his disciples used mathematics and geometry to describe the structure of the universe. Although some of these mathematical links took on mystical importance for Pythagoras and his followers, their numerical explanation of the cosmos had a significant impact on the early stages of scientific thought.

Philosophy is not solely the domain of smart but unconventional thinkers, as is commonly assumed. It's what everyone does when they're not occupied with their daily lives and have time to think about what life and the cosmos are all about. We humans are inherently inquisitive animals who can't help but wonder about our surroundings and our part in it. We also have a significant intellectual faculty that allows us to argue as well as just wonder. We may not know it, yet everytime we reason, we are thinking philosophically. Philosophy is not so much about finding solutions to basic concerns as it is about the process of seeking to find these answers via reasoning rather than blindly accepting conventional ideas or traditional authority.

In ancient Greece and China, the earliest philosophers were intellectuals who were dissatisfied with the accepted explanations offered by religion and custom and sought solutions with reasonable arguments. And, much as we would talk our ideas with friends and colleagues, they shared theirs with one another, even establishing "schools" to teach not just the conclusions they had reached, but how they had arrived at them. They encouraged their pupils to dispute and critique ideas in order to refine them and develop new and distinct ones. A common misperception is that the lonely philosopher arrives at his findings in solitude, although this is rarely the case. New ideas come via debate and the inspection, analysis, and critique of others' ideas.

Socrates was the archetypal philosopher in this regard. He left no papers or even huge concepts as the outcomes of his pondering. Indeed, he took satisfaction in being the smartest of men, despite the fact that he recognised he didn't know anything. His legacy was the debate and discussion tradition he developed, of probing other people's beliefs in order to obtain a better knowledge and extract underlying truths. Plato's writings, almost often in the form of dialogues, feature Socrates as a key figure. Many later philosophers used dialogues to illustrate their views, providing arguments and counterarguments rather than just stating their reasoning and conclusions. When a philosopher delivers his views to the world, he is likely to be received with "Yes, but..." or "What if..." comments rather than wholehearted acceptance.

In reality, philosophers have violently clashed on nearly every topic of philosophy. Plato and his disciple Aristotle, for example, had drastically opposing views on basic philosophical issues, and their differing perspectives have split philosophers ever since. This, in turn, has sparked additional debate and generated new ideas.

The Origins Of Western Philosophy

The work of Greek philosophers in the fifth and sixth centuries may be traced back to the origins of Western philosophy. These thinkers, later described as what was before, began to scrutinize their surroundings. Rather than blaming their circumstances on the Greek gods, these thinkers sought better reasonable explanations for the earth, the universe, and their own existence.

This was natural philosophy. Which was before philosophers wondered where everything originated from, what everything was made of, how nature could be mathematically defined, and how the existence of multiplicity in nature could be explained. They were looking for a primordial principle known as archê, which was the fundamental substance of the cosmos. Because hardly everything in the cosmos appears the same or continues in the same precise condition, pre-Socratic thinkers concluded that the archê included principles of change.

Introduction

What Is Philosophy?

Doesn't the question itself sound philosophical? But what does that actually mean? What exactly is philosophy?

Philosophy literally means "love of wisdom." Indeed, a desire of wisdom drives philosophers to investigate basic concerns about who we are and why we are here. On the surface, philosophy appears to be a social science. However, as you read this book, you will learn that it is so much more. Philosophy touches on every subject you can think of. It's not simply a group of old Greek men asking each other the same questions over and over (though it has its fair share of that as well). Philosophy has highly practical applications, ranging from ethical issues presented in government policy to the logic forms necessary in computer programming.

Philosophy allows us to investigate ideas such as the purpose of life, knowledge, morality, reality, the presence of God, consciousness, politics, religion, economics, art, and linguistics—philosophy has no boundaries!

There are six primary subjects that philosophy deals with in a general sense:

- Metaphysics: The study of reality and the cosmos.
- Logic: How to Construct a Sound Argument
- Epistemology: The study of knowledge and how it is acquired.
- Aesthetics: The study of art and beauty.
- Politics: The study of political rights, governance, and citizens' roles.
- Ethics: The study of morals and the proper way to live

one's life.

If you've ever thought to yourself, "Oh, philosophy. If you're thinking, "I'll never grasp that stuff," don't worry. This is the philosophy crash course you've always wanted. Finally, you'll be able to open your thoughts without your eyes tearing up.

CHAPTER ONE

George Santayana

Santayana's heritage is rooted in the Spanish diplomatic society with its stress on high education and familiarity with the world community. He was born in Madrid, Spain, on 16 December 1863. His father, Agustín Santayana, was born in 1812. The father studied law and practiced for a short time before entering the colonial service for posting to the Philippines. While studying law, Agustín served an apprenticeship to a professional painter of the school of Goya and a number of his paintings remain in the private possession of the family. He translated four Senecan tragedies into Spanish, wrote an unpublished book about the island of Mindanao, had an extensive library, and made three trips around the world. In 1845, he became the governor of Batang, a small island in the Philippines. He took over the governorship from the recently deceased José Borrás y Bofarull, who was the father of Josefina Borrás, later to become Agustín's wife in 1861 and the mother of George Santayana. His mother, Josefina Sturgis (formerly Josefina Borrás y Carbonell), was born in Scotland and was the daughter of a Spanish diplomat. Previously she married

George Sturgis (d. 1857), a Boston merchant, whose early death left her alone with children in Manila. There were five children from this first marriage, three of whom survived infancy. She promised her first husband to raise the children in Boston where she moved her family. During a holiday in Spain, Josefina met Agustín again, and they were married in 1861. He was fifty years of age and she was probably thirty-five. In 1863, Santayana was christened Jorge Agustín Nicolás Ruiz de Santayana y Borrás. His half sister, Susan, insisted that he be called "George," after her Boston father. Santayana, in turn, always referred to his sister in the Spanish, "Susana."

1863–1886. Santayana lived eight years in Spain, forty years in Boston, and forty years in Europe. In his autobiography, *Persons and* Places, Santayana divides his life into three phases. The background (1863–1886) encompasses his childhood in Spain through his undergraduate years at Harvard. The second period (1886–1912) is that of the Harvard graduate student and professor with a trans-Atlantic penchant for traveling to Europe. The third period (1912–1952) is the retired professor writing and traveling in Europe and eventually establishing Rome as his home.

The family moved from Madrid to Ávila where Santayana spent his boyhood. In 1869, Santayana's mother left Spain in order to raise the Sturgis children in Boston, keeping her pledge to her first husband. In 1872, his father realized the opportunities for his son were better in Boston, and he moved there with his son. Finding Boston inhospitable, puritanical, and cold, the father returned alone to Ávila within a few months. The separation between father and mother was permanent. In 1888 Agustín wrote to Josefina: "When we were married I felt as if it were written that I should be reunited with you, yielding to the force of destiny. Strange marriage, this of ours! So you say, and so it is in fact. I love you very much, and you too have cared for me, yet we do not live together" (*Persons and Places*, 9).

Until his father's death (1893), Santayana regularly corresponded with his father and he visited him after Santayana's first year at Harvard College. In Boston, Santayana's family spoke only Spanish in their home. Santayana first attended Mrs. Welchman's Kindergarten to learn English from the younger children, then he was a student at the Boston Latin School, and he completed his B.A. and Ph.D. at Harvard College (1882–1889), including eighteen months of study in Germany on a Walker Fellowship. His undergraduate years at Harvard reveal an energetic student with an active social life. He was a member of eleven organizations including *The Lampoon* (largely as a cartoonist), the *Harvard Monthly* (a founding member), the Philosophical Club (President), and the Hasty Pudding.

Some scholars conclude that Santayana was an active homosexual based on allusions in Santayana's early poetry (McCormick, 49–52) and Santayana's association with known homosexual and bisexual friends. Santayana provides no clear indication of his sexual preferences, and he never married. Attraction to both women and men seems apparent in his undergraduate and graduate correspondence. The one documented comment about his homosexuality occurs when he was sixty-five. After a discussion of A. E. Housman's poetry and homosexuality, Santayana remarked, "I think I must have been that way in my Harvard days — although I was unconscious of it at the time" (Cory, *Santayana: The Later Years*, 40). Because of

Santayana's well-known frankness, many scholars consider Santayana a latent homosexual based on this evidence.

1886–1912. Santayana received his Ph.D. from Harvard in 1889 and became a faculty member at Harvard University (1889–1912) and eventually a central figure in the era now called Classical American Philosophy. He was a highly respected and popular teacher, and his students included poets (Conrad Aiken, T. S. Eliot, Robert Frost, Wallace Stevens), journalists and writers (Walter Lippmann, Max Eastman, Van Wyck Brooks), professors (Samuel Eliot Morison, Harry Austryn Wolfson), a Supreme Court Justice (Felix Frankfurter), many diplomats (including his friend Bronson Cutting), and a university president (James B. Conant). He retired from Harvard in 1912 at the age of forty-eight and lived the remainder of his life in England and Europe, never returning to the U.S. and rejecting academic posts offered at a number of universities, including Harvard, Columbia, and Cambridge.

Santayana cherished academic life for its freedom to pursue intellectual interests and curiosity, but he found that many aspects of being a professor infringed on that freedom. Faculty meetings and university committees seemed primarily to be partisan heat over false issues, so he rarely attended them. The general corporate and businesslike adaptation of universities was increasingly less conducive to intellectual development and growth. He expressed concern about the evolving Harvard goal of producing muscular intellectuals to lead America as statesmen in business and government. Were not delight and celebration also a central aspect of education? He wrote to a friend in 1892, expressing the hope that his academic life would be "resolutely unconventional" and noted that he could only be a professor *per accidens*, saying that "I would rather beg than be one essentially" (GS to H. W. Abbot, Stoughton Hall, Harvard, 15 February 1892. Columbia).

In 1893, Santayana experienced a *metanoia*, a change of heart. Gradually he altered his style of life from that of an active student turned professor to one focused on the imaginative celebration of life. In doing so, he began planning for his early retirement, finding university life increasingly less conducive to intellectual pursuits and delight in living. Three events preceded his *metanoia*: the unexpected death of a young student, witnessing his father's death, and the marriage of his sister Susana. Santayana's reflections on these events led to the ancient wisdom that acceptance of the tragic leads to a lyrical release. "Cultivate imagination, love it, give it endless forms, but do not let it deceive you. Enjoy the world, travel over it, and learn its ways, but do not let it hold you … . To possess things and persons in idea is the only pure good to be got out of them; to possess them physically or legally is a burden and a snare (*Persons and Places*, 427–28)."

Increasingly, naturalism and the lyrical cry of human imagination became the focal points of Santayana's life and thought. Pragmatism, as developed by Peirce and James, was an undercurrent in his naturalism, particularly as an approach to how we ascertain knowledge, but there are aspects of his naturalism more aligned with European and Greek thought that presage developments in the late twentieth century. His naturalism had its historical roots primarily in Aristotle and Spinoza and its contemporary background in James's pragmatism and Royce's idealism. His focus on and celebration of creative imagination in all human endeavors (particularly in art, philosophy, religion, literature, and science) is one of Santayana's major contributions to American thought. This focus, along with his Spanish heritage, Catholic upbringing, and European suspicion of American industry, set him apart in the Harvard Yard.

Santayana's strong interest in literature and aesthetics is evident throughout this early period, but by 1904, his attention turned almost fully to philosophical pursuits. During this period his publications include: *Lotze's System of Philosophy* (dissertation), *Sonnets and Other Verses* (1894), *The Sense of Beauty* (1896), *Lucifer: A Theological Tragedy* (1899), *Interpretations of Poetry and Religion* (1900), *A Hermit of Carmel, and Other Poems* (1901), *The Life of Reason* (five books, 1905–1906), *Three Philosophical Poets: Lucretius, Dante, and Goethe* (1910).

In May 1911, Santayana formally announced his long-planned retirement from Harvard. President Lowell asked him to reconsider. By now Santayana was a highly recognized philosopher, cultural critic, poet, and teacher, and his desire to be free from academic confinement was also well known. Lowell indicated he was open to any arrangement that provided Santayana the time he desired for writing and for travel in Europe. Initially Santayana agreed to alternate years in Europe and the U.S., but in 1912, his resolve to retire overtook his sense of obligation to Harvard. The year before his retirement, he had presented at least six lectures at a variety of universities including Berkeley, Wisconsin, Columbia, and Williams. His books were selling well and his publishers were asking for more. Two major universities were courting him. At forty-eight, he left Harvard to become a full-time writer and to escape the academic professionalism that nurtured a university overgrown with "thistles of trivial and narrow scholarship."

1912–1952. As Santayana sailed for Europe, his mother died, apparently of Alzheimer's disease. Always attentive to his family, Santayana visited her weekly, then daily, during his last years at Harvard. Knowing his mother's death was imminent, he arranged for Josephine, his half sister, to live in Spain with Susana, who previously had married a well-to-do Ávilan. An inheritance of $10,000 from his mother, coupled with his steady income from publications and his early planning, made retirement easier. He arranged for his half brother, Robert, to manage his finances with the agreement that upon Santayana's death, Robert or his heirs would receive the bulk of Santayana's estate. Hence, in January 1912, at age forty-eight, Santayana was free from the constraints of university regimen and expectations and, more importantly, free to write, to travel, and to choose his residence and country.

Harvard attempted to bring him back to the United States, offering him several professorships beginning in 1917. As late as 1929, he was offered the Norton Chair in Poetry, one of Harvard's most respected chairs. In 1931, he received an invitation from Brown University, and Harvard later asked him to accept the William James Lecturer in Philosophy, a newly established honorary post. But Santayana never returned to Harvard or to America. Believing that the academic life was not a place for him to cultivate intellectual achievement or scholarly work, Santayana also refused academic appointments both at Oxford University and Cambridge University.

At first, Santayana planned to reside in Europe, and after numerous exploratory trips to several cities, he decided on Paris. However, while he was in England, World War I broke out and he was unable to return to the mainland.

First, he lived in London and then primarily at Oxford and Cambridge. After the war, he was more of a traveling scholar, and his principal locales included Paris, Madrid, Ávila, the Riviera, Florence, and Rome. By the late 1920s, he settled principally in Rome, and during the summers, he often retreated to Cortina d'Ampezzo in Northern Italy to write and to escape the heat. Because of his success as a writer, he assisted friends and scholars when they found themselves in need of financial support. For example, when Bertrand Russell was unable to find a teaching post in the U.S. or England because of his views regarding pacifism and marriage, Santayana displayed a characteristic generosity in his plan to make an anonymous gift to Bertrand Russell of the $25,000 royalty earnings from *The Last Puritan*, at the rate of $5,000 per year, in the letter to George Sturgis (15 July 1937). Despite the fact that he and Russell disagreed radically both politically and philosophically, his memory of their earlier friendship and his regard for Russell's genius moved him to compassion for Russell's financial plight.

The rise of Mussolini in the 1930s initially seemed positive to Santayana. He viewed the Italian civil society as chaotic and thought Mussolini might bring order where needed. But Santayana soon noted the rise of a tyrant. Trying to leave Italy by train for Switzerland, he was not permitted to cross the border because he did not have the proper papers. With most of his funds coming from the United States and England, his case was complicated by his Spanish citizenship and his age. He returned to Rome, and on 14 October 1941 he entered the Clinica della Piccola Compagna di Maria, a hospital-clinic run by a Catholic order of nuns, where he lived until his death eleven years later. This arrangement was not unusual. The hospital periodically received distinguished guests and cared for them in an assisted-living environment. Santayana died of cancer on 26 September 1952.

Santayana asked that he be buried in unconsecrated ground, affirming his naturalism to the end. However, the only such cemetery ground in Rome was reserved for criminals. The Spanish Consulate at Rome would not permit Santayana to be buried in such a place and provided the "Panteon de la Obra Pia espanola" in the Campo Verano cemetery as a suitable burial ground, turning it into a memorial for the lifelong Spanish citizen. At the graveside, Daniel Cory read lines from Santayana's "The Poet's Testament," a poem affirming his naturalistic outlook:

I give back to the earth what the earth gave,
All to the furrow, nothing to the grave.
The candle's out, the spirit's vigil spent;
Sight may not follow where the vision went.

In the United States, Wallace Stevens commemorated his teacher in "To an Old Philosopher in Rome."

Total grandeur of a total edifice,
Chosen by an inquisitor of structures
For himself. He stops upon this threshold,
As if the design of all his words takes form
And frame from thinking and is realized.

Philosophy, Literature, and Culture

Throughout his life, Santayana's literary achievements are evident. As an eight-year-old Spaniard, he wrote *Un matrimonio* (A Married Couple), describing the trip of a newly married couple that meets the Queen of Spain. Later in Boston, he wrote a poetic parody of *The Aeneid*; "A Short

History of the Class of '82"; and "Lines on Leaving the Bedford St. Schoolhouse." His first book, *Sonnets and Other Verses* (1894), is a book of poems, not philosophy. And, until the turn of the century, much of his intellectual life was directed to the writing of verse and drama. He was a principal figure in making modernism possible but was not a modernist in poetry or literature. His naturalism and emphasis on constructive imagination influenced both T. S. Eliot and Wallace Stevens. Eliot's notion of the "objective correlative" is drawn from Santayana, and Stevens follows Santayana in his refined naturalism by incorporating both Platonism and Christianity without any nostalgia for God or dogma.

Santayana was among the leaders in transforming the American literary canon, dislodging the dominant Longfellow, Lowell, Whittier, Holmes, Bryant canon. Santayana's essay "The Genteel Tradition in American Philosophy" (presented to the Philosophical Union of the University of California in 1911) greatly affected Van Wyck Brooks's *America's Coming-of-Age*, a book that set the tone for modernism. Brooks drew on Santayana's essay, adapting Santayana's idea of two Americas to fit his notion of an America split between highbrow and lowbrow culture.

By the turn of the century, Santayana's interests largely centered on his philosophical inquiries, and although he never abandoned writing poetry, he no longer considered it his central work. Even so, some of his most moving poetry came later and was inspired by the trench warfare and casualties of World War I: "A Premonition: Cambridge, October, 1913"; "The Undergraduate Killed in Battle: Oxford, 1915"; "Sonnet: Oxford, 1916"; and "The Darkest Hour: Oxford, 1917." Throughout his life, even near death, he recited and translated long fragments of Horace, Racine,

Leopardi, and others.

The relationships between literature, art, religion and philosophy are prominent themes throughout Santayana's writings. *The Sense of Beauty* (1896) is a primary source for the study of aesthetics. Philip Blair Rice wrote in the foreword to the 1955 Modern Library edition: "To say that aesthetic theory in America reached maturity with *The Sense of Beauty* is in no way an overstatement. Only John Dewey's *Art as Experience* has competed with it in the esteem of philosophical students of aesthetics and has approached its suggestiveness for artists, critics and the public which takes a thoughtful interest in the arts." Santayana's groundbreaking approach to aesthetics is emphasized in Arthur Danto's "Introduction" to the 1988 critical edition. Danto writes that Santayana brings "beauty down to earth" by treating it as a subject for science and giving it a central role in human conduct, in contrast to the preceding intellectualist tradition of aesthetics. "The exaltation of emotion and the naturalization of beauty — *especially* of beauty — imply a revolutionary impulse for a book it takes a certain violent act of historical imagination to recover" (*Sense of Beauty*, xxviii). This naturalistic approach to aesthetics is expanded in his philosophical explication of art found in *The Life of Reason: Reason in Art* (1905).

In 1900, Santayana's *Interpretations of Poetry and Religion* develops his view that religion and poetry are expressive celebrations of life. Each in its own right is of great value, but if either is mistaken for science, the art of life is lost along with the beauty of poetry and religion. Science provides explanations of natural phenomena, but poetry and religion are festive celebrations of human life born of consciousness generated from the interaction of one's psyche (the natural structure and heritable traits of one's physical body) and the physical environment. As expressions of human values, poetry and religion are identical in origin. Understanding the naturalistic base for poetry and religion and valuing their expressive character enable one to appreciate them without being hoodwinked: "poetry loses its frivolity and ceases to demoralise, while religion surrenders its illusions and ceases to deceive" (172). Interestingly, his father expressed similar views in his letters to his son, providing the genesis of his son's reflections, and this conclusion is expressed as late as the 1946 publication of *The Idea of Christ in the Gospels* where Santayana presents the idea of Christ as poetic and imaginative, contrasted with attempts at historical, factual accounts of the Christ figure. The impact of Santayana's view was significant, and Henry James (after reading *Interpretations of Poetry and Religion*) wrote that he would "crawl across London" if need be to meet Santayana.

Three Philosophical Poets (1910) was the first volume of the Harvard Studies in Comparative Literature. Santayana employs a naturalistic account of poetry and philosophy, attempting to combine comparative structures with as few embedded parochial assumptions as possible while making explicit our material boundness to particular worlds and perspectives. His analyses of Lucretius, Dante, and Goethe are described by one biographer as "a classical work and one of the few written in America to be genuinely comparative in conception and execution, for its absence of national bias and its intellectual, linguistic, and aesthetic range" (McCormick, 193).

Initially, Santayana appears optimistic about the youthful America. In his Berkeley lecture, "The Genteel Tradition in American Philosophy," he declared "the

American Will inhabits the sky-scraper; the American Intellect inhabits the colonial mansion." ("The Genteel Tradition in American Philosophy," Triton Edition, vol. VII. P. 129.) European transcendentalism and Calvinism are the American intellectual traditions, but they no longer suit the American drive for success in industry, business, and football. Hence, the youthful willfulness of the country has outrun the old wits, but there remains a chance for wisdom and energy to be coupled in a future coherent and rich tradition, and he sees the beginnings of such a tradition in James's pragmatism.

Within a decade, he is less optimistic. *Character and Opinion in the United States* (1920) is his valediction to America. It includes frank, intellectual portraits of his Harvard colleagues and of American culture. From his residence in Cambridge, he praises the English emphasis on social cooperation and personal integrity and contrasts them with America where "You must wave, you must cheer, you must push with the irresistible crowd; otherwise you will feel like a traitor, a soulless outcast, a deserted ship high and dry on the shore ... . This national faith and morality are vague in idea, but inexorable in spirit; they are the gospel of work and the belief in progress. By them, in a country where all men are free, every man finds that what most matters has been settled beforehand" (211).

Santayana's standing as a literary figure reached its zenith with the publication of *The Last Puritan* (1936). *The Last Puritan* is Santayana's only novel, and it was an international success. It was compared positively with Goethe's *Wilhelm Meister*, Pater's *Marius*, and Mann's *The Magic Mountain*. Its provenance lies in the 1890s when Santayana began a series of sketches on college life that, broadened through his experience and travel, resulted in

The Last Puritan. Essentially, it is about the life and early death of an American youth, Oliver Alden, who is sadly restricted by his Puritanism. Santayana draws a sharp contrast with the European Mario, who delights in all matters without a narrow moralism. Mario is a carefree, naturally gifted and likeable young man who by American standards appears too focused on the peripheral aspects of life: travel, opera, love affairs, and architecture. And the American perspective is embodied in the tragic hero, Oliver Alden, who is the last Puritan. He does what is right, based on his duties to his family, school, and friends. Life is a slow, powerful flow of tasks and responsibilities. He is intelligent and knows there is more than obligation, and he senses his guilt at not being able to achieve the natural abundant life, but knowing this only nourishes his Puritanism and causes him to feel guilty about being guilty. In a charming scene in the novel, Oliver introduces Mario to Professor Santayana at Harvard. Oliver is a dedicated student and football player, thoroughly a first rate American taking matters seriously and doing his best. After only a short visit with the Professor, Mario, it is decided by Santayana, does not need to take a course from the Professor. Mario already has the natural, instinctual approach of a cultivated person. Oliver, on the other hand, knows he must work to achieve his goal, which will be only a succession of goals, and ends tragically. Santayana's Hispanic and Catholic background play a central role in his critique of American life: too bound by past traditions and obligations that are not understood or rooted in one's own culture.

The fear that Santayana's autobiography would be lost or destroyed during World War II, led Scribner's, the publisher, to conspire with the U.S. Department of State, the Vatican, and the Spanish government to bring the manuscript of the first part (*Persons and Places*) out of Rome *sub rosa*, despite the Italian government's refusal to allow any mail to the U.S. The manuscript for the second part (*The Middle Span*, 1945) also was conveyed surreptitiously to New York. The third part (*My Host the World*, 1953) was published after Santayana's death. His autobiography provides the basis for understanding the development of his philosophy

Development of Santayana's Philosophy

In his autobiography, *Persons and Places*, Santayana describes the development of his thought as a movement from the idealisms of boyhood to the intellectual materialism of a traveling student, and finally to the complete, naturalistic outlook of the adult Santayana. He emphasizes the continuity of his life and beliefs, contrasting what may appear to be disparate views with the overall unity of his thought: "The more I change the more I am the same person" (*Persons and Places*, 159).

As a young man of the nineteenth century, he was influenced by the idealism of the age and of his age, but he claims to have always been a realist or naturalist at heart.

But those ideal universes in my head did not produce any firm convictions or actual duties. They had nothing to do with the wretched poverty-stricken real world in which I was condemned to live. That the real was rotten and only the imaginary at all interesting seemed to me axiomatic. That was too sweeping; yet allowing for the rash generalisations of youth, it is still what I think. My philosophy has never changed. (*Persons and Places*, 167)

Hence he notes, that in spite "of my religious and other day-dreams, I was at bottom a young realist; I knew I was dreaming, and so was awake. A sure proof of this was that I was never anxious about what those dreams would have involved if they had been true. I never had the least touch of superstition" (*Persons and Places*, 167). Santayana cites poems, "To the Moon" and "To the Host," written when he was fifteen or sixteen, as revealing this early realism, and he quotes from memory one stanza of "At the Church Door" where the realistic sentiment is the same (*Persons and Places*, 169).

By the time he was a traveling student seeing the world in Germany, England, and Spain his "intellectual materialism" was firmly established with little change in his religious affections.

From the boy dreaming awake in the church of the Immaculate Conception, to the travelling student seeing the world in Germany, England, and Spain there had been no great change in sentiment.

I was still "at the church door". Yet in belief, in the clarification of my philosophy, I had taken an important step. I no longer wavered between alternative views of the world, to be put on or taken off like alternative plays at the theatre. I now saw that there was only one possible play, the actual history of nature and of mankind, although there might well be ghosts among the characters and soliloquies among the speeches. Religions, all religions, and idealistic philosophies, all idealistic philosophies, were the soliloquies and the ghosts. They might be eloquent and profound. Like Hamlet's soliloquy they might be excellent reflective criticisms of the play as a whole. Nevertheless they were only parts of it, and their value as criticisms lay entirely in their fidelity to the facts, and to the sentiments which those facts aroused in the critic. (*Persons and Places*, 169)

The full statement and development of his materialism did not occur until later in his life. It was certainly in place by the time of *Scepticism and Animal Faith* (1923) but not fully so at the time of *The Life of Reason* (1905). The influence of the Harvard philosophers, particularly James and Royce is evident in Santayana's thought, but he was hardly a mere follower and often advanced his philosophy more along European and Greek lines rather than the American tradition, which he thought was both too derivative and too tied to the advancement of business and capitalism.

The move from Harvard marked not only a geographical shift but a philosophical one as well. Henry Levinson in *Santayana, Pragmatism, and the Spiritual Life* provides a well-balanced account of this gradual but distinctive move from the Harvard philosophical mentality. Leaving Harvard also meant that Santayana abandoned the view of a philosopher as a public, philosophical statesman and of language as being representative. This philosophical turn placed makes him a forerunner of many issues in the next two centuries. Removing himself, literally and philosophically, from the American scene, Santayana increasingly came to believe that the "brimstone" sensibility of pragmatism was wrong-headed (*Character and Opinion in the United States*, 53). A major aspect of this sensibility was the view that philosophers must be engaged fundamentally in social and cultural policy formulation, and if they are not, they are not pulling their civic weight. In this fashion, Santayana believes the pragmatists came to belie "the genuinely expressive, poetic, meditative, and festive character of their vocation" (Levinson,165). A condition that James took seriously in his "On a Certain Blindness in Human Beings," suggesting that the world of practical responsibility fosters a blindness to multiplural ways of living that can only be escaped by catching sight of "the world of impersonal worths as such" — "only your mystic, your dreamer, or your insolent loafer or tramp can afford so sympathetic an occupation" (James, *Talks to Teachers on Psychology and to Students on Some of Life's Ideals*, 141). Interestingly, America's imperialistic actions toward the Philippines during the Spanish-American War sparked James' remarks; this was a war that had a much deeper ancestral and historical aspect for Santayana and led to his poem, "Young Sammy's First Wild Oats." Whether connected or not, Santayana later came to identify himself as an intellectual vagabond or tramp, not isolated in the specific perspectives of an ideology, hosted by the world, and devoted to spiritual disciplines that "appear irresponsible to philosophers hoping to command representative or some otherwise privileged authority at the center of society" (Levinson, 167).

Building on his naturalism, institutional pragmatism, social realism, and poetic religion, Santayana on leaving Harvard moves even farther from the role of philosophical statesman by removing the representative authority of language from the quest for a comprehensive synthesis, by narrowing the line between literature and philosophy (as he had earlier done between religion and poetry), and by wrestling more with the influence of James than of Emerson. Santayana's stay in Oxford during the Great War led to his famous counter to Wilson's war to end all wars: "Only the dead have seen the end of war." (*Soliloquies in England and Later Soliloquies*, 102)

Santayana's message is clear: The epistemological project that Russell's *Problems* epitomizes is diseased. The renewed quest to establish unmediated Knowledge of Reality simply leads to "intellectual cramp" (*Soliloquies*, 216). Philosophy has itself become spiritually *disordered* by blinding its practitioners from their traditional and proper task, which is to celebrate the good life. If the spiritual disciplines of philosophy are to thrive, philosophers have to take off the bandages of epistemology and metaphysics altogether, accept the finite and fallible status of their knowledge claims, and get on with confessing their belief in the things that make life worth living (Levinson, 204).

Leaving Harvard and America enabled Santayana to develop his naturalism.

Naturalism

Scepticism and Animal Faith (1923) introduces Santayana's mature naturalism. In summary, he maintains that knowledge and belief are not the result of reasoning. They are inescapable beliefs essential for action. Epistemological foundationalism is a futile approach to knowledge. A more promising approach is to discern the underlying belief structures assumed in animal action and imposed by natural circumstances. The foundations for this approach are rooted in Aristotle's concept of activity and the pragmatic approach to action and knowledge. Explanations of natural events are the proper purview of scientists, while explications of the meaning and value of action may be the proper sphere of historians and philosophers. Even so, both scientific explanations and philosophical explications are based in the natural world. Meaning and value are generated by the interaction of our physical makeup, which

Santayana calls "psyche," and our material environment.

Santayana's critique of epistemological foundationalism is as unique as his heritage. With Spanish irony, he structures his argument after Descartes' *Meditations* but arrives at an anti-foundationalist conclusion. Drawing attention to what is given in an instant of awareness (the smallest conceivable moment of consciousness), he maintains that any knowledge or recognition found in such an instant would have to be characterized by a concept (or "essence" to use Santayana's term). Concepts cannot be limited to particular instances; rather the particular object is seen as an instance of the concept (essence). Thus, pursuing doubt to its ultimate end, one is confined by the "solipsism of the present moment." That is, in a single instant of awareness there can be no knowledge or belief, since both require concepts not bounded by a moment of awareness. Hence, the ultimate end of doubt, an instance of awareness, is empty. It is the vacant awareness of a given without a basis for belief, knowledge or action. Santayana concludes that if one attempts to find the bedrock of certainty, one may rest his claim only after he has, at least theoretically, recognized that knowledge is composed of instances of awareness that in themselves do not contain the prerequisites for knowledge, e.g., concepts, universals, or essences. That both skepticism and proofs against skepticism lead nowhere is precisely Santayana's point.

Philosophy must begin *in medias res* (in the middle of things), in action itself, where there is an instinctive and arational belief in the natural world: "animal faith." For Santayana, animal faith is the arational basis for any knowledge claims. It is the nether world of biological order operating through our physical, non-conscious being generating beliefs that are "radically incapable of proof"

(*Scepticism*, 35).

In rising out of passive intuition, I pass, by a vital constitutional necessity, to belief in discourse, in experience, in substance, in truth and in spirit. All these objects may conceivably be illusory. Belief in them however, is not grounded on a prior probability, but all judgements of probability are grounded on them. They express a rational instinct or instinctive reason, the waxing faith of an animal living in a world which he can observe and sometimes remodel. (*Scepticism*, 308–309)

He describes these prejudices as "animal" in an effort to emphasize our biological base and community. This emphasis is similar to Wittgenstein's reference to convictions that are beyond being justified or unjustified as "something animal" (*On Certainty* 359). Ours is a long-standing primitive credulity, and our most basic beliefs are those of an animal creed: "that there is a world, that there is a future, that things sought can be found, and things seen can be eaten" (*Scepticism* 180).

Santayana (like Hume, Wittgenstein, and Strawson) holds there are certain inevitable beliefs; they are inescapable given nature and our individual physical history. And like Wittgenstein, he maintains that these beliefs are various and variable. They are determined by the interplay between environment and psyche, i.e., between our natural conditions and the inherited, physical "organisation of the animal" (the psyche). That we now inescapably believe in external objects and the general reliability of inductive reasoning, for example, is a result of physical history and the natural conditions of our world and ourselves. Since these beliefs are relative to our physical histories, if our history and biological order had been different, our natural beliefs would also be different.

The environment determines the occasions on which intuitions arise, the psyche — the inherited organisation of the animal — determines their form, and ancient conditions of life on Earth no doubt determined which psyches should arise and prosper; and probably many forms of intuition, unthinkable to man, express the facts and the rhythms of nature to other animal minds (*Scepticism*, 88).

By displacing privileged mentalistic accounts with his pragmatic naturalism, Santayana challenges then prevailing structures in both American and English philosophies.

Santayana explicates the primary distinguishable characteristics of our knowledge in his four-book *Realms of Being*. Believing that philosophical terminology should have historical roots, Santayana employed classical terminology for these characteristics: matter, essence, spirit, and truth. And although these terms are central to many philosophical traditions, he views his work as "a revision of the categories of common sense, faithful in spirit to orthodox human tradition, and endeavouring only to clarify those categories and disentangle the confusions that inevitably arise ..." (*Realms* 826).

Within Santayana's naturalism, the origins of all events in the world are arbitrary, temporal, and contingent. Matter (by whatever name it is called) is the principle of existence. It is "often untoward, and an occasion of imperfection or conflict in things." (*Realm of Matter*, v) Hence, a "sour moralist" may consider it evil, but, according to Santayana, if one takes a wider view "matter would seem a good ... because it is the principle of existence: it is all things in their potentiality and therefore the condition of all their excellence or possible perfection." (*Realm of Matter*, v) Matter is the non-discursive, natural foundation for all that is. In itself, it is neither good nor evil but may be perceived as such when viewed from the vested interest of animal life. Latent animal interests convert matter's non-discernible, neutral face to a smile or frown. But "moral values cannot preside over nature." (*Realm of Matter*, 134) Principled values are the products of natural forces: "The germination, definition, and prevalence of any good must be grounded in nature herself, not in human eloquence." (*Realm of Matter*, 131) From the point of view of origins, therefore, the realm of matter is the matrix and the source of everything: it is nature, the sphere of genesis, the universal mother.

"Essence" is Santayana's term for concepts and meanings. He draws on Aristotle's notion of essence but removes all capacities for producing effects. An essence is a universal, an object of thought, not a material force. However, consciousness of an essence is generated by the interaction of a psyche and the material environment. Hence, matter remains as the origin of existence and the arena of action, and the realm of essence encompasses all possible thought.

"Truth," if some disinterested observer could ascertain it, would constitute all the essences that genuinely characterize the natural world and all activities within it. Since all living beings have natural interests and preferences, no such knowledge of truth can exist. All conscious beings must ascertain belief about truth based on the success of actions that sustain life and permit periods of delight and joy.

Santayana uses the term "spirit" to mean consciousness or awareness. As early as 19 April 1909, Santayana wrote to his sister that he was writing a brand new system of philosophy to be called "The realms of Being" — "not the mineral vegetable and animal, but something far more metaphysical, namely Essence, Matter, and Consciousness. It will not be a long book, but very technical." When the book was published in the 1930s, he had added his notion of truth and substituted "spirit" for "consciousness." From his perspective, the substitution did not alter the meaning of consciousness but rather captured an entire tradition of philosophical and religious inquiry as well as borrowed associated ideas from eastern religions. But to the consternation of traditional views, many found the identity of spirit with consciousness a troublesome idea. And so they should, for with this identity Santayana removes the spiritual from the field of agency as well as from being an alternative way of living. Santayana's approach is therefore in direct contrast with those who think of spirit as causing action or as fostering a particular lifestyle. Following the tracks of Aristotle, he makes the spiritual life one form of culminating experiences arising from fulfilling activity.

Awareness evolved through the natural development of the physical world, and he demurs to scientific accounts for explanations of that development. Almost poetically, he sees spirit as emerging in moments of harmony between the psyche and the environment. Such harmony is temporary, and the disorganized natural forces permit spirit to arise "only spasmodically, to suffer and to fail. For just as the birth of spirit is joyous, because some nascent harmony evokes it, so the rending or smothering of that harmony, if not sudden, imposes useless struggles and suffering" (*Birth of Reason*, 53). Accepting the world's insecure equilibrium enables one to celebrate the birth of spirit. Reasoning, particularly reasoning associated with action, is a signal of the nascent activities of the psyche working to harmonize its actions with the environment, and if successful, reason permits individual and social organization to prosper while spirit leads to the delight of imagination and artistry.

Some commentators characterize Santayana as an epiphenomenalist, and there are some commonalities, specifically the view that spirit is not efficacious. But there also are considerable differences. Santayana does not characterize his view as one-way interactionism, primarily because he does not think of spirit as an object to be acted upon. Spirit is rather a distinguishable aspect of thought, generated in activity, and may be viewed more as a relational property. Santayana sometimes speaks of spirit and essence as supervening on material events. But lacking the distinctions of contemporary philosophy, it is difficult to characterize Santayana's philosophy of mind accurately. His view of consciousness is more celebrational, as opposed to being a burden or eliciting action. Spirit is "precisely the voice of order in nature, the music, as full of light as of motion, of joy as of peace, that comes with an even partial and momentary perfection in some vital rhythm" (*Birth of Reason*, 53).

Santayana's account of spirit and essence may lead one to wonder how Santayana can be included as a pragmatist, and this classification is accurate only if one includes an extended notion of pragmatic naturalism. For Santayana, explanations of human life, including reason and spirit, lie within the sciences. The nature of truth simply is correspondence with what is, but since humans, nor any other conscious being, are able to see beyond the determinant limits of their nature and environment, pragmatism becomes the test of truth rather than correspondence. In short, the nature of truth is correspondence while the test of truth is pragmatic. If an explanation continues to bear fruit over the long run, then it is accepted as truth until it is replaced by a better explanation. In this, Santayana's account of pragmatic truth is more closely aligned with Peirce's conception than that of James or Dewey, including a tripartite account of knowledge consisting of the subject, symbol, and object. Pragmatism is properly focused on scientific inquiry and explanations, and it is severely limited, even useless, in spiritual and aesthetic matters. Pragmatism is rooted in animal life, the need to know the world in a way that fosters successful action. If all life were constituted only by successful or unsuccessful activities, one's fated circumstances would govern. But consciousness makes liberation possible and brings delight and festivity in material circumstances.

Santayana's anti-foundationalism, non-reductive materialism, and pragmatic naturalism coupled with his emphasis on the spiritual life and his view of philosophy as literature anticipated many developments in philosophy and literary criticism that occurred in the latter half of the twentieth century, and these served as a challenge to the more humanistic naturalisms of John Dewey and other American naturalists. These views also provide the foundation for his view of ethics, political philosophy, and the spiritual life.

Ethics, Politics, and the Spiritual Life

Santayana's moral philosophy is based on his naturalism. Most commentators classify Santayana as an extreme moral relativist who maintains that all individual moral perspectives have equal standing and are based on the heritable traits and environmental circumstances of individuals. This naturalistic approach applies to all living organisms. Nature does not establish a moral hierarchy of goods between animal populations nor between individual animals. However, this same moral relativism is also the basis for Santayana's claim that the good of individual animals is clear and is subject to naturalistic or biological investigation.

Two tenets of his ethics are (1) the forms of the good are diverse, and (2) the good of each animal is definite and final. The moral terrain of animals, viewed from a neutral perspective, places all animal interests and goods as equal. Each good stems from heritable physical traits and is shaped by adaptations to the environment. Concluding that the "forms of the good are divergent," Santayana holds that the good for each animal may differ, depending on the nature of the psyche and the circumstances, and may be different for an individual animal in different times and environments. There is no one good for all, or even for an individual.

Seen as a whole, animal goods are not logically or morally ordered, they are natural, morally neutral forces. But no living being can observe all interests with such neutrality. Situated in a particular place and time with heritable traits, all living beings have interests originating from their physiology and physical environment. For Santayana, one may reasonably note that a neutral observer could view all moral perspectives as equal, but such a view must be balanced by the understanding that no animal stands on neutral ground. There is a polarity between the ideal neutral, objective understanding of behavior on the one hand and the committed and vested interest of particular living beings on the other hand. One may recognize that every animal good has its own standing, and one may respect that ideal, but "the right of alien natures to pursue their proper aims can never abolish our right to pursue ours" (*Persons and Places*, 179).

Santayana's second moral insight is that for each animal the good is definite and final. There are specific goods for each animal depending on the specific heritable traits and interests of the psyche and on the specific circumstances of the environment. Self-knowledge, then, is the distinguishing moral mark. The extent to which one knows one's interests, their complexity and centrality, will determine whether one can achieve a good life, provided the environment is accommodating. Santayana's philosophy rests on his naturalism and on his humane and sympathetic appreciation for the excellence of each life. But from the perspective of autobiography, Santayana's clear notion of self-knowledge, in the sense of the Greeks, is his most distinguishing mark. For Santayana, "integrity or self-definition is and remains first and fundamental in morals ..." (*Persons and Places* 170).

Self-knowledge requires a critical appreciation of one's culture and physical inheritance, and the ability to shape one's life in streams of conflicting goods within oneself and within one's community. Although this position is common to many considerations of political philosophy, Santayana's approach to politics was much more conservative than that normally associated with the founders of American pragmatism, such as James and Dewey.

Santayana's political conservatism is founded on his naturalism and his emphasis on self-realization and spirituality. He is concerned that liberal democracy may not provide a consistent basis for individual freedom and spirituality. The twin fears of private anarchy and public uniformity are the grounds for his criticisms of democracy, and his account of social justice focuses on the individual rather than the society. Santayana's inattentiveness to social inequality is perhaps understandable in the context of his naturalism where the final cause is the "authority of things." His basic contention that individual suffering is the worse feature of human life, not social inequality, causes him to focus more on the natural dilemmas of the individual rather than on social action. Coupling this argument with the view that all institutions, including governments, are inextricably rooted in their culture and background perhaps makes it understandable that he would not readily see how particular views of social inequality could be transferred readily from one culture to another. In addition, Santayana's European and particularly Spanish background influenced his attitudes toward social action. His repeated "Latin" perspective caused him to look with considerable suspicion toward forcing Anglo-Saxon outlooks on other cultures. Yet, in individual matters he was remarkably forthcoming as when he provided financial support to numerous friends, often of quite different philosophical, literary, and political persuasions than his own.

Within the natural order every living entity stands on the same natural ground bathing equally in the impartial light of nature. No one can claim a central place above others. But each entity also has an embodied set of values, and the art of life is to structure one's environment in such a fashion as to best realize those embodied values, i.e., to place in harmony the natural forces of one's life and one's environment.

American democracy has an exacting challenge. Lacking the time to live in the mind, Americans use quantity as a justification for lack of quality in their achievements. Quantity is potentially infinite and assures unrivaled busyness, but is it worth it? No, according to Santayana, if self-realization is the goal of individual life. Of course, circumstances make it difficult, perhaps impossible, for some individuals to order their lives reasonably and attain the practical wisdom to achieve individual happiness. America's economic success would appear to make this possible for many, but to succeed Americans must abandon servility to mechanism and economics. What is needed is a life made free by a recovery of the capacity to have a vision of the good life (*Persons and Places*, xxxiv). According to Santayana, the fanatic is a person who has lost sight of their goals and redoubled their efforts. To supplant this busy, blind, relentlessly quantitative existence, we must regain sight of our goals. Individual life should be structured in light of those goals.

Santayana's focus is on the individual, and the role of the state is to protect and to enable the individual to flourish. The goal is not something far off to be worked toward. It is not a task to be accomplished and then supplanted by another task, as is often the case with American enterprise does. Rather it is the celebration of life in its festivities. It is Aristotle's practical wisdom: structuring individual life as it is, living it joyfully, and assuring that one's commitments are conducive to the delights of the intellect and consistent with the demands of the time and tradition. It is the exercise of one's free choice, shaping one's life through material well-being, but doing so to appreciate the poetic, dramatic quality of our own existence. To rush through life and die without the joy of living, that is the tragedy of American life.

For some, though perhaps not for many, the spiritual life will be an organizing good. The cultural background for the spiritual life is the religious life, primarily as found within the Catholic Church and informed by the late nineteenth century and early twentieth century accounts of Eastern religions. But Santayana is not interested in an historical or doctrinal explication of the elements of traditional religion, rather the philosophical task is to discern the elements giving rise to such traditional views, and, in his own case, to explicate the aspects of these origins without the dogmatism of traditional religious belief.

Introducing the concept of a spiritual life led some to see an inherent conflict between Santayana's life of reason and the spiritual life. In a letter to Milton Karl Munitz (23 July 1939), Santayana explains the different perspectives of the life of reason and the spiritual life:

I admit gladly that religion (= the "Spiritual life") is a natural interest, to be collated within the life of reason with every other interest; but it is an interest in the ultimate, an adjustment to life, death, science, and politics; and though cultivated specially by certain minds at certain hours, it has no moral or natural claim to predominance. The races and ages in which it is absent will inevitably regard it as unnecessary and obstructive, because they tend to arrange their moral economy without religion at all. Those to whom religion is absorbing (e.g., the Indians) will on the contrary think a moral economy inferior in which no place and no influence is given to the monition of ultimate facts. I think you would not find my two voices inharmonious (I agree that they are different in pitch) if you did not live in America in the XXth century when the "dominance of the foreground" is so pronounced. The dominance of the distance or background would impose a different synthesis. (*Works*, v. 5, book 6, 254)

If the spiritual life was considered a dominating or guiding influence in structuring one's life, the way

Santayana views reason, then one would be forced to choose between the life of reason and the life of the spirit as a monk or a nun must choose between the life of the world and that of the religious order. But for Santayana, no such conflict exists; spirituality is not choosing a way of living over an extended period of time. Indeed, any effort to choose such a life would be short lived, since the spiritual life is a life of receptivity to all that comes in the moment while suspending animal interests. Suspending one's specific natural interests, such as eating or sleeping, for any extended period would be both detrimental and tragic.

Consciousness essentially is only awareness, an attention to what is given, rather than being an instrument in reshaping the world. Consciousness, emerging late in the evolutionary pathway, is a flowering of happy circumstances that celebrates what is given, and when truly recognized, does only that. It is joyful, delighting in what is presented, and not troubled by where it leads or what it means. This is not to restate Santayana's view poetically but rather to convey that Santayana characterizes consciousness, itself, as poetic rather than as a means to an action or as a way of implementing an action. The more dower, moralistic, and evangelical aspects of religion he saw as confused efforts to make religion a science, a social club, or a political movement. Spirit, or consciousness, is momentary, fleeting, and depends on the physical forces of our bodies and environment in order to exist. Shaping one's life to enhance these spiritual, fleeting moments, extending them as long as is practical, is one of the delights of living for some people, but it is certainly not a goal for all, nor should it be.

CHAPTER TWO

HANNAH ARENDT

Hannah Arendt, one of the leading political thinkers of the twentieth century, was born in 1906 in Hanover and died in New York in 1975. In 1924, after having completed her high school studies, she went to Marburg University to study with Martin Heidegger. The encounter with Heidegger, with whom she had a brief but intense love-affair, had a lasting influence on her thought. After a year of study in Marburg, she moved to Freiburg University where she spent one semester attending the lectures of Edmund Husserl. In the spring of 1926 she went to Heidelberg University to study with Karl Jaspers, a philosopher with whom she established a long-lasting intellectual and personal friendship. She completed her doctoral dissertation, entitled Der Liebesbegriff bei Augustin (hereafter LA) under Jaspers's supervision in 1929. She was forced to flee Germany in 1933 as a result of Hitler's rise to power, and after a brief stay in Prague and Geneva she moved to Paris where for six years (1933–39) she worked for a number of Jewish refugee organisations. In 1936 she separated from her first husband, Günther Stern, and started to live with Heinrich Blücher, whom she married in 1940. During her stay in Paris she continued to work on her biography of Rahel Varnhagen, which was not published until 1957 (hereafter RV). In 1941 she was forced to leave France and moved to New York with her husband and mother. In New York she soon became part of an influential circle of writers and intellectuals gathered around the journal Partisan Review. During the post-war period she lectured at a number of American universities, including Princeton, Berkeley and Chicago, but was most closely associated with the New School for Social Research, where she was a professor of political philosophy until her death in 1975. In 1951 she published The Origins of Totalitarianism (hereafter OT), a major study of the Nazi and Stalinist regimes that soon became a classic, followed by The Human Condition in 1958 (hereafter HC), her most important philosophical work. In 1961 she attended the trial of Adolf Eichmann in Jerusalem as a reporter for The New Yorker magazine, and two years later published Eichmann in Jerusalem (hereafter EJ), which caused a deep controversy in Jewish circles. The same year saw the publication of On Revolution (hereafter OR), a comparative analysis of the American and French revolutions. A number of important essays were also published during the 1960s and early 1970s: a first collection was entitled Between Past and Future (hereafter BPF), a second Men in Dark Times (hereafter MDT), and a third Crises of the Republic (hereafter CR). At the time of her death in 1975, she had completed the first two volumes on Thinking and Willing of her last major philosophical work, The Life of the Mind, which was published posthumously in 1978 (hereafter LM). The third volume, on Judging, was left unfinished, but some background material and lecture notes were published in 1982 under the title Lectures on Kant's Political Philosophy (hereafter LKPP). Hannah Arendt was one of the seminal political thinkers of the twentieth century. The power and originality of her thinking was evident in works such as The Origins of Totalitarianism, The Human Condition, On Revolution and The Life of the Mind. In these works and in numerous essays she grappled with the most crucial political events of her time, trying to grasp their meaning and historical import, and showing how they affected our categories of moral and political judgment. What was required, in her view, was a new framework that could enable us to come to terms with the twin horrors of the twentieth century, Nazism and Stalinism. She provided such framework in her book on totalitarianism, and went on to develop a new set of philosophical categories that could illuminate the human condition and provide a fresh perspective on the nature of political life. Although some of her works now belong to the classics of the Western tradition of political thought, she has always remained difficult to classify. Her political philosophy cannot be characterized in terms of the traditional categories of conservatism, liberalism, and socialism. Nor can her thinking be assimilated to the recent revival of communitarian political thought, to be found, for example, in the writings of A. MacIntyre, M. Sandel, C. Taylor and M. Walzer. Her name has been invoked by a number of critics of the liberal tradition, on the grounds that she presented a vision of politics that stood in opposition some key liberal principles. There are many strands of Arendt's thought that could justify such a claim, in particular, her critique of representative democracy, her stress on civic engagement and political deliberation, her separation of morality from politics, and her praise of the revolutionary tradition. However, it would be a mistake to view Arendt as an anti-liberal thinker. Arendt was in fact a stern defender of constitutionalism and the rule of law, an advocate of fundamental human rights (among which she included not only the right to life, liberty, and freedom of expression, but also the right to action and to opinion), and a critic of all forms of political community based on traditional ties and customs, as well as those based on religious, ethnic, or racial identity. Arendt's political thought cannot, in this sense, be identified either with the liberal tradition or with the claims advanced by a number of its critics. Arendt did not conceive of politics as a means for the satisfaction of individual preferences, nor as a way to integrate individuals around a shared conception of the good. Her conception of politics is based instead on the idea of active citizenship, that is, on the value and importance of civic engagement and collective deliberation about all matters affecting the political community. If there is a tradition of thought with which Arendt can be identified, it is the classical tradition of civic republicanism originating in Aristotle and embodied in the writings of Machiavelli, Montesquieu, Jefferson, and Tocqueville. According to this tradition politics finds its authentic expression whenever citizens gather together in a public space to deliberate and decide about matters of collective concern. Political activity is valued not because it may lead to agreement or to a shared conception of the good, but because it enables each citizen to exercise his or her powers of agency, to develop the capacities for judgment and to attain by concerted action some measure of political efficacy. In what follows, we reconstruct Arendt's political philosophy along four major themes: (1) her conception of modernity, (2) her theory of action, (3) her theory of judgment, and (4) her conception of citizenship. 3. Arendt's Conception of Modernity In her major philosophical work, The Human Condition, and in some of the essays collected in Between Past and Future, Arendt articulated a fairly negative conception of modernity. In these writings Arendt is primarily concerned with the losses incurred as a result of the eclipse of tradition, religion, and authority, but she offers a number of illuminating suggestions with respect to the resources that the modern age can still provide to address questions of meaning, identity, and value. For Arendt modernity is characterized by the loss of the world, by which she means the restriction or elimination of the public sphere of action and speech in favor of the private world of introspection and the private pursuit of economic interests. Modernity is the age of mass society, of the rise of the social out of a previous distinction between the public and the private, and of the victory of animal laborans over homo faber and the classical conception of man as zoon politikon. Modernity is the age of bureaucratic administration and anonymous labor, rather than politics and action, of elite domination and the manipulation of public opinion. It is the age when totalitarian forms of government, such as Nazism and Stalinism, have emerged as a result of the institutionalization of terror and violence. It is the age where history as a "natural process" has replaced history as a fabric of actions and events, where homogeneity and conformity have replaced plurality and freedom, and where isolation and loneliness have eroded human solidarity and all spontaneous forms of living together. Modernity is the age where the past no longer carries any certainty of evaluation, where individuals, having lost their traditional standards and values, must search for new grounds of human community as such. This is Arendt's vision of modernity, a vision which, at first sight, appears quite stark and unredeeming. It is worth pointing out, however, that Arendt's negative appraisal of modernity was shaped by her experience of totalitarianism in the twentieth century, and that her work provides a number of important insights that may help us to address certain problematic features of the modern age. In her political writings, and especially in The Origins of Totalitarianism, Arendt claimed that the phenomenon of totalitarianism has broken the continuity of Occidental history, and has rendered meaningless most of our moral and political categories. The break in our tradition has become irrevocable after the tragic events of the twentieth century and the triumph of totalitarian movements East and West. In the form of Stalinism and Nazism, totalitarianism has exploded the established categories of political thought and the accepted standards of moral judgment, and has thereby broken the continuity of our history. Faced with the tragic events of the Holocaust and the Gulag, we can no longer go back to traditional concepts and values, so as to explain the unprecedented by means of precedents, or to understand the monstrous by means of the familiar. The burden of our time must be faced without the aid of tradition, or as Arendt once put it, "without a bannister" (RPW, 336). Our inherited concepts and criteria for judgment have been dissolved under the impact of modern political events, and the task now is to re-establish the meaning of the past outside the framework of any tradition, since none have retained their original validity. It is the past, then, and not tradition, that Arendt attempts to preserve from the rupture in modern time-consciousness. Only by reappropriating the past by means of what Arendt called "the deadly impact of new thoughts" (MDT, 201) can we hope to restore meaning to the present and throw some light on the contemporary situation. The hermeneutic strategy that Arendt employed to re-establish a link with the past is indebted to both Walter Benjamin and Martin Heidegger. From Benjamin she took the idea of a fragmentary historiography, one that seeks to identify the moments of rupture, displacement and dislocation in history. Such fragmentary historiography enables one to recover the lost potentials of the past in the hope that they may find actualization in the present. From Heidegger she took the idea of a deconstructive reading of the Western philosophical tradition, one that seeks to uncover the original meaning of our categories and to liberate them from the distorting incrustations of tradition. Such deconstructive hermeneutics enables one to recover those primordial experiences (Urphaenomene) which have been occluded or forgotten by the philosophical tradition, and thereby to recover the lost origins of our philosophical concepts and categories. By relying on these two hermeneutic strategies Arendt hopes to redeem from the past its lost or "forgotten treasure," that is, those fragments from the past that might still be of significance to us. In her view it is no longer possible, after the collapse of tradition, to save the past as a whole; the task, rather, is to redeem from oblivion those elements of the past that are still able to illuminate our situation. To re-establish a linkage with the past is not an antiquarian exercise; on the contrary, without the critical reappropriation of the past our temporal horizon becomes disrupted, our experience precarious, and our identity more fragile. In Arendt's view, then, it is necessary to redeem from the past those moments worth preserving, to save those fragments from past treasures that are significant for us. Only by means of this critical reappropriation can we discover the past anew, endow it with relevance and meaning for the present, and make it a source of inspiration for the future. This critical reappropriation is facilitated, in part, by the fact that after the rupture in modern time-consciousness the past may "open up to us with unexpected freshness and tell us things no one has yet had ears to hear" (BPF, 94). The breakdown of tradition may in fact provide the great chance to look upon the past "with eyes undistorted by any tradition, with a directness which has disappeared from Occidental reading and hearing ever since Roman civilization submitted to the authority of Greek thought" (BPF, 28–9). Arendt's return to the original experience of the Greek polis represents, in this sense, an attempt to break the fetters of a worn-out tradition and to rediscover a past over which tradition has no longer a claim. Against tradition Arendt sets the criterion of genuineness, against the authoritative that which is forgotten, concealed, or displaced at the margins of history. Only by operating against the grain of traditionalism and the claims of conventional historiography can the past be made meaningful again, provide sources of illumination for the present, and yield its treasures to those who search for them with "new thoughts" and saving acts of remembrance. Arendt articulates her conception of modernity around a number of key features: these are world alienation, earth alienation, the rise of the social, and the victory of animal laborans. World alienation refers to the loss of an intersubjectively constituted world of experience and action by means of which we establish our self-identity and an adequate sense of reality. Earth alienation refers to the attempt to escape from the confines of the earth; spurred by modern science and technology, we have searched for ways to overcome our earth-bound condition by setting out on the exploration of space, by attempting to recreate life under laboratory conditions, and by trying to extend our given life-span. The rise of the social refers to the expansion of the market economy from the early modern period and the ever increasing accumulation of capital and social wealth. With the rise of the social everything has become an object of production and consumption, of acquisition and exchange; moreover, its constant expansion has resulted in the blurring of the distinction between the private and the public. The victory of animal laborans refers to the triumph of the values of labor over those of homo faber and of man as zoon politikon. All the values characteristic of the world of fabrication — permanence, stability, durability — as well as those characteristic of the world of action and speech — freedom, plurality, solidarity — are sacrificed in favor of the values of life, productivity and abundance. Arendt identifies two main stages in the emergence of modernity: the first, from the sixteenth to the nineteenth century, corresponds to world alienation and the rise of the social, the second, from the beginning of the twentieth century, corresponds to earth alienation and the victory of animal laborans. She also identifies a number of causes: the discovery of America and the corresponding shrinking of the earth, the waves of expropriation started during the Reformation, the invention of the telescope challenging the adequacy of the senses, the rise of modern science and philosophy and subsequently of a conception of man as part of a process of Nature and History, and the expansion of the realm of the economy, of the production and accumulation of social wealth. Arendt's interpretation of modernity can be criticized on a number of grounds. We focus attention here on two categories employed by Arendt, those of nature, and the social. With respect to the category of nature, Arendt oscillates between two contrasting accounts. According to the first account, the modern age, by elevating labor, the most natural of human activities, to the highest position within the vita activa, has brought us too close to nature. Instead of building and preserving the human artifice and creating public spaces for action and deliberation, we are reduced to engage in the activity of sheer survival and in the production of things that are by definition perishable. According to the second account, however, the modern age is characterized by a growing artificiality, by the rejection of anything that is not man-made. Arendt cites the fact that natural processes, including that of life itself, have been recreated artificially by means of scientific experiment, that our natural environment has been extensively transformed and in some instances entirely replaced by technology, and that we have searched for ways to overcome our natural condition as earth-bound creatures by setting out on the exploration of space and envisaging the possibility of inhabiting other planets. All this leads to a situation where nothing around us will be a naturally given event, object, or process, but will instead be the product of our instruments and the will to refashion the world in our image. These two accounts are difficult to reconcile, since in the former we have nature intruding upon and even destroying the human artifice, while in the latter we have art (techne) expanding upon and replacing everything natural or merely given. The result is to endow nature with an ambiguous status, since in the former case the victory of animal laborans indicates our subjection to natural processes, while in the latter case the expansion of scientific knowledge and of technological mastery indicates the overcoming of all natural limits. The modern world would thus appear to be too natural and too artificial, too much under the dominance of labor and the life-process of the species, as well as too much under the dominance of techne. With respect to the second category, that of the social, Arendt was unable to account for certain important features of the modern world. Arendt identifies the social with all those activities formerly restricted to the private sphere of the household and having to do with the necessities of life. Her claim is that, with the tremendous expansion of the economy from the end of the eighteenth century, all such activities have taken over the public realm and transformed it into a sphere for the satisfaction of our material needs. Society has thus invaded and conquered the public realm, turning it into a function of what previously were private needs and concerns, and has thereby destroyed the boundary separating the public and the private. Arendt also claims that with the expansion of the social realm the tripartite division of human activities has been undermined to the point of becoming meaningless. In her view, once the social realm has established its monopoly, the distinction between labor, work and action is lost, since every effort is now expended on reproducing our material conditions of existence. Obsessed with life, productivity, and consumption, we have turned into a society of laborers and jobholders who no longer appreciate the values associated with work, nor those associated with action. From this brief account it is clear that Arendt's concept of the social plays a crucial role in her assessment of modernity. I would argue, however, that it blinds her to many important issues and leads her to a series of questionable judgments. In the first place, Arendt's characterization of the social is overly restricted. She claims that the social is the realm of labor, of biological and material necessity, of the reproduction of our condition of existence. She also claims that the rise of the social coincides with the expansion of the economy from the end of the eighteenth century. However, having identified the social with the growth of the economy in the past two centuries, Arendt cannot characterize it in terms of a subsistence model of simple reproduction (Benhabib 2003, Ch. 6; Bernstein 1986, Ch. 9; Hansen 1993, Ch. 3; Parekh 1981, Ch. 8). Secondly, Arendt's identification of the social with the activities of the household is responsible for a major shortcoming in her analysis of the economy. She is, in fact, unable to acknowledge that a modern capitalist economy constitutes a structure of power with a highly asymmetric distribution of costs and rewards. By relying on the misleading analogy of the household, she maintains that all questions pertaining to the economy are pre-political, and thus ignores the crucial question of economic power and exploitation (Bernstein 1986, Ch. 9; Hansen 1993, Ch. 3; Parekh 1981, Ch. 8; Pitkin 1998; Pitkin 1994, Ch. 10, Hinchman and Hinchman; Wolin 1994, Ch. 11, Hinchman and Hinchman). Finally, by insisting on a strict separation between the private and the public, and between the social and the political, she is unable to account for the essential connection between these spheres and the struggles to redraw their boundaries. Today many so-called private issues have become public concerns, and the struggle for justice and equal rights has extended into many spheres. By insulating the political sphere from the concerns of the social, and by maintaining a strict distinction between the public and the private, Arendt is unable to account for some of the most important achievements of modernity — the extension of justice and equal rights, and the redrawing of the boundaries between the public and the private (Benhabib 2003, Ch. 6; Bernstein 1986, Ch. 9; Dietz 2002, Ch. 5; Pitkin 1998; Pitkin 1995, Ch. 3, Honig; Zaretsky

1997, Ch. 8, Calhoun and McGowan). 4. Arendt's Theory of Action Arendt's theory of action and her revival of the ancient notion of praxis represent one of the most original contributions to twentieth century political thought. By distinguishing action (praxis) from fabrication (poiesis), by linking it to freedom and plurality, and by showing its connection to speech and remembrance, Arendt is able to articulate a conception of politics in which questions of meaning and identity can be addressed in a fresh and original manner. Moreover, by viewing action as a mode of human togetherness, Arendt is able to develop a conception of participatory democracy which stands in direct contrast to the bureaucratized and elitist forms of politics so characteristic of the modern epoch. In what follows, we focus on some of the key components of Arendt's theory of action, such as freedom, plurality and disclosure. We then examine the links between action and narrative, the importance of remembrance, and of what may be called "communities of memory." We then show the connection between action, power and the space of appearance. Lastly, we look at the remedies for the unpredictability and irreversibility of action, namely, the power of promise and the power to forgive. 4.1 Action, Freedom, and Plurality Action, the only activity that goes on directly between men without the intermediary of things or matter, corresponds to the human condition of plurality ... this plurality is specifically the condition — not only the conditio sine qua non, but the conditio per quam — of all political life. (HC, 7) For Arendt, action is one of the fundamental categories of the human condition and constitutes the highest realization of the vita activa. Arendt analyzes the vita activa via three categories which correspond to the three fundamental activities of our being-in-the-world: labor, work, and action. Labor is the activity which is tied to the human condition of life, work the activity which is tied to the condition of worldliness, and action the activity tied to the condition of plurality. For Arendt each activity is autonomous, in the sense of having its own distinctive principles and of being judged by different criteria. Labor is judged by its ability to sustain human life, to cater to our biological needs of consumption and reproduction, work is judged by its ability to build and maintain a world fit for human use, and action is judged by its ability to disclose the identity of the agent, to affirm the reality of the world, and to actualize our capacity for freedom. Although Arendt considers the three activities of labor, work and action equally necessary to a complete human life, in the sense that each contributes in its distinctive way to the realization of our human capacities, it is clear from her writings that she takes action to be the differentia specifica of human beings, that which distinguishes them from both the life of animals (who are similar to us insofar as they need to labor to sustain and reproduce themselves) and the life of the gods (with whom we share, intermittently, the activity of contemplation). In this respect the categories of labor and work, while significant in themselves, must be seen as counterpoints to the category of action, helping to differentiate and highlight the place of action within the order of the vita activa. The two central features of action are freedom and plurality. By freedom Arendt does not mean the ability to choose among a set of possible alternatives (the freedom of choice so dear to the liberal tradition) or the faculty of liberum arbitrium which, according to Christian doctrine, was given to us by God. Rather, by freedom Arendt means the capacity to begin, to start something new, to do the unexpected, with which all human beings are endowed by virtue of being born. Action as the realization of freedom is therefore rooted in natality, in the fact that each birth represents a new beginning and the introduction of novelty in the world. To be sure, Arendt recognizes that all activities are in some way related to the phenomenon of natality, since both labor and work are necessary to create and preserve a world into which new human beings are constantly born. However, of the three activities, action is the one most closely connected with natality, because by acting individuals re-enact the miracle of beginning inherent in their birth. For Arendt, the beginning that each of us represents by virtue of being born is actualized every time we act, that is, every time we begin something new. As she puts it: "the new beginning inherent in birth can make itself felt in the world only because the newcomer possesses the capacity of beginning something anew, that is, of acting " (HC, 9). Arendt also stresses the fact that since action as beginning is rooted in natality, since it is the actualization of freedom, it carries with it the capacity to perform miracles, that is, to introduce what is totally unexpected. "It is in the nature of beginning" — she claims — "that something new is started which cannot be expected from whatever may have happened before. This character of startling unexpectedness is inherent in all beginnings ... The fact that man is capable of action means that the unexpected can be expected from him, that he is able to perform what is infinitely improbable. And this again is possible only because each man is unique, so that with each birth something uniquely new comes into the world " (HC, 177–8). The birth of every individual is thus the promise of a new beginning: to act means to be able to disclose one's self and to do the unanticipated; and it is entirely in keeping with this conception that most of the concrete examples of action in the modern age that Arendt discusses are cases of revolutions and popular uprisings. Her claim is that "revolutions are the only political events which confront us directly and inevitably with the problem of beginning," (OR, 21) since they represent the attempt to found a new political space, a space where freedom can appear as a worldly reality. The favorite example for Arendt is the American Revolution, because there the act of foundation took the form of a constitution of liberty. Her other examples are the revolutionary clubs of the French Revolution, the Paris Commune of 1871, the creation of Soviets during the Russian Revolution, the French Resistance to Hitler in the Second World War, and the Hungarian revolt of 1956. In all these cases individual men and women had the courage to interrupt their routine activities, to step forward from their private lives in order to create a public space where freedom could appear, and to act in such a way that the memory of their deeds could become a source of inspiration for the future. In doing so, according to Arendt, they rediscovered the truth known to the ancient Greeks that action is the supreme blessing of human life, that which bestows significance to the lives of individuals. In the book On Revolution Arendt devotes much attention to the rediscovery of this truth by those who participated in the American Revolution. In her view the Founding Fathers, although they might have pretended that they longed for private life and engaged in politics only out of a sense of duty, made clear in their letters and recollections that they had discovered unexpected delights in action and had acquired a taste for public freedom and for earning distinction among their peers. Plurality, to which we may now turn, is the other central feature of action. For if to act means to take the initiative, to introduce the novum and the unexpected into the world, it also means that it is not something that can be done in isolation from others, that is, independently of the presence of a plurality of actors who from their different perspectives can judge the quality of what is being enacted. In this respect action needs plurality in the same way that performance artists need an audience; without the presence and acknowledgment of others, action would cease to be a meaningful activity. Action, to the extent that it requires appearing in public, making oneself known through words and deeds, and eliciting the consent of others, can only exist in a context defined by plurality. Arendt establishes the connection between action and plurality by means of an anthropological argument. In her view just as life is the condition that corresponds to the activity of labor and worldliness the condition that corresponds to the activity of work, so plurality is the condition that corresponds to action. She defines plurality as "the fact that men, not Man, live on the earth and inhabit the world," and says that it is the condition of human action "because we are all the same, that is, human, in such a way that nobody is ever the same as anyone else who ever lived, lives, or will live " (HC, 7–8). Plurality thus refers both to equality and distinction, to the fact that all human beings belong to the same species and are sufficiently alike to understand one another, but yet no two of them are ever interchangeable, since each of them is an individual endowed with a unique biography and perspective on the world. It is by virtue of plurality that each of us is capable of acting and relating to others in ways that are unique and distinctive, and in so doing of contributing to a network of actions and relationships that is infinitely complex and unpredictable. This network of actions is what makes up the realm of human affairs, that space where individuals relate directly without the intermediary of things or matter — that is, through language. Let us examine briefly this connection between action and language. In The Human Condition Arendt stresses repeatedly that action is primarily symbolic in character and that the web of human relationships is sustained by communicative interaction (HC, 178–9, 184–6, 199–200). We may formulate it as follows. Action entails speech: by means of language we are able to articulate the meaning of our actions and to coordinate the actions of a plurality of agents. Conversely, speech entails action, not only in the sense that speech itself is a form of action, or that most acts are performed in the manner of speech, but in the sense that action is often the means whereby we check the sincerity of the speaker. Thus, just as action without speech runs the risk of being meaningless and would be impossible to coordinate with the actions of others, so speech without action would lack one of the means by which we may confirm the veracity of the speaker. As we shall see, this link between action and speech is central to Arendt's characterization of power, that potential which springs up between people when they act "in concert," and which is actualized "only where word and deed have not parted company, where words are not empty and deeds not brutal, where words are not used to veil intentions but to disclose realities, and deeds are not used to violate and destroy but to establish relations and create new realities " (HC, 200). 4.2 Action and Speech as Disclosure Let us now turn to an examination of the disclosing power of action and speech. In the opening section of the chapter on action in The Human Condition Arendt discusses one of its central functions, namely, the disclosure of the identity of the agent. In action and speech, she maintains, individuals reveal themselves as the unique individuals they are, disclose to the world their distinct personalities. In terms of Arendt's distinction, they reveal "who" they are as distinct to "what" they are — the latter referring to individual abilities and talents, as well as deficiencies and shortcomings, which are traits all human beings share. Neither labor nor work enable individuals to disclose their identities, to reveal "who" they are as distinct from "what" they are. In labor the individuality of each person is submerged by being bound to a chain of natural necessities, to the constraints imposed by biological survival. When we engage in labor we can only show our sameness, the fact that we all belong to the human species and must attend to the needs of our bodies. In this sphere we do indeed "behave," "perform roles," and "fulfill functions," since we all obey the same imperatives. In work there is more scope for individuality, in that each work of art or production bears the mark of its maker; but the maker is still subordinate to the end product, both in the sense of being guided by a model, and in the sense that the product will generally outlast the maker. Moreover, the end product reveals little about the maker except the fact that he or she was able to make it. It does not tell us who the creator was, only that he or she had certain abilities and talents. It is thus only in action and speech, in interacting with others through words and deeds, that individuals reveal who they personally are and can affirm their unique identities. Action and speech are in this sense very closely related because both contain the answer to the question asked of every newcomer: "Who are you?" This disclosure of the "who" is made possible by both deeds and words, but of the two it is speech that has the closest affinity to revelation. Without the accompaniment of speech, action would lose its revelatory quality and could no longer be identified with an agent. It would lack, as it were, the conditions of ascription of agency. 4.3 Action, Narrative, and Remembrance We have seen, then, how through action and speech individuals are able to disclose their identities, to reveal their specific uniqueness — their who — as distinct from their personal abilities and talents — their what. However, while engaging in speech and action individuals can never be sure what kind of self they will reveal. Only retrospectively, that is, only through the stories that will arise from their deeds and performances, will their identity become fully manifest. The function of the storyteller is thus crucial not only for the preservation of the doings and sayings of actors, but also for the full disclosure of the identity of the actor. The narratives of a storyteller, Arendt claims, "tell us more about their subjects, the 'hero' in the center of each story, than any product of human hands ever tells us about the master who produced it" (HC, 184). Without a Plato to tell us who Socrates was, what his conversations with fellow Athenian citizens were like, without a Thucydides to set down Pericles' Funeral Speech and refashion it in his powerful and dramatic style, we would not have known what made Socrates and Pericles such outstanding personalities, nor would the reason for their uniqueness have been made fully manifest. Indeed, it is one of Arendt's most important claims that the meaning of action itself is dependent upon the articulation retrospectively given to it by historians and narrators. Storytelling, or the weaving of a narrative out of the actions and pronouncements of individuals, is partly constitutive of their meaning, because it enables the retrospective articulation of their significance and import, both for the actors themselves and for the spectators. Being absorbed by their immediate aims and concerns, not aware of the full implications of their actions, actors are often not in a position to assess the true significance of their doings, or to be fully aware of their own motives and intentions. Only when action has run a certain course, and its relationship to other actions has unfolded, can its significance be made fully manifest and be embodied in a narrative, whether of poets or historians. The fact that this narrative is temporally deferred, that it is at some distance from the events it describes, is one of the reasons why it can provide further insight into the motives and aims of the actors. Narratives can thus provide a measure of truthfulness and a greater degree of significance to the actions of individuals. But they also preserve the memory of deeds through time, and in so doing, they enable these deeds to become sources of inspiration for the future, that is, models to be imitated, and, if possible, surpassed. One of the principal drawbacks of action, Arendt maintains, is to be extremely fragile, to be subject to the erosion of time and to forgetfulness; unlike the products of the activity of work, which acquire a measure of permanence by virtue of their sheer facticity, deeds and words do not survive their enactment unless they are remembered. Remembrance alone, the retelling of deeds as stories, can save the lives and deeds of actors from oblivion and futility. And it is precisely for this reason, Arendt points out, that the Greeks valued poetry and history so highly, because they rescued the glorious (as well as the less glorious) deeds of the past for the benefit of future generations (HC, 192 ff; BPF, 63–75). It was the poet's and the historian's political function to preserve the memory of past actions and to make them a source of instruction for the future. Homer was known as the "educator of Hellas," since he immortalized for all those who came after him the events of the Trojan War; Thucydides, in his History of the Peloponnesian War, told a story of human ambition and folly, of courage and unchecked greed, of ruthless struggle and inevitable defeat. In their work the past became a repository of instruction, of actions to be emulated as well as deeds to be shunned. Through their narratives the fragility and perishability of human action was overcome and made to outlast the lives of their doers and the limited life-span of their contemporaries. However, to be preserved, such narratives needed in turn an audience, that is, a community of hearers who became the transmitters of the deeds that had been immortalized. As Sheldon Wolin has aptly put it, "audience is a metaphor for the political community whose nature is to be a community of remembrance" (Wolin 1977, 97). In other words, behind the actor stands the storyteller, but behind the storyteller stands a community of memory. It was one of the primary functions of the polis to be precisely such a community, to preserve the words and deeds of its citizens from oblivion and the ravages of time, and thereby to leave a testament for future generations. The Greek polis, beyond making possible the sharing of words and deeds and multiplying the occasions to win immortal fame, was meant to remedy the frailty of human affairs. It did this by establishing a framework where action and speech could be recorded and transformed into stories, where every citizen could be a witness and thereby a potential narrator. What the polis established, then, was a space where organized remembrance could take place, and where, as a result, the mortality of actors and the fragility of human deeds could be partially overcome. 4.4 Action, Power, and the Space of Appearance The metaphor of the polis recurs constantly in the writings of Arendt. This is indeed a 'metaphor' because in employing this term Arendt is not simply referring to the political institutions of the Greek city-states, bounded as they were to their time and circumstance, but to all those instances in history where a public realm of action and speech was set up among a community of free and equal citizens. "The polis, properly speaking, is not the city-state in its physical location; it is the organization of the people as it arises out of acting and speaking together, and its true space lies between people living together for this purpose, no matter where they happen to be" (HC, 198). Thus the famous motto: "Wherever you go, you will be a polis" expressed the conviction among the Greek colonists that the kind of political association they had set up originally could be reproduced in their new settlements, that the space created by the "sharing of words and deeds" could find its proper location almost anywhere. For Arendt, therefore, the polis stands for the space of appearance, for that space "where I appear to others as others appear to me, where men exist not merely like other living or inanimate things, but to make their appearance explicitly." Such public space of appearance can be always recreated anew wherever individuals gather together politically, that is, "wherever men are together in the manner of speech and action" (HC, 198–9). However, since it is a creation of action, this space of appearance is highly fragile and exists only when actualized through the performance of deeds or the utterance of words. Its peculiarity, as Arendt says, is that "unlike the spaces which are the work of our hands, it does not survive the actuality of the movement which brought it into being, but disappears not only with the dispersal of men — as in the case of great catastrophes when the body politic of a people is destroyed — but with the disappearance or arrest of the activities themselves. Wherever people gather together, it is potentially there, but only potentially, not necessarily and not forever" (HC, 199). The space of appearance must be continually recreated by action; its existence is secured whenever actors gather together for the purpose of discussing and deliberating about matters of public concern, and it disappears the moment these activities cease. It is always a potential space that finds its actualization in the actions and speeches of individuals who have come together to undertake some common project. It may arise suddenly, as in the case of revolutions, or it may develop slowly out of the efforts to change some specific piece of legislation or policy. Historically, it has been recreated whenever public spaces of action and deliberation have been set up, from town hall meetings to workers' councils, from demonstrations and sit-ins to struggles for justice and equal rights. This capacity to act in concert for a public-political purpose is what Arendt calls power. Power needs to be distinguished from strength, force, and violence (CR, 143–55). Unlike strength, it is not the property of an individual, but of a plurality of actors joining together for some common political purpose. Unlike force, it is not a natural phenomenon but a human creation, the outcome of collective engagement. And unlike violence, it is based not on coercion but on consent and rational persuasion. For Arendt, power is a sui generis phenomenon, since it is a product of action and rests entirely on persuasion. It is a product of action because it arises out of the concerted activities of a plurality of agents, and it rests on persuasion because it consists in the ability to secure the consent of others through unconstrained discussion and debate. Its only limitation is the existence of other people, but this limitation, she notes, "is not accidental, because human power corresponds to the condition of plurality to begin with" (HC, 201). It is actualized in all those cases where action is undertaken for communicative (rather than strategic or instrumental) purposes, and where speech is employed to disclose our intentions and to articulate our motives to others. Arendt maintains that the legitimacy of power is derived from the initial getting together of people, that is, from the original pact of association that establishes a political community, and is reaffirmed whenever individuals act in concert through the medium of speech and persuasion. For her "power needs no justification, being inherent in the very existence of political communities; what it does need is legitimacy ... Power springs up whenever people get together and act in concert, but it derives its legitimacy from the initial getting together rather than from any action that then may follow" (CR, 151). Beyond appealing to the past, power also relies for its continued legitimacy on the rationally binding commitments that arise out of a process of free and undistorted communication. Because of this, power is highly independent of material factors: it is sustained not by economic, bureaucratic or military means, but by the power of common convictions that result from a process of fair and unconstrained deliberation. Power is also not something that can be relied upon at all times or accumulated and stored for future use. Rather, it exists only as a potential which is actualized when actors gather together for political action and public deliberation. It is thus closely connected to the space of appearance, that public space which arises out of the actions and speeches of individuals. Indeed, for Arendt, "power is what keeps the public realm, the potential space of appearance between acting and speaking men, in existence." Like the space of appearance, power is always "a power potential and not an unchangeable, measurable and reliable entity like force or strength ... [it] springs up between men when they act together and vanishes the moment they disperse" (HC, 200). Power, then, lies at the basis of every political community and is the expression of a potential that is always available to actors. It is also the source of legitimacy of political and governmental institutions, the means whereby they are transformed and adapted to new circumstances and made to respond to the opinions and needs of the citizens. "It is the people's support that lends power to the institutions of a country, and this support is but the continuation of the consent that brought the laws into existence to begin with ... All political institutions are manifestations and materializations of power; they petrify and decay as soon as the living power of the people ceases to uphold them" (CR, 140). The legitimacy of political institutions is dependent on the power, that is, the active consent of the people; and insofar as governments may be viewed as attempts to preserve power for future generations by institutionalizing it, they require for their vitality the continuing support and active involvement of all citizens. 4.5 Action, Unpredictability, and Irreversibility The discussion of Arendt's theory of action so far has stressed a number of features, chief among which is action's capacity to disclose the identity of the agent, to enable freedom to appear and be actualized as a worldly reality, to create and sustain a public space of appearance, and to make possible the generation of power. We have also emphasized the importance of narrative and remembrance, of the retrospective articulation of the meaning of action by means of storytelling and its preservation through a community of memory. In conclusion, we examine two other features of action, namely, unpredictability and irreversibility, and their respective remedies, the power of promise and the power to forgive. Action is unpredictable because it is a manifestation of freedom, of the capacity to innovate and to alter situations by engaging in them; but also, and primarily, because it takes place within the web of human relationships, within a context defined by plurality, so that no actor can control its final outcome. Each actor sets off processes and enters into the inextricable web of actions and events to which all other actors also contribute, with the result that the outcome can never be predicted from the intentions of any particular actor. The open and unpredictable nature of action is a consequence of human freedom and plurality: by acting we are free to start processes and bring about new events, but no actor has the power to control the consequences of his or her deeds. Another and related reason for the unpredictability of action is that its consequences are boundless: every act sets in motion an unlimited number of actions and reactions which have literally no end. As Arendt puts it: "The reason why we are never able to foretell with certainty the outcome and end of any action is simply that action has no end" (HC, 233). This is because action "though it may proceed from nowhere, so to speak, acts into a medium where every action becomes a chain reaction and where every process is the cause of new processes ... the smallest act in the most limited circumstances bears the seed of the same boundlessness, because one deed, and sometimes one word, suffices to change every constellation" (HC, 190). Closely connected to the boundlessness and unpredictability of action is its irreversibility. Every action sets off processes which cannot be undone or retrieved in the way, say, we are able to undo a faulty product of our hands. If one builds an artifact and is not satisfied with it, it can always be destroyed and recreated again. This is impossible where action is concerned, because action always takes place within an already existing web of human relationships, where every action becomes a reaction, every deed a source of future deeds, and none of these can be stopped or subsequently undone. The consequences of each act are thus not only unpredictable but also irreversible; the processes started by action can neither be controlled nor be reversed. The remedy which the tradition of Western thought has proposed for the unpredictability and irreversibility of action has consisted in abstaining from action altogether, in the withdrawal from the sphere of interaction with others, in the hope that one's freedom and integrity could thereby be preserved. Platonism, Stoicism and Christianity elevated the sphere of contemplation above the sphere of action, precisely because in the former one could be free from the entanglements and frustrations of action. Arendt's proposal, by contrast, is not to turn one's back on the realm of human affairs, but to rely on two faculties inherent in action itself, the faculty of forgiving and the faculty of promising. These two faculties are closely connected, the former mitigating the irreversibility of action by absolving the actor from the unintended consequences of his or her deeds, the latter moderating the uncertainty of its outcome by binding actors to certain courses of action and thereby setting some limit to the unpredictability of the future. Both faculties are, in this respect, connected to temporality: from the standpoint of the present forgiving looks backward to what has happened and absolves the actor from what was unintentionally done, while promising looks forward as it seeks to establish islands of security in an otherwise uncertain and unpredictable future. Forgiving enables us to come to terms with the past and liberates us to some extent from the burden of irreversibility; promising allows us to face the future and to set some bounds to its unpredictability. As Arendt puts it: “Without being forgiven, released from the consequences of what we have done, our capacity to act would, as it were, be confined to one single deed from which we could never recover; we would remain the victims of its consequences forever.” On the other hand, “without being bound to the fulfillment of promises, we would never be able to keep our identities; we would be condemned to wander helplessly and without direction in the darkness of each man’s lonely heart” (HC, 237). Both faculties, in this sense, depend on plurality, on the presence and acting of others, for no one can forgive himself and no one can feel bound by a promise made only to one’s self. At the same time, both faculties are an expression of human freedom, since without the faculty to undo what we have done in the past, and without the ability to control at least partially the processes we have started, we would be the victims “of an automatic necessity bearing all the marks of inexorable laws” (HC, 246). 5. Arendt’s Theory of Judgment One of the most enduring contributions of Arendt’s political thought is to be found in her reflections on judgment which were to occupy the last years of her life. Together with the theory of action, her unfinished theory of judgment represents her central legacy to twentieth century political thought. We now explore some of the key aspects of her theory of judgment, and will examine its place in the architectonic of Arendt’s theory of politics. 5.1 Judgment: Two Models Arendt’s theory of judgment was never developed as systematically or extensively as her theory of action. She intended to complete her study of the life of the mind by devoting the third volume to the faculty of judgment, but was not able to do so because of her untimely death in 1975. What she left was a number of reflections scattered in the first two volumes on Thinking and Willing (LM, vol. I; vol. II), a series of lectures on Kant's political philosophy delivered at the New School for Social Research in the Fall of 1970 (LKPP), an essay entitled "Thinking and Moral Considerations" written at the time she was composing The Life of the Mind (TMC, 417–46), and two articles included in Between Past and Future where judgment and opinion are treated in relation to culture and taste ("The Crisis in Culture" – BPF, 197–226) and with respect to the question of truth ("Truth and Politics" – BPF, 227–64). However, these writings do not present a unified theory of judgment but, rather, two distinct models, one based on the standpoint of the actor, the other on the standpoint of the spectator, which are somewhat at odds with each other. Arendt's writings on the theme of judgment can be seen to fall into two more or less distinct phases, an early one in which judgment is the faculty of political actors acting in the public realm, and a later one in which it is the privilege of non-participating spectators, primarily poets and historians, who seek to understand the meaning of the past and to reconcile us to what has happened. In this later formulation Arendt is no longer concerned with judging as a feature of political life as such, as the faculty which is exercised by actors in order to decide how to act in the public realm, but with judgment as a component in the life of the mind, the faculty through which the privileged spectators can recover meaning from the past and thereby reconcile themselves to time and, retrospectively, to tragedy. In addition to presenting us with two models of judgment which stand in tension with each other, Arendt did not clarify the status of judgment with respect to two of its philosophical sources, Aristotle and Kant. The two conceptions seem to pull in opposite directions, the Aristotelian toward a concern with the particular, the Kantian toward a concern with universality and impartiality. It would appear, therefore, that Arendt's theory of judgment not only incorporates two models, the actor's — judging in order to act — and the spectator's — judging in order to cull meaning from the past — but that the philosophical sources it draws upon are somewhat at odds with each other. 5.2 Judgment and the Vita Contemplativa Arendt's concern with judgment as the faculty of retrospective assessment that allows meaning to be redeemed from the past originated in her attempt to come to terms with the twin political tragedies of the twentieth century, Nazism and Stalinism. Faced with the horrors of the extermination camps and what is now termed the Gulag, Arendt strove to understand these phenomena in their own terms, neither deducing them from precedents nor placing them in some overarching scheme of historical necessity. This need to come to terms with the traumatic events of the twentieth century, and to understand them in a manner that does not explain them away but faces them in all their starkness and unprecedentedness, is something to which Arendt returns again and again. Our inherited framework for judgment fails us "as soon as we try to apply it honestly to the central political experiences of our own time" (UP, 379). Even our ordinary common-sense judgment is rendered ineffective, since "we are living in a topsy-turvy world, a world where we cannot find our way by abiding by the rules of what once was common sense" (UP, 383). The crisis in understanding is therefore coeval with a crisis in judgment, insofar as understanding for Arendt is "so closely related to and interrelated with judging that one must describe both as the subsumption of something particular under a universal rule" (UP, 383). Once these rules have lost their validity we are no longer able to understand and to judge the particulars, that is, we are no longer able to subsume them under our accepted categories of moral and political thought. Arendt, however, does not believe that the loss of these categories has brought to an end our capacity to judge; on the contrary, since human beings are distinguished by their capacity to begin anew, they are able to fashion new categories and to formulate new standards of judgment for the events that have come to pass and for those that may emerge in the future. For Arendt, therefore, the enormity and unprecedentedness of totalitarianism have not destroyed, strictly speaking, our ability to judge; rather, they have destroyed our accepted standards of judgment and our conventional categories of interpretation and assessment, be they moral or political. And in this situation the only recourse is to appeal to the imagination, which allows us to view things in their proper perspective and to judge them without the benefit of a pre-given rule or universal. For Arendt, the imagination enables us to create the distance which is necessary for an impartial judgment, while at the same time allowing for the closeness that makes understanding possible. In this way it makes possible our reconciliation with reality, even with the tragic reality of the twentieth century. Arendt's participation at the trial of Eichmann in the early sixties made her once more aware of the need to come to terms with a reality that initially defied human comprehension. How could such an ordinary, law-abiding, and all-too-human individual have committed such atrocities? The impact of the trial also forced her to raise another problem concerning judgment, namely, whether we are entitled to presuppose "an independent human faculty, unsupported by law and public opinion, that judges anew in full spontaneity every deed and intent whenever the occasion arises" (PRD, 187). 5.3 Judgment and the Wind of Thought Arendt returned to this issue in The Life of the Mind, a work which was meant to encompass the three faculties of thinking, willing, and judging. In the introduction to the first volume she declared that the immediate impulse to write it came from attending the Eichmann trial in Jerusalem, while the second, equally important motive, was to provide an account of our mental activities that was missing from her previous work on the vita activa. It was Eichmann's absence of thinking, his "thoughtlessness," that struck her most, because it was responsible in her view for his inability to judge in those circumstances where judgment was most needed. "It was this absence of thinking," she wrote, "that awakened my interest. Is evil-doing ... possible in default of not just 'base motives' ... but of any motives whatever ... Might the problem of good and evil, our faculty for telling right from wrong, be connected with our faculty of thought?" (LM, vol. I, 4–5). Arendt attempted a reply by connecting the activity of thinking to that of judging in a twofold manner. First, thinking — the silent dialogue of me and myself — dissolves our fixed habits of thought and the accepted rules of conduct, and thus prepares the way for the activity of judging particulars without the aid of pre-established universals. It is not that thinking provides judgment with new rules for subsuming the particular under the universal. Rather, it loosens the grip of the universal over the particular, thereby releasing judgment from ossified categories of thought and conventional standards of assessment. It is in times of historical crisis that thinking ceases to be a marginal affair, because by undermining all established criteria and values, it prepares the individual to judge for him or herself instead of being carried away by the actions and opinions of the majority. The second way in which Arendt connected the activity of thinking with that of judging is by showing that thinking, by actualizing the dialogue of me and myself which is given in consciousness, produces conscience as a by-product. This conscience, unlike the voice of God or what later thinkers called lumen naturale, gives no positive prescriptions; it only tells us what not to do, what to avoid in our actions and dealings with others, as well as what to repent of. Arendt notes in this context that Socrates' dictum "It is better to suffer wrong than to do wrong," and his proposition that "It would be better for me that my lyre or a chorus I directed should be out of tune and loud with discord, and that multitudes of men should disagree with me, rather than that I, being one, should be out of harmony with myself and contradict me," derive their validity from the idea that there is a silent partner within ourselves to whom we render account of our actions (TMC, 29–30; 35). What we fear most is the anticipation of the presence of this partner (i.e., our conscience) who awaits us at the end of the day. Arendt also remarks that thinking, as the actualization of the difference given in consciousness, "is not a prerogative of the few but an ever-present faculty in everybody; by the same token, inability to think is not a failing of the many who lack brain power, but an ever-present possibility for everybody" (LM, vol. I, 191). For those who do engage in thinking, however, conscience emerges as an inevitable by-product. As the side-effect of thinking, conscience has its counterpart in judgment as the by-product of the liberating activity of thought. If conscience represents the inner check by which we evaluate our actions, judgment represents the outer manifestation of our capacity to think critically. Both faculties relate to the question of right and wrong, but while conscience directs attention to the self, judgment directs attention to the world. In this respect, judgment makes possible what Arendt calls "the manifestation of the wind of thought" in the sphere of appearance. 5.4 Judgment and Kant's Aesthetics The foregoing account has explored the way in which Arendt attempted to connect the activity of thinking to our capacity to judge. To be sure, this connection of thinking and judging seems to operate only in emergencies, in those exceptional moments where individuals, faced with the collapse of traditional standards, must come up with new ones and judge according to their own autonomous values. There is, however, a second, more elaborated view of judgment which does not restrict it to moments of crisis, but which identifies it with the capacity to think representatively, that is, from the standpoint of everyone else. Arendt called this capacity to think representatively an "enlarged mentality," adopting the same terms that Kant employed in his Third Critique to characterize aesthetic judgment. It is to this work that we must now turn our attention, since Arendt based her theory of political judgment on Kant's aesthetics rather than on his moral philosophy. At first sight this might seem a puzzling choice, since Kant himself based his moral and political philosophy on practical reason and not on our aesthetic faculties. Arendt, however, claimed that the Critique of Judgment contained Kant's unwritten political philosophy, and that the first part of it, the "Critique of Aesthetic Judgment," was the most fruitful basis on which to build a theory of political judgment, since it dealt with the world of appearances from the point of view of the judging spectator and took as its starting point the faculty of taste, understood as a faculty of concrete and embodied subjects (BPF, 219–20). For Arendt the capacity to judge is a specifically political ability insofar as it enables individuals to orient themselves in the public realm and to judge the phenomena that are disclosed within it from a standpoint that is relatively detached and impartial. She credits Kant with having dislodged the prejudice that judgments of taste lie altogether outside the political realm, since they supposedly concern only aesthetic matters. She believes, in fact, that by linking taste to that wider manner of thinking which Kant called an "enlarged mentality" the way was opened to a revaluation of judgment as a specific political ability, namely, as the ability to think in the place of everybody else. It is only in Kant's Critique of Judgment that we find a conception of judgment as the ability to deal with particulars in their particularity, that is, without subsuming them under a pre-given universal, but actively searching the universal out of the particular. Kant formulated this distinction as that between determinant and reflective judgments. For him judgment in general is the faculty of thinking the particular as contained under the universal. If the universal, (the rule, principle, or law) is given, then the judgment which subsumes the particular under it is determinant. If, however, only the particular is given and the universal has to be found for it, then the judgment is reflective. For Kant determinant judgments were cognitive, while reflective judgments were non-cognitive. Reflective judgment is seen as the capacity to ascend from the particular to the universal without the mediation of determinate concepts given in advance; it is reasoning about particulars in their relation to the universal rather than reasoning about universals in their relation to the particular. In the case of aesthetic judgment this means that one can understand and apply the universal predicate of beauty only through experiencing a particular object that exemplifies it. Thus, upon encountering a flower, a unique landscape, or a particular painting, one is able to say that it is an example of beauty, that it possesses "exemplary validity." For Arendt this notion of exemplary validity is not restricted to aesthetic objects or to individuals who exemplified certain virtues. Rather, she wants to extend this notion to events in the past that carry a meaning beyond their sheer enactment, that is, to events that could be seen as exemplary for those who came after. It is here that aesthetic judgment joins with the retrospective judgment of the historian. The American and French Revolutions, the Paris Commune, the Russian soviets, the German revolutionary councils of 1918–19, the Hungarian uprising of 1956, all these events possess the kind of exemplary validity that makes them of universal significance, while still retaining their own specificity and uniqueness. Thus, by attending to these events in their particularity the historian or judging spectator is able to illuminate their universal import and thereby preserve them as "examples" for posterity. For Arendt it is the spectators who have the privilege of judging impartially and disinterestedly, and in doing so they exercise two crucial faculties, imagination and common sense. Imagination is the faculty of representing in one's mind that which has already appeared to one's senses. Through the imagination one can represent objects that are no longer present and thus establish the distance necessary for an impartial judgment. Once this distancing has occurred, one is in a position to reflect upon these representations from a number of different perspectives, and thereby to reach a judgment about the proper value of an object. The other faculty that spectators have to appeal to is common sense or sensus communis, since without it they could not share their judgments or overcome their individual idiosyncrasies. Kant believed that for our judgments to be valid we must transcend our private or subjective conditions in favor of public and intersubjective ones, and we are able to do this by appealing to our community sense, our sensus communis. The criterion for judgment, then, is communicability, and the standard for deciding whether our judgments are indeed communicable is to see whether they could fit with the sensus communis of others. Arendt points out that the emphasis on the communicability of judgments of taste, and the correlative notion of an enlarged mentality, link up effortlessly with Kant's idea of a united mankind living in eternal peace. She argues that "It is by virtue of this idea of mankind, present in every single man, that men are human, and they can be called civilized or humane to the extent that this idea becomes the principle not only of their judgments but of their actions. It is at this point that actor and spectator become united; the maxim of the actor and the maxim, the 'standard,' according to which the spectator judges the spectacle of the world, become one" (LKPP, 75). In her reflections on Kant's Third Critique Arendt acknowledges the links between the standpoint of the actor and that of the spectator. Let us now examine the way in which judgment operates from the standpoint of the actor. 5.5 Judgment and the Vita Activa Arendt presented a model of judgment in the essays “The Crisis in Culture” and “Truth and Politics” which could be characterized as far more ‘political’ than the one presented so far. In these essays, in fact, she treated judgment as a faculty that enables political actors to decide what courses of action to undertake in the public realm, what kind of objectives are most appropriate or worth pursuing, as well as who to praise or blame for past actions or for the consequences of past decisions. In this model judgment is viewed as a specifically political ability, namely, as “the ability to see things not only from one’s own point of view but from the perspective of all those who happen to be present,” and as being “one of the fundamental abilities of man as a political being insofar as it enables him to orient himself in the public realm, in the common world” (BPF, 221). Arendt claims that “the Greeks called this ability [to judge] phronesis, or insight, and they considered it the principal virtue or excellence of the statesman in distinction from the wisdom of the philosopher. The difference between this judging insight and speculative thought lies in that the former has its roots in what we usually call common sense, which the latter constantly transcends. Common sense ... discloses to us the nature of the world insofar as it is a common world; we owe to it the fact that our strictly private and ‘subjective’ five senses and their sensory data can adjust themselves to a non-subjective and ‘objective’ world which we have in common and share with others. Judging is one, if not the most, important activity in which this sharing-the-world-with-others comes to pass” (BPF, 221). Moreover, in discussing the non-coercive character of judgment, the fact that it can only appeal to but never force the agreement of others, she claims that “this ‘wooing’ or persuading corresponds closely to what the Greeks called peithein, the convincing and persuading speech which they regarded as the typically political form of people talking with one another" (BPF, 222). Some commentators have claimed that there is a contradiction in Arendt's employment of the Aristotelian notion of phronesis alongside Kant's idea of an "enlarged mentality," since they supposedly pull in opposite directions, the former toward a concern with the particular, the latter toward universality and impartiality. However, this contradiction is more apparent than real, since Kant's theory of aesthetic judgment is a theory of reflective judgment, that is, of those judgments where the universal is not given but must be searched out of the particular. In this respect the theory of aesthetic judgment to which Arendt appeals does have close affinities with Aristotle's notion of phronesis: both are concerned with the judgment of particulars qua particulars, not with their subsumption under universal rules. If a distinction is to be made, it has more to do with the mode of asserting validity: In Aristotle phronesis is the privilege of a few experienced individuals (the phronimoi) who, over time, have shown themselves to be wise in practical matters; the only criterion of validity is their experience and their past record of judiciuos actions. In the case of judgments of taste, on the other hand, individuals have to appeal to the judgments and opinions of others, and thus the validity of their judgments rests on the consent they can elicit from a community of differently situated subjects. For Arendt the validity of political judgment depends on our ability to think "representatively," that is, from the standpoint of everyone else, so that we are able to look at the world from a number of different perspectives. And this ability, in turn, can only be acquired and tested in a public forum where individuals have the opportunity to exchange their opinions on particular matters and see whether they accord with the opinions of others. In this respect the process of opinion formation is never a solitary activity; rather, it requires a genuine encounter with different opinions so that a particular issue may be examined from every possible standpoint until, as she puts it, "it is flooded and made transparent by the full light of human comprehension" (BPF, 242). Debate and discussion, and the capacity to enlarge one's perspective, are indeed crucial to the formation of opinions that can claim more than subjective validity; individuals may hold personal opinions on many subject matters, but they can form representative opinions only by enlarging their standpoint to incorporate those of others. As Arendt says: Political thought is representative. I form an opinion by considering a given issue from different viewpoints, by making present to my mind the standpoints of those who are absent; that is, I represent them ... The more people's standpoints I have present in my mind while I am pondering a given issue, and the better I can imagine how I would feel and think if I were in their place, the stronger will be my capacity for representative thinking and the more valid my final conclusions, my opinion. (BPF, 241) Opinions, in fact, are never self-evident. In matters of opinion, but not in matters of truth, "our thinking is truly discursive, running, as it were, from place to place, from one part of the world to another, through all kinds of conflicting views, until it finally ascends from these particularities to some impartial generality" (BPF, 242). In this respect one is never alone while forming an opinion; as Arendt notes, "even if I shun all company or am completely isolated while forming an opinion, I am not simply together only with myself in the solitude of philosophical thought; I remain in this world of universal interdependence, where I can make myself the representative of everybody else" (BPF, 242). 5.6 Judgment and Validity The representative character of judgment and opinion has important implications for the question of validity. Arendt always stressed that the formation of valid opinions requires a public space where individuals can test and purify their views through a process of mutual debate and enlightenment. She was, however, quite opposed to the idea that opinions should be measured by the standard of truth, or that debate should be conducted according to strict scientific standards of validity. In her view, truth belongs to the realm of cognition, the realm of logic, mathematics and the strict sciences, and carries always an element of coercion, since it precludes debate and must be accepted by every individual in possession of her rational faculties. Set against the plurality of opinions, truth has a despotic character: it compels universal assent, leaves the mind little freedom of movement, eliminates the diversity of views and reduces the richness of human discourse. In this respect, truth is anti-political, since by eliminating debate and diversity it eliminates the very principles of political life. As Arendt writes, "The trouble is that factual truth, like all other truth, peremptorily claims to be acknowledged and precludes debate, and debate constitutes the very essence of political life. The modes of thought and communication that deal with truth, if seen from the political perspective, are necessarily domineering; they don't take into account other people's opinions, and taking these into account is the hallmark of all strictly political thinking" (BPF, 241). Arendt's defense of opinion is motivated not just by her belief that truth leaves no room for debate or dissent, or for the acknowledgment of difference, but also by her conviction that our reasoning faculties can only flourish in a dialogic context. She cites Kant's remark that "the external power that deprives man of the freedom to communicate his thoughts publicly deprives him at the same time of his freedom to think," and underlines the fact that for Kant the only guarantee of the correctness of our thinking is that "we think, as it were, in community with others to whom we communicate our thoughts as they communicate theirs to us" (BPF, 234–5). She also quotes Madison's statement that "the reason of man, like man himself, is timid and cautious when left alone, and acquires firmness and confidence in proportion to the number with which it is associated" (BPF, 234). The appeal to Kant and Madison is meant to vindicate the power and dignity of opinion against those thinkers, from Plato to Hobbes, who saw it as mere illusion, as a confused or inadequate grasp of the truth. For Arendt opinion is not a defective form of knowledge that should be transcended or left behind as soon as one is in possession of the truth. Rather, it is a distinct form of knowledge which arises out of the collective deliberation of citizens, and which requires the use of the imagination and the capacity to think "representatively." By deliberating in common and engaging in "representative thinking" citizens are in fact able to form opinions that can claim intersubjective validity. It is important to stress that Arendt does not want to dismiss the philosophers' attempt to find universal or absolute standards of knowledge and cognition, but to check their desire to impose those standards upon the sphere of human affairs, since they would eliminate its plurality and essential relativity. The imposition of a single or absolute standard into the domain of praxis would do away with the need to persuade others of the relative merits of an opinion, to elicit their consent to a specific proposal, or to obtain their agreement with respect to a particular policy. Indeed, for Arendt the imposition of such a standard would mean that individuals would no longer be required to exercise their judgment, develop their imagination, or cultivate an "enlarged mentality," since they would no longer need to deliberate in common. Strict demonstration, rather than persuasive argumentation, would then become the only legitimate form of discourse. Now, we must be careful not to impute to Arendt the view that truth has no legitimate role to play in politics or in the sphere of human affairs. She does indeed assert that "All truths — not only the various kinds of rational truth but also factual truth — are opposed to opinion in their mode of asserting validity" (BPF, 239), since they all carry an element of compulsion. However, she is only preoccupied with the negative consequences of rational truth when applied to the sphere of politics and collective deliberation, while she defends the importance of factual truth for the preservation of an accurate account of the past and for the very existence of political communities. Factual truth, she writes, "is always related to other people: it concerns events and circumstances in which many are involved; it is established by witnesses and depends upon testimony ... It is political by nature." It follows, therefore, that "facts and opinions, though they must be kept apart, are not antagonistic to each other; they belong to the same realm. Facts inform opinions, and opinions, inspired by different interests and passions, can differ widely and still be legitimate as long as they respect factual truth. Freedom of opinion is a farce unless factual information is guaranteed and the facts themselves are not in dispute. In other words, factual truth informs political thought just as rational truth informs philosophical speculation" (BPF, 238). The relationship between facts and opinions is thus one of mutual entailment: if opinions were not based on correct information and the free access to all relevant facts they could scarcely claim any validity. And if they were to be based on fantasy, self-deception, or deliberate falsehood, then no possibility of genuine debate and argumentation could be sustained. Both factual truth and the general habit of truth-telling are therefore basic to the formation of sound opinions and to the flourishing of political debate. Moreover, if the record of the past were to be destroyed by organized lying, or be distorted by an attempt to rewrite history, political life would be deprived of one of its essential and stabilizing elements. In sum, both factual truth and the practice of truth-telling are essential to political life. The antagonism for Arendt is between rational truth and well-grounded opinion, since the former does not allow for debate and dissent, while the latter thrives on it. Arendt's defense of opinion must therefore be understood as a defense of political deliberation, and of the role that persuasion and dissuasion play in all matters affecting the political community. Against Plato and Hobbes, who denigrated the role of opinion in political matters, Arendt reasserts the value and importance of political discourse, of deliberation and persuasion, and thus of a politics that acknowledges difference and the plurality of opinions. 6. Arendt's Conception of Citizenship In this last section, we reconstruct Arendt's conception of citizenship around two themes: (1) the public sphere, and (2) political agency and collective identity, and to highlight the contribution of Arendt's conception to a theory of democratic citizenship. 6.1 Citizenship and the Public Sphere For Arendt the public sphere comprises two distinct but interrelated dimensions. The first is the space of appearance, a space of political freedom and equality which comes into being whenever citizens act in concert through the medium of speech and persuasion. The second is the common world, a shared and public world of human artifacts, institutions and settings which separates us from nature and which provides a relatively permanent and durable context for our activities. Both dimensions are essential to the practice of citizenship, the former providing the spaces where it can flourish, the latter providing the stable background from which public spaces of action and deliberation can arise. For Arendt the reactivation of citizenship in the modern world depends upon both the recovery of a common, shared world and the creation of numerous spaces of appearance in which individuals can disclose their identities and establish relations of reciprocity and solidarity. There are three features of the public sphere and of the sphere of politics in general that are central to Arendt's conception of citizenship. These are, first, its artificial or constructed quality; second, its spatial quality; and, third, the distinction between public and private interests. As regards the first feature, Arendt always stressed the artificiality of public life and of political activities in general, the fact that they are man-made and constructed rather than natural or given. She regarded this artificiality as something to be celebrated rather than deplored. Politics for her was not the result of some natural predisposition, or the realization of the inherent traits of human nature. Rather, it was a cultural achievement of the first order, enabling individuals to transcend the necessities of life and to fashion a world within which free political action and discourse could flourish. The stress on the artificiality of politics has a number of important consequences. For example, Arendt emphasized that the principle of political equality does not rest on a theory of natural rights or on some natural condition that precedes the constitution of the political realm. Rather, it is an attribute of citizenship which individuals acquire upon entering the public realm and which can be secured only by democratic political institutions. Another consequence of Arendt's stress on the artificiality of political life is evident in her rejection of all neo-romantic appeals to the volk and to ethnic identity as the basis for political community. She maintained that one's ethnic, religious, or racial identity was irrelevant to one's identity as a citizen, and that it should never be made the basis of membership in a political community. Arendt's emphasis on the formal qualities of citizenship made her position rather distant from those advocates of participation in the 1960s who saw it in terms of recapturing a sense of intimacy, of warmth and authenticity. For Arendt political participation was important because it permitted the establishment of relations of civility and solidarity among citizens. She claimed that the ties of intimacy and warmth can never become political since they represent psychological substitutes for the loss of the common world. The only truly political ties are those of civic friendship and solidarity, since they make political demands and preserve reference to the world. For Arendt, therefore, the danger of trying to recapture the sense of intimacy and warmth, of authenticity and communal feelings is that one loses the public values of impartiality, civic friendship, and solidarity. The second feature stressed by Arendt has to do with the spatial quality of public life, with the fact that political activities are located in a public space where citizens are able to meet one another, exchange their opinions and debate their differences, and search for some collective solution to their problems. Politics, for Arendt, is a matter of people sharing a common world and a common space of appearance so that public concerns can emerge and be articulated from different perspectives. In her view, it is not enough to have a collection of private individuals voting separately and anonymously according to their private opinions. Rather, these individuals must be able to see and talk to one another in public, to meet in a public-political space, so that their differences as well as their commonalities can emerge and become the subject of democratic debate. This notion of a common public space helps us to understand how political opinions can be formed which are neither reducible to private, idiosyncratic preferences, on the one hand, nor to a unanimous collective opinion, on the other. Arendt herself distrusted the term "public opinion," since it suggested the mindless unanimity of mass society. In her view representative opinions could arise only when citizens actually confronted one another in a public space, so that they could examine an issue from a number of different perspectives, modify their views, and enlarge their standpoint to incorporate that of others. Political opinions, she claimed, can never be formed in private; rather, they are formed, tested, and enlarged only within a public context of argumentation and debate. Another implication of Arendt's stress on the spatial quality of politics has to do with the question of how a collection of distinct individuals can be united to form a political community. For Arendt the unity that may be achieved in a political community is neither the result of religious or ethnic affinity, not the expression of some common value system. Rather, the unity in question can be attained by sharing a public space and a set of political institutions, and engaging in the practices and activities which are characteristic of that space and those institutions. A further implication of Arendt's conception of the spatial quality of politics is that since politics is a public activity, one cannot be part of it without in some sense being present in a public space. To be engaged in politics means actively participating in the various public forums where the decisions affecting one's community are taken. Arendt's insistence on the importance of direct participation in politics is thus based on the idea that, since politics is something that needs a worldly location and can only happen in a public space, then if one is not present in such a space one is simply not engaged in politics. This public or world-centered conception of politics lies also at the basis of the third feature stressed by Arendt, the distinction between public and private interests. According to Arendt, political activity is not a means to an end, but an end in itself; one does not engage in political action to promote one's welfare, but to realize the principles intrinsic to political life, such as freedom, equality, justice, and solidarity. In a late essay entitled "Public Rights and Private Interests" (PRPI) Arendt discusses the difference between one's life as an individual and one's life as a citizen, between the life spent on one's own and the life spent in common with others. She argues that our public interest as citizens is quite distinct from our private interest as individuals. The public interest is not the sum of private interests, nor their highest common denominator, nor even the total of enlightened self-interests. In fact, it has little to do with our private interests, since it concerns the world that lies beyond the self, that was there before our birth and that will be there after our death, a world that finds embodiment in activities and institutions with their own intrinsic purposes which might often be at odds with our short-term and private interests. The public interest refers, therefore, to the interests of a public world which we share as citizens and which we can pursue and enjoy only by going beyond our private self-interest. 6.2 Citizenship, Agency, and Collective Identity Arendt's participatory conception of citizenship provides the best starting point for addressing both the question of the constitution of collective identity and that concerning the conditions for the exercise of effective political agency. With respect to the first claim, it is important to note that one of the crucial questions at stake in political discourse is the creation of a collective identity, a "we" to which we can appeal when faced with the problem of deciding among alternative courses of action. Since in political discourse there is always disagreement about the possible courses of action, the identity of the "we" that is going to be created through a specific form of action becomes a central question. By engaging in this or that course of action we are, in fact, entering a claim on behalf of a "we," that is, we are creating a specific form of collective identity. Political action and discourse are, in this respect, essential to the constitution of collective identities. This process of identity-construction, however, is never given once and for all and is never unproblematic. Rather, it is a process of constant renegotiation and struggle, a process in which actors articulate and defend competing conceptions of cultural and political identity. Arendt's participatory conception of citizenship is particularly relevant in this context since it articulates the conditions for the establishment of collective identities. Once citizenship is viewed as the process of active deliberation about competing identities, its value resides in the possibility of establishing forms of collective identity that can be acknowledged, tested, and transformed in a discursive and democratic fashion. With respect to the second claim, concerning the question of political agency, it is important to stress the connection that Arendt establishes between political action, understood as the active engagement of citizens in the public realm, and the exercise of effective political agency. This connection between action and agency is one of the central contributions of Arendt's participatory conception of citizenship. According to Arendt, the active engagement of citizens in the determination of the affairs of their community provides them not only with the experience of public freedom and public happiness, but also with a sense of political agency and efficacy

Hannah Arendt, one of the leading political thinkers of the twentieth century, was born in 1906 in Hanover and died in New York in 1975. In 1924, after having completed her high school studies, she went to Marburg University to study with Martin Heidegger. The encounter with Heidegger, with whom she had a brief but intense love-affair, had a lasting influence on her thought. After a year of study in Marburg, she moved to Freiburg University where she spent one semester attending the lectures of Edmund Husserl. In the spring of 1926 she went to Heidelberg University to study with Karl Jaspers, a philosopher with whom she established a long-lasting intellectual and personal friendship. She completed her doctoral dissertation, entitled *Der Liebesbegriff bei Augustin* (hereafter LA) under Jaspers's supervision in 1929. She was forced to flee Germany in 1933 as a result of Hitler's rise to power, and after a brief stay in Prague and Geneva she moved to Paris where for six years (1933–39) she worked for a number of Jewish refugee organisations. In 1936 she separated from her first husband, Günther

Stern, and started to live with Heinrich Blücher, whom she married in 1940. During her stay in Paris she continued to work on her biography of *Rahel Varnhagen*, which was not published until 1957 (hereafter RV). In 1941 she was forced to leave France and moved to New York with her husband and mother. In New York she soon became part of an influential circle of writers and intellectuals gathered around the journal *Partisan Review*. During the post-war period she lectured at a number of American universities, including Princeton, Berkeley and Chicago, but was most closely associated with the New School for Social Research, where she was a professor of political philosophy until her death in 1975. In 1951 she published *The Origins of Totalitarianism* (hereafter OT), a major study of the Nazi and Stalinist regimes that soon became a classic, followed by *The Human Condition* in 1958 (hereafter HC), her most important philosophical work. In 1961 she attended the trial of Adolf Eichmann in Jerusalem as a reporter for *The New Yorker* magazine, and two years later published *Eichmann in Jerusalem* (hereafter EJ), which caused a deep controversy in Jewish circles. The same year saw the publication of *On Revolution* (hereafter OR), a comparative analysis of the American and French revolutions. A number of important essays were also published during the 1960s and early 1970s: a first collection was entitled *Between Past and Future* (hereafter BPF), a second *Men in Dark Times* (hereafter MDT), and a third *Crises of the Republic* (hereafter CR). At the time of her death in 1975, she had completed the first two volumes on *Thinking* and *Willing* of her last major philosophical work, *The Life of the Mind*, which was published posthumously in 1978 (hereafter LM). The third volume, on *Judging*, was left unfinished, but some background material and lecture notes were published in 1982 under the title *Lectures on Kant's Political Philosophy* (hereafter LKPP).

Hannah Arendt was one of the seminal political thinkers of the twentieth century. The power and originality of her thinking was evident in works such as *The Origins of Totalitarianism, The Human Condition, On Revolution* and *The Life of the Mind*. In these works and in numerous essays she grappled with the most crucial political events of her time, trying to grasp their meaning and historical import, and showing how they affected our categories of moral and political judgment. What was required, in her view, was a new framework that could enable us to come to terms with the twin horrors of the twentieth century, Nazism and Stalinism. She provided such framework in her book on totalitarianism, and went on to develop a new set of philosophical categories that could illuminate the human condition and provide a fresh perspective on the nature of political life.

Although some of her works now belong to the classics of the Western tradition of political thought, she has always remained difficult to classify. Her political philosophy cannot be characterized in terms of the traditional categories of conservatism, liberalism, and socialism. Nor can her thinking be assimilated to the recent revival of communitarian political thought, to be found, for example, in the writings of A. MacIntyre, M. Sandel, C. Taylor and M. Walzer. Her name has been invoked by a number of critics of the liberal tradition, on the grounds that she presented a vision of politics that stood in opposition some key liberal principles. There are many strands of Arendt's thought that could justify such a claim, in particular, her critique of representative democracy, her stress on civic engagement and political deliberation, her separation of morality from politics, and her praise of the revolutionary tradition. However, it would be a mistake to view Arendt as an anti-liberal thinker. Arendt was in fact a stern defender of constitutionalism and the rule of law, an advocate of fundamental human rights (among which she included not only the right to life, liberty, and freedom of expression, but also the right to action and to opinion), and a critic of all forms of political community based on traditional ties and customs, as well as those based on religious, ethnic, or racial identity.

Arendt's political thought cannot, in this sense, be identified either with the liberal tradition or with the claims advanced by a number of its critics. Arendt did not conceive of politics as a means for the satisfaction of individual preferences, nor as a way to integrate individuals around a shared conception of the good. Her conception of politics is based instead on the idea of active citizenship, that is, on the value and importance of civic engagement and collective deliberation about all matters affecting the political community. If there is a tradition of thought with which Arendt can be identified, it is the classical tradition of civic republicanism originating in Aristotle and embodied in the writings of Machiavelli, Montesquieu, Jefferson, and Tocqueville. According to this tradition politics finds its authentic expression whenever citizens gather together in a public space to deliberate and decide about matters of collective concern. Political activity is valued not because it may lead to agreement or to a shared conception of the good, but because it enables each citizen to exercise his or her powers of agency, to develop the capacities for judgment and to attain by concerted action some measure of political efficacy.

In what follows, we reconstruct Arendt's political philosophy along four major themes: (1) her conception of modernity, (2) her theory of action, (3) her theory of judgment, and (4) her conception of citizenship.

Arendt's Conception of Modernity

In her major philosophical work, *The Human Condition*, and in some of the essays collected in *Between Past and Future*, Arendt articulated a fairly negative conception of modernity. In these writings Arendt is primarily concerned with the losses incurred as a result of the eclipse of tradition, religion, and authority, but she offers a number of illuminating suggestions with respect to the resources that the modern age can still provide to address questions of meaning, identity, and value.

For Arendt modernity is characterized by the *loss of the world*, by which she means the restriction or elimination of the public sphere of action and speech in favor of the private world of introspection and the private pursuit of economic interests. Modernity is the age of mass society, of the rise of the *social* out of a previous distinction between the public and the private, and of the victory of *animal laborans* over *homo faber* and the classical conception of man as *zoon politikon*. Modernity is the age of bureaucratic administration and anonymous labor, rather than politics and action, of elite domination and the manipulation of public opinion. It is the age when totalitarian forms of government, such as Nazism and Stalinism, have emerged as a result of the institutionalization of terror and violence. It is the age where history as a "natural process" has replaced history as a fabric of actions and events, where homogeneity and conformity have replaced plurality and freedom, and where isolation and loneliness have eroded human solidarity and all spontaneous forms of living together. Modernity is the age where the past no longer carries any certainty of evaluation, where individuals, having lost their traditional standards and values, must search for new grounds of human community as such.

This is Arendt's vision of modernity, a vision which, at first sight, appears quite stark and unredeeming. It is worth pointing out, however, that Arendt's negative appraisal of modernity was shaped by her experience of totalitarianism in the twentieth century, and that her work provides a number of important insights that may help us to address certain problematic features of the modern age. In her political writings, and especially in *The Origins of Totalitarianism*, Arendt claimed that the phenomenon of totalitarianism has broken the continuity of Occidental history, and has rendered meaningless most of our moral and political categories. The break in our tradition has become irrevocable after the tragic events of the twentieth century and the triumph of totalitarian movements East and West. In the form of Stalinism and Nazism, totalitarianism has exploded the established categories of political thought and the accepted standards of moral judgment, and has thereby broken the continuity of our history. Faced with the tragic events of the Holocaust and the Gulag, we can no longer go back to traditional concepts and values, so as to explain the unprecedented by means of precedents, or to understand the monstrous by means of the familiar. The burden of our time must be faced without the aid of tradition, or as Arendt once put it, "without a bannister" (RPW, 336). Our inherited concepts and criteria for judgment have been dissolved under the impact of modern political events, and the task now is to re-establish the meaning of the past outside the framework of any tradition, since none have retained their original validity. It is the past, then, and not tradition, that Arendt attempts to preserve from the rupture in modern time-consciousness. Only by reappropriating the past by means of what Arendt called "the deadly impact of new thoughts" (MDT, 201) can we hope to restore meaning to the present and throw some light on the contemporary situation.

The hermeneutic strategy that Arendt employed to re-establish a link with the past is indebted to both Walter Benjamin and Martin Heidegger. From Benjamin she took the idea of a fragmentary historiography, one that seeks to identify the moments of rupture, displacement and dislocation in history. Such fragmentary historiography enables one to recover the lost potentials of the past in the hope that they may find actualization in the present. From Heidegger she took the idea of a deconstructive reading of the Western philosophical tradition, one that seeks to uncover the original meaning of our categories and to liberate them from the distorting incrustations of tradition. Such deconstructive hermeneutics enables one to recover those primordial experiences (*Urphaenomene*) which have been occluded or forgotten by the philosophical tradition, and thereby to recover the lost origins of our philosophical concepts and categories.

By relying on these two hermeneutic strategies Arendt hopes to redeem from the past its lost or "forgotten treasure," that is, those fragments from the past that might still be of significance to us. In her view it is no longer possible, after the collapse of tradition, to save the past as a whole; the task, rather, is to redeem from oblivion those elements of the past that are still able to illuminate our situation. To re-establish a linkage with the past is not an antiquarian exercise; on the contrary, without the critical reappropriation of the past our temporal horizon becomes disrupted, our experience precarious, and our identity more fragile. In Arendt's view, then, it is necessary to redeem from the past those moments worth preserving, to save those fragments from past treasures that are significant for us. Only by means of this critical reappropriation can we discover the past anew, endow it with relevance and meaning for the present, and make it a source of inspiration for the future.

This critical reappropriation is facilitated, in part, by the fact that after the rupture in modern time-consciousness the past may "open up to us with unexpected freshness and tell us things no one has yet had ears to hear" (BPF, 94). The breakdown of tradition may in fact provide the great chance to look upon the past "with eyes undistorted by any tradition, with a directness which has disappeared from Occidental reading and hearing ever since Roman civilization submitted to the authority of Greek thought" (BPF, 28–9).

Arendt's return to the original experience of the Greek *polis* represents, in this sense, an attempt to break the fetters of a worn-out tradition and to rediscover a past over which tradition has no longer a claim. Against tradition Arendt sets the criterion of genuineness, against the authoritative that which is forgotten, concealed, or displaced at the margins of history. Only by operating against the grain of traditionalism and the claims of conventional historiography can the past be made meaningful again, provide sources of illumination for the present, and yield its treasures to those who search for them with "new thoughts" and saving acts of remembrance.

Arendt articulates her conception of modernity around a number of key features: these are *world alienation*, *earth alienation*, the rise of the *social*, and the victory of *animal laborans*. World alienation refers to the loss of an intersubjectively constituted world of experience and action by means of which we establish our self-identity and an adequate sense of reality. Earth alienation refers to the attempt to escape from the confines of the earth; spurred by modern science and technology, we have searched for ways to overcome our earth-bound condition by setting out on the exploration of space, by attempting to recreate life under laboratory conditions, and by trying to extend our given life-span. The rise of the social refers to the expansion of the market economy from the early modern period and the ever increasing accumulation of capital and social wealth. With the rise of the social everything has become an object of production and consumption, of acquisition and exchange; moreover, its constant expansion has resulted in the blurring of the distinction between the private and the public. The victory of *animal laborans* refers to the triumph of the values of labor over those of *homo faber* and of man as *zoon politikon*. All the values characteristic of the world of fabrication — permanence, stability, durability — as well as those characteristic of the world of action and speech — freedom, plurality, solidarity — are sacrificed in favor of the values of life, productivity and abundance.

Arendt identifies two main stages in the emergence of modernity: the first, from the sixteenth to the nineteenth century, corresponds to world alienation and the rise of the social, the second, from the beginning of the twentieth century, corresponds to earth alienation and the victory of *animal laborans*. She also identifies a number of causes:

the discovery of America and the corresponding shrinking of the earth, the waves of expropriation started during the Reformation, the invention of the telescope challenging the adequacy of the senses, the rise of modern science and philosophy and subsequently of a conception of man as part of a process of Nature and History, and the expansion of the realm of the economy, of the production and accumulation of social wealth.

Arendt's interpretation of modernity can be criticized on a number of grounds. We focus attention here on two categories employed by Arendt, those of *nature*, and the *social*. With respect to the category of nature, Arendt oscillates between two contrasting accounts. According to the first account, the modern age, by elevating labor, the most natural of human activities, to the highest position within the *vita activa*, has brought us too close to nature. Instead of building and preserving the human artifice and creating public spaces for action and deliberation, we are reduced to engage in the activity of sheer survival and in the production of things that are by definition perishable. According to the second account, however, the modern age is characterized by a growing artificiality, by the rejection of anything that is not man-made. Arendt cites the fact that natural processes, including that of life itself, have been recreated artificially by means of scientific experiment, that our natural environment has been extensively transformed and in some instances entirely replaced by technology, and that we have searched for ways to overcome our natural condition as earth-bound creatures by setting out on the exploration of space and envisaging the possibility of inhabiting other planets. All this leads to a situation where nothing around us will be a naturally given event, object, or process, but will instead be the product of our instruments and the will to refashion the world in our image.

These two accounts are difficult to reconcile, since in the former we have nature intruding upon and even destroying the human artifice, while in the latter we have art (*techne*) expanding upon and replacing everything natural or merely given. The result is to endow nature with an ambiguous status, since in the former case the victory of *animal laborans* indicates our subjection to natural processes, while in the latter case the expansion of scientific knowledge and of technological mastery indicates the overcoming of all natural limits. The modern world would thus appear to be too natural and too artificial, too much under the dominance of labor and the life-process of the species, as well as too much under the dominance of *techne*.

With respect to the second category, that of the social, Arendt was unable to account for certain important features of the modern world. Arendt identifies the social with all those activities formerly restricted to the private sphere of the household and having to do with the necessities of life. Her claim is that, with the tremendous expansion of the economy from the end of the eighteenth century, all such activities have taken over the public realm and transformed it into a sphere for the satisfaction of our material needs. Society has thus invaded and conquered the public realm, turning it into a function of what previously were private needs and concerns, and has thereby destroyed the boundary separating the public and the private. Arendt also claims that with the expansion of the social realm the tripartite division of human activities has been undermined to the point of becoming meaningless. In her view, once the social realm has established its monopoly, the distinction between labor, work and action is lost, since every effort is now expended on reproducing our material conditions of existence. Obsessed with life, productivity, and consumption, we have turned into a society of laborers and jobholders who no longer appreciate the values associated with work, nor those associated with action.

From this brief account it is clear that Arendt's concept of the social plays a crucial role in her assessment of modernity. I would argue, however, that it blinds her to many important issues and leads her to a series of questionable judgments. In the first place, Arendt's characterization of the social is overly restricted. She claims that the social is the realm of labor, of biological and material necessity, of the reproduction of our condition of existence. She also claims that the rise of the social coincides with the expansion of the economy from the end of the eighteenth century. However, having identified the social with the growth of the economy in the past two centuries, Arendt cannot characterize it in terms of a subsistence model of simple reproduction (Benhabib 2003, Ch. 6; Bernstein 1986, Ch. 9; Hansen 1993, Ch. 3; Parekh 1981, Ch. 8). Secondly, Arendt's identification of the social with the activities of the household is responsible for a major shortcoming in her analysis of the economy. She is, in fact, unable to acknowledge that a modern capitalist economy constitutes a structure of power with a highly asymmetric distribution of costs and rewards. By relying on the misleading analogy of the household, she maintains that all questions pertaining to the economy are pre-political, and thus ignores the crucial question of economic power and exploitation (Bernstein 1986, Ch. 9; Hansen 1993, Ch. 3; Parekh 1981, Ch. 8; Pitkin 1998; Pitkin 1994, Ch. 10,

Hinchman and Hinchman; Wolin 1994, Ch. 11, Hinchman and Hinchman). Finally, by insisting on a strict separation between the private and the public, and between the social and the political, she is unable to account for the essential connection between these spheres and the struggles to redraw their boundaries. Today many so-called private issues have become public concerns, and the struggle for justice and equal rights has extended into many spheres. By insulating the political sphere from the concerns of the social, and by maintaining a strict distinction between the public and the private, Arendt is unable to account for some of the most important achievements of modernity — the extension of justice and equal rights, and the redrawing of the boundaries between the public and the private (Benhabib 2003, Ch. 6; Bernstein 1986, Ch. 9; Dietz 2002, Ch. 5; Pitkin 1998; Pitkin 1995, Ch. 3, Honig; Zaretsky 1997, Ch. 8, Calhoun and McGowan).

Arendt's Theory of Action

Arendt's theory of action and her revival of the ancient notion of *praxis* represent one of the most original contributions to twentieth century political thought. By distinguishing action (*praxis*) from fabrication (*poiesis*), by linking it to freedom and plurality, and by showing its connection to speech and remembrance, Arendt is able to articulate a conception of politics in which questions of meaning and identity can be addressed in a fresh and original manner. Moreover, by viewing action as a mode of human togetherness, Arendt is able to develop a conception of participatory democracy which stands in direct contrast to the bureaucratized and elitist forms of politics so characteristic of the modern epoch.

In what follows, we focus on some of the key components of Arendt's theory of action, such as freedom, plurality and disclosure. We then examine the links between action and narrative, the importance of remembrance, and of what may be called "communities of memory." We then show the connection between action, power and the space of appearance. Lastly, we look at the remedies for the unpredictability and irreversibility of action, namely, the power of promise and the power to forgive.

Action, Freedom, and Plurality

Action, the only activity that goes on directly between men without the intermediary of things or matter, corresponds to the human condition of plurality ... this plurality is specifically the condition — not only the *conditio sine qua non*, but the *conditio per quam* — of all political life. (HC, 7)

For Arendt, action is one of the fundamental categories of the human condition and constitutes the highest realization of the *vita activa*. Arendt analyzes the *vita activa* via three categories which correspond to the three fundamental activities of our being-in-the-world: labor, work, and action. Labor is the activity which is tied to the human condition of life, work the activity which is tied to the condition of worldliness, and action the activity tied to the condition of plurality. For Arendt each activity is autonomous, in the sense of having its own distinctive principles and of being judged by different criteria. Labor is judged by its ability to sustain human life, to cater to our biological needs of consumption and reproduction, work is judged by its ability to build and maintain a world fit for human use, and action is judged by its ability to disclose the identity of the agent, to affirm the reality of the world, and to actualize our capacity for freedom.

Although Arendt considers the three activities of labor, work and action equally necessary to a complete human life, in the sense that each contributes in its distinctive way to the realization of our human capacities, it is clear from her writings that she takes action to be the *differentia specifica* of human beings, that which distinguishes them from both the life of animals (who are similar to us insofar as they need to labor to sustain and reproduce themselves) and the life of the gods (with whom we share, intermittently, the activity of contemplation). In this respect the categories of labor and work, while significant in themselves, must be seen as counterpoints to the category of action, helping to differentiate and highlight the place of action within the order of the *vita activa*.

The two central features of action are **freedom** and **plurality**. By freedom Arendt does not mean the ability to choose among a set of possible alternatives (the freedom of choice so dear to the liberal tradition) or the faculty of *liberum arbitrium* which, according to Christian doctrine, was given to us by God. Rather, by freedom Arendt means the capacity to begin, to start something new, to do the unexpected, with which all human beings are endowed by virtue of being born. Action as the realization of freedom is therefore rooted in *natality*, in the fact that each birth represents a new beginning and the introduction of novelty in the world.

To be sure, Arendt recognizes that all activities are in some way related to the phenomenon of natality, since both labor and work are necessary to create and preserve a world into which new human beings are constantly born. However, of the three activities, action is the one most closely connected with natality, because by acting individuals re-enact the miracle of beginning inherent in their birth. For Arendt, the beginning that each of us represents by virtue of being born is actualized every time we act, that is, every time we begin something new. As she puts it: "the new beginning inherent in birth can make itself felt in the world only because the newcomer possesses the capacity of beginning something anew, that is, of acting " (HC, 9).

Arendt also stresses the fact that since action as beginning is rooted in natality, since it is the actualization of freedom, it carries with it the capacity to perform miracles, that is, to introduce what is totally unexpected. "It is in the nature of beginning" — she claims — "that something new is started which cannot be expected from whatever may have happened before. This character of startling unexpectedness is inherent in all beginnings ... The fact that man is capable of action means that the unexpected can be expected from him, that he is able to perform what is infinitely improbable. And this again is possible only because each man is unique, so that with each birth something uniquely new comes into the world " (HC, 177–8).

The birth of every individual is thus the promise of a new beginning: to act means to be able to disclose one's self and to do the unanticipated; and it is entirely in keeping with this conception that most of the concrete examples of action in the modern age that Arendt discusses are cases of revolutions and popular uprisings. Her claim is that "revolutions are the only political events which confront us directly and inevitably with the problem of beginning," (OR, 21) since they represent the attempt to found a new political space, a space where freedom can appear as a worldly reality. The favorite example for Arendt is the American Revolution, because there the act of foundation took the form of a constitution of liberty. Her other examples are the revolutionary clubs of the French Revolution, the Paris Commune of 1871, the creation of Soviets during the Russian Revolution, the French Resistance to Hitler in the Second World War, and the Hungarian revolt of 1956. In all these cases individual men and women had the courage to interrupt their routine activities, to step forward from their private lives in order to create a public space where freedom could appear, and to act in such a way that the memory of their deeds could become a source of inspiration for the future. In doing so, according to Arendt, they rediscovered the truth known to the ancient Greeks that action is the supreme blessing of human life, that which bestows significance to the lives of individuals.

In the book *On Revolution* Arendt devotes much attention to the rediscovery of this truth by those who participated in the American Revolution. In her view the Founding Fathers, although they might have pretended that they longed for private life and engaged in politics only out of a sense of duty, made clear in their letters and recollections that they had discovered unexpected delights in action and had acquired a taste for public freedom and for earning distinction among their peers.

Plurality, to which we may now turn, is the other central feature of action. For if to act means to take the initiative, to introduce the *novum* and the unexpected into the world, it also means that it is not something that can be done in isolation from others, that is, independently of the presence of a plurality of actors who from their different perspectives can judge the quality of what is being enacted. In this respect action needs plurality in the same way that performance artists need an audience; without the presence and acknowledgment of others, action would cease to be a meaningful activity. Action, to the extent that it requires appearing in public, making oneself known through words and deeds, and eliciting the consent of others, can only exist in a context defined by plurality.

Arendt establishes the connection between action and plurality by means of an anthropological argument. In her view just as *life* is the condition that corresponds to the activity of labor and *worldliness* the condition that corresponds to the activity of work, so *plurality* is the condition that corresponds to action. She defines plurality as "the fact that men, not Man, live on the earth and inhabit the world," and says that it is the condition of human action "because we are all the same, that is, human, in such a way that nobody is ever the same as anyone else who ever lived, lives, or will live " (HC, 7–8). Plurality thus refers both to *equality* and *distinction*, to the fact that all human beings belong to the same species and are sufficiently alike to understand one another, but yet no two of them are ever interchangeable, since each of them is an individual endowed with a unique biography and perspective on the world.

It is by virtue of plurality that each of us is capable of acting and relating to others in ways that are unique and distinctive, and in so doing of contributing to a network of actions and relationships that is infinitely complex and unpredictable. This network of actions is what makes up the realm of human affairs, that space where individuals relate directly without the intermediary of things or matter — that is, through language. Let us examine briefly this connection between action and language.

In *The Human Condition* Arendt stresses repeatedly that action is primarily symbolic in character and that the web of human relationships is sustained by communicative interaction (HC, 178–9, 184–6, 199–200). We may formulate it as follows. *Action entails speech*: by means of language we are able to articulate the meaning of our actions and to coordinate the actions of a plurality of agents. Conversely, *speech entails action*, not only in the sense that speech itself is a form of action, or that most acts are performed in the manner of speech, but in the sense that action is often the means whereby we check the sincerity of the speaker. Thus, just as action without speech runs the risk of being meaningless and would be impossible to coordinate with the actions of others, so speech without action would lack one of the means by which we may confirm the veracity of the speaker. As we shall see, this link between action and speech is central to Arendt's characterization of power, that potential which springs up between people when they act "in concert," and which is actualized "only where word and deed have not parted company, where words are not empty and deeds not brutal, where words are not used to veil intentions but to disclose realities, and deeds are not used to violate and destroy but to establish relations and create new realities " (HC, 200).

Action and Speech as Disclosure

Let us now turn to an examination of the disclosing power of action and speech. In the opening section of the chapter on action in *The Human Condition* Arendt discusses one of its central functions, namely, the disclosure of the identity of the agent. In action and speech, she maintains, individuals reveal themselves as the unique individuals they are, disclose to the world their distinct personalities. In terms of Arendt's distinction, they reveal "who" they are as distinct to "what" they are — the latter referring to individual abilities and talents, as well as deficiencies and shortcomings, which are traits all human beings share. Neither labor nor work enable individuals to disclose their identities, to reveal "who" they are as distinct from "what" they are. In labor the individuality of each person is submerged by being bound to a chain of natural necessities, to the constraints imposed by biological survival. When we engage in labor we can only show our sameness, the fact that we all belong to the human species and must attend to the needs of our bodies. In this sphere we do indeed "behave," "perform roles," and "fulfill functions," since we all obey the same imperatives. In work there is more scope for individuality, in that each work of art or production bears the mark of its maker; but the maker is still subordinate to the end product, both in the sense of being guided by a model, and in the sense that the product will generally outlast the maker. Moreover, the end product reveals little about the maker except the fact that he or she was able to make it. It does not tell us who the creator was, only that he or she had certain abilities and talents. It is thus only in action and speech, in interacting with others through words and deeds, that individuals reveal who they personally are and can affirm their unique identities. Action and speech are in this sense very closely related because both contain the answer to the question asked of every newcomer: "Who are you?" This disclosure of the "who" is made possible by both deeds and words, but of the two it is speech that has the closest affinity to revelation. Without the accompaniment of speech, action would lose its revelatory quality and could no longer be identified with an agent. It would lack, as it were, the conditions of ascription of agency.

4.3 Action, Narrative, and Remembrance

We have seen, then, how through action and speech individuals are able to disclose their identities, to reveal their specific uniqueness — their *who* — as distinct from their personal abilities and talents — their *what*. However, while engaging in speech and action individuals can never be sure what kind of self they will reveal. Only retrospectively, that is, only through the stories that will arise from their deeds and performances, will their identity become fully manifest. The function of the storyteller is thus crucial not only for the preservation of the doings and sayings of actors, but also for the full disclosure of the identity of the actor. The narratives of a storyteller, Arendt claims, "tell us more about their subjects, the 'hero' in the center of each story, than any product of human hands ever tells us about the master who produced it" (HC, 184). Without a Plato to tell us who Socrates was, what his conversations with fellow Athenian citizens were like, without a Thucydides to set down Pericles' Funeral Speech and refashion it in his powerful and dramatic style, we would not have known what made Socrates and Pericles such outstanding personalities, nor would the reason for their uniqueness have been made fully manifest. Indeed, it is one of Arendt's most important claims that the meaning of action itself is dependent upon the articulation retrospectively given to it by historians and narrators.

Storytelling, or the weaving of a narrative out of the actions and pronouncements of individuals, is partly constitutive of their meaning, because it enables the retrospective articulation of their significance and import, both for the actors themselves and for the spectators. Being absorbed by their immediate aims and concerns, not aware of the full implications of their actions, actors are often not in a position to assess the true significance of their doings, or to be fully aware of their own motives and intentions. Only when action has run a certain course, and its relationship to other actions has unfolded, can its significance be made fully manifest and be embodied in a narrative, whether of poets or historians. The fact that this narrative is temporally deferred, that it is at some distance from the events it describes, is one of the reasons why it can provide further insight into the motives and aims of the actors.

Narratives can thus provide a measure of truthfulness and a greater degree of significance to the actions of individuals. But they also preserve the memory of deeds through time, and in so doing, they enable these deeds to become sources of inspiration for the future, that is, models to be imitated, and, if possible, surpassed. One of the principal drawbacks of action, Arendt maintains, is to be extremely fragile, to be subject to the erosion of time and to forgetfulness; unlike the products of the activity of work, which acquire a measure of permanence by virtue of their sheer facticity, deeds and words do not survive their enactment unless they are remembered. Remembrance alone, the retelling of deeds *as* stories, can save the lives and deeds of actors from oblivion and futility. And it is precisely for this reason, Arendt points out, that the Greeks valued poetry and history so highly, because they rescued the glorious (as well as the less glorious) deeds of the past for the benefit of future generations (HC, 192 ff; BPF, 63–75). It was the poet's and the historian's political function to preserve the memory of past actions and to make them a source of instruction for the future. Homer was known as the "educator of Hellas," since he immortalized for all those who came after him the events of the Trojan War; Thucydides, in his *History of the Peloponnesian War*, told a story of human ambition and folly, of courage and unchecked greed, of ruthless struggle and inevitable defeat. In their work the past became a repository of instruction, of actions to be emulated as well as deeds to be shunned. Through their narratives the fragility and perishability of human action was overcome and made to outlast the lives of their doers and the limited life-span of their contemporaries.

However, to be preserved, such narratives needed in turn an audience, that is, a community of hearers who became the transmitters of the deeds that had been immortalized. As Sheldon Wolin has aptly put it, "audience is a metaphor for the political community whose nature is to be a community of remembrance" (Wolin 1977, 97). In other words, behind the actor stands the storyteller, but behind the storyteller stands a *community of memory*.

It was one of the primary functions of the *polis* to be precisely such a community, to preserve the words and deeds of its citizens from oblivion and the ravages of time, and thereby to leave a testament for future generations. The Greek *polis*, beyond making possible the sharing of words and deeds and multiplying the occasions to win immortal fame, was meant to remedy the frailty of human affairs. It did this by establishing a framework where action and speech could be recorded and transformed into stories, where every citizen could be a witness and thereby a potential narrator. What the *polis* established, then, was a space where *organized remembrance* could take place, and where, as a result, the mortality of actors and the fragility of human deeds could be partially overcome.

Action, Power, and the Space of Appearance

The metaphor of the *polis* recurs constantly in the writings of Arendt. This is indeed a 'metaphor' because in employing this term Arendt is not simply referring to the political institutions of the Greek city-states, bounded as they were to their time and circumstance, but to all those instances in history where a public realm of action and speech was set up among a community of free and equal citizens. "The *polis*, properly speaking, is not the city-state in its physical location; it is the organization of the people as it arises out of acting and speaking together, and its true space lies between people living together for this purpose, no matter where they happen to be" (HC, 198). Thus the famous motto: "Wherever you go, you will be a *polis*" expressed the conviction among the Greek colonists that the kind of political association they had set up originally could be reproduced in their new settlements, that the space created by the "sharing of words and deeds" could find its proper location almost anywhere.

For Arendt, therefore, the *polis* stands for the **space of appearance**, for that space "where I appear to others as others appear to me, where men exist not merely like other living or inanimate things, but to make their appearance explicitly." Such public space of appearance can be always recreated anew wherever individuals gather together politically, that is, "wherever men are together in the manner of speech and action" (HC, 198–9). However, since it is a creation of action, this space of appearance is highly fragile and exists only when actualized through the performance of deeds or the utterance of words. Its peculiarity, as Arendt says, is that "unlike the spaces which are the work of our hands, it does not survive the actuality of the movement which brought it into being, but disappears not only with the dispersal of men — as in the case of great catastrophes when the body politic of a people is destroyed — but with the disappearance or arrest of the activities themselves. Wherever people gather together, it is potentially there, but only potentially, not necessarily and not forever" (HC, 199).

The space of appearance must be continually recreated by action; its existence is secured whenever actors gather together for the purpose of discussing and deliberating about matters of public concern, and it disappears the moment these activities cease. It is always a potential space that finds its actualization in the actions and speeches of individuals who have come together to undertake some common project. It may arise suddenly, as in the case of revolutions, or it may develop slowly out of the efforts to change some specific piece of legislation or policy. Historically, it has been recreated whenever public spaces of action and deliberation have been set up, from town hall meetings to workers' councils, from demonstrations and sit-ins to struggles for justice and equal rights.

This capacity to act in concert for a public-political purpose is what Arendt calls **power**. Power needs to be distinguished from strength, force, and violence (CR, 143–55). Unlike strength, it is not the property of an individual, but of a plurality of actors joining together for some common political purpose. Unlike force, it is not a natural phenomenon but a human creation, the outcome of collective engagement. And unlike violence, it is based not on coercion but on consent and rational persuasion.

For Arendt, power is a *sui generis* phenomenon, since it is a product of action and rests entirely on persuasion. It is a product of action because it arises out of the concerted activities of a plurality of agents, and it rests on persuasion because it consists in the ability to secure the consent of others through unconstrained discussion and debate. Its only limitation is the existence of other people, but this limitation, she notes, "is not accidental, because human power corresponds to the condition of plurality to begin with" (HC, 201). It is actualized in all those cases where action is undertaken for communicative (rather than strategic or instrumental) purposes, and where speech is employed to disclose our intentions and to articulate our motives to others.

Arendt maintains that the legitimacy of power is derived from the initial getting together of people, that is, from the original pact of association that establishes a political community, and is reaffirmed whenever individuals act in concert through the medium of speech and persuasion. For her "power needs no justification, being inherent in the very existence of political communities; what it does need is legitimacy ... Power springs up whenever people get together and act in concert, but it derives its legitimacy from the initial getting together rather than from any action that then may follow" (CR, 151).

Beyond appealing to the past, power also relies for its continued legitimacy on the rationally binding commitments that arise out of a process of free and undistorted communication. Because of this, power is highly independent of material factors: it is sustained not by economic, bureaucratic or military means, but by the power of common convictions that result from a process of fair and unconstrained deliberation.

Power is also not something that can be relied upon at all times or accumulated and stored for future use. Rather, it exists only as a potential which is actualized when actors gather together for political action and public deliberation. It is thus closely connected to the space of appearance, that public space which arises out of the actions and speeches of individuals. Indeed, for Arendt, "power is what keeps the public realm, the potential space of appearance between acting and speaking men, in existence." Like the space of appearance, power is always "a power potential and not an unchangeable, measurable and reliable entity like force or strength ... [it] springs up between men when they act together and vanishes the moment they disperse" (HC, 200).

Power, then, lies at the basis of every political community and is the expression of a potential that is always available to actors. It is also the source of legitimacy of political and governmental institutions, the means whereby they are transformed and adapted to new circumstances and made to respond to the opinions and needs of the citizens. "It is the people's support that lends power to the institutions of a country, and this support is but the continuation of the consent that brought the laws into existence to begin with ... All political institutions are manifestations and materializations of power; they petrify and decay as soon as the living power of the people ceases to uphold them" (CR, 140).

The legitimacy of political institutions is dependent on the power, that is, the active consent of the people; and insofar as governments may be viewed as attempts to preserve power for future generations by institutionalizing it, they require for their vitality the continuing support and active involvement of all citizens.

Action, Unpredictability, and Irreversibility

The discussion of Arendt's theory of action so far has stressed a number of features, chief among which is action's capacity to disclose the identity of the agent, to enable freedom to appear and be actualized as a worldly reality, to create and sustain a public space of appearance, and to make possible the generation of power. We have also emphasized the importance of narrative and remembrance, of the retrospective articulation of the meaning of action by means of storytelling and its preservation through a community of memory. In conclusion, we examine two other features of action, namely, **unpredictability** and **irreversibility**, and their respective remedies, the power of promise and the power to forgive.

Action is unpredictable because it is a manifestation of freedom, of the capacity to innovate and to alter situations by engaging in them; but also, and primarily, because it takes place within the web of human relationships, within a context defined by plurality, so that no actor can control its final outcome. Each actor sets off processes and enters into the inextricable web of actions and events to which all other actors also contribute, with the result that the outcome can never be predicted from the intentions of any particular actor. The open and unpredictable nature of action is a consequence of human freedom and plurality: by acting we are free to start processes and bring about new events, but no actor has the power to control the consequences of his or her deeds.

Another and related reason for the unpredictability of action is that its consequences are boundless: every act sets in motion an unlimited number of actions and reactions which have literally no end. As Arendt puts it: "The reason why we are never able to foretell with certainty the outcome and end of any action is simply that action has no end" (HC, 233). This is because action "though it may proceed from nowhere, so to speak, acts into a medium where every action becomes a chain reaction and where every process is the cause of new processes ... the smallest act in the most limited circumstances bears the seed of the same boundlessness, because one deed, and sometimes one word, suffices to change every constellation" (HC, 190).

Closely connected to the boundlessness and unpredictability of action is its irreversibility. Every action sets off processes which cannot be undone or retrieved in the way, say, we are able to undo a faulty product of our hands. If one builds an artifact and is not satisfied with it, it can always be destroyed and recreated again. This is impossible where action is concerned, because action always takes place within an already existing web of human relationships, where every action becomes a reaction, every deed a source of future deeds, and none of these can be stopped or subsequently undone. The consequences of each act are thus not only unpredictable but also irreversible; the processes started by action can neither be controlled nor be reversed.

The remedy which the tradition of Western thought has proposed for the unpredictability and irreversibility of action has consisted in abstaining from action altogether, in the withdrawal from the sphere of interaction with others, in the hope that one's freedom and integrity could thereby be preserved. Platonism, Stoicism and Christianity elevated the sphere of contemplation above the sphere of action, precisely because in the former one could be free from the entanglements and frustrations of action. Arendt's proposal, by contrast, is not to turn one's back on the realm of human affairs, but to rely on two faculties inherent in action itself, the faculty of **forgiving** and the faculty of **promising**. These two faculties are closely connected, the former mitigating the irreversibility of action by absolving the actor from the unintended consequences of his or her deeds, the latter moderating the uncertainty of its outcome by binding actors to certain courses of action and thereby setting some limit to the unpredictability of the future. Both faculties are, in this respect, connected to *temporality*: from the standpoint of the present forgiving looks backward to what has happened and absolves the actor from what was unintentionally done, while promising looks forward as it seeks to establish islands of security in an otherwise uncertain and unpredictable future.

Forgiving enables us to come to terms with the past and liberates us to some extent from the burden of irreversibility; promising allows us to face the future and to set some bounds to its unpredictability. As Arendt puts it: "Without being forgiven, released from the consequences of what we have done, our capacity to act would, as it were, be confined to one single deed from which we could never recover; we would remain the victims of its consequences forever." On the other hand, "without being bound to the fulfillment of promises, we would never be able to keep our identities; we would be condemned to wander helplessly and without direction in the darkness of each man's lonely heart" (HC, 237). Both faculties, in this sense, depend on *plurality*, on the presence and acting of others, for no one can forgive himself and no one can feel bound by a promise made only to one's self. At the same time, both faculties are an expression of human *freedom*, since without the faculty to undo what we have done in the past, and without the ability to control at least partially the processes we have started, we would be the victims "of an automatic necessity bearing all the marks of inexorable laws" (HC, 246).

Arendt's Theory of Judgment

One of the most enduring contributions of Arendt's political thought is to be found in her reflections on judgment which were to occupy the last years of her life. Together with the theory of action, her unfinished theory of judgment represents her central legacy to twentieth century political thought. We now explore some of the key aspects of her theory of judgment, and will examine its place in the architectonic of Arendt's theory of politics.

Judgment: Two Models

Arendt's theory of judgment was never developed as systematically or extensively as her theory of action. She intended to complete her study of the life of the mind by devoting the third volume to the faculty of judgment, but was not able to do so because of her untimely death in 1975. What she left was a number of reflections scattered in the first two volumes on *Thinking* and *Willing* (LM, vol. I; vol. II), a series of lectures on Kant's political philosophy delivered at the New School for Social Research in the Fall of 1970 (LKPP), an essay entitled "Thinking and Moral Considerations" written at the time she was composing *The Life of the Mind* (TMC, 417–46), and two articles included in *Between Past and Future* where judgment and opinion are treated in relation to culture and taste ("The Crisis in Culture" – BPF, 197–226) and with respect to the question of truth ("Truth and Politics" – BPF, 227–64). However, these writings do not present a unified theory of judgment but, rather, two distinct models, one based on the standpoint of the actor, the other on the standpoint of the spectator, which are somewhat at odds with each other. Arendt's writings on the theme of judgment can be seen to fall into two more or less distinct phases, an early one in which judgment is the faculty of political actors acting in the public realm, and a later one in which it is the privilege of non-participating spectators, primarily poets and historians, who seek to understand the meaning of the past and to reconcile us to what has happened. In this later formulation Arendt is no longer concerned with judging as a feature of political life as such, as the faculty which is exercised by actors in order to decide how to act in the public realm, but with judgment as a component in the life of the mind, the faculty through which the privileged spectators can recover meaning from the past and thereby reconcile themselves to time and, retrospectively, to tragedy.

In addition to presenting us with two models of judgment which stand in tension with each other, Arendt did not clarify the status of judgment with respect to two of its philosophical sources, Aristotle and Kant. The two conceptions seem to pull in opposite directions, the Aristotelian toward a concern with the particular, the Kantian toward a concern with universality and impartiality.

It would appear, therefore, that Arendt's theory of judgment not only incorporates two models, the actor's — judging in order to act — and the spectator's — judging in order to cull meaning from the past — but that the philosophical sources it draws upon are somewhat at odds with each other.

Judgment and the Vita Contemplativa

Arendt's concern with judgment as the faculty of retrospective assessment that allows meaning to be redeemed from the past originated in her attempt to come to terms with the twin political tragedies of the twentieth century, Nazism and Stalinism. Faced with the horrors of the extermination camps and what is now termed the Gulag, Arendt strove to understand these phenomena in their own terms, neither deducing them from precedents nor placing them in some overarching scheme of historical necessity. This need to come to terms with the traumatic events of the twentieth century, and to understand them in a manner that does not explain them away but faces them in all their starkness and unprecedentedness, is something to which Arendt returns again and again. Our inherited framework for judgment fails us "as soon as we try to apply it honestly to the central political experiences of our own time" (UP, 379). Even our ordinary common-sense judgment is rendered ineffective, since "we are living in a topsy-turvy world, a world where we cannot find our way by abiding by the rules of what once was common sense" (UP, 383).

The crisis in understanding is therefore coeval with a crisis in judgment, insofar as understanding for Arendt is "so closely related to and interrelated with judging that one must describe both as the subsumption of something particular under a universal rule" (UP, 383). Once these rules have lost their validity we are no longer able to understand and to judge the particulars, that is, we are no longer able to subsume them under our accepted categories of moral and political thought. Arendt, however, does not believe that the loss of these categories has brought to an end our capacity to judge; on the contrary, since human beings are distinguished by their capacity to begin anew, they are able to fashion new categories and to formulate new standards of judgment for the events that have come to pass and for those that may emerge in the future.

For Arendt, therefore, the enormity and unprecedentedness of totalitarianism have not destroyed, strictly speaking, our ability to judge; rather, they have destroyed our accepted standards of judgment and our conventional categories of interpretation and assessment, be they moral or political. And in this situation the only recourse is to appeal to the *imagination*, which allows us to view things in their proper perspective and to judge them without the benefit of a pre-given rule or universal. For Arendt, the imagination enables us to create the distance which is necessary for an impartial judgment, while at the same time allowing for the closeness that makes understanding possible. In this way it makes possible our reconciliation with reality, even with the tragic reality of the twentieth century.

Arendt's participation at the trial of Eichmann in the early sixties made her once more aware of the need to come to terms with a reality that initially defied human comprehension. How could such an ordinary, law-abiding, and all-too-human individual have committed such atrocities? The impact of the trial also forced her to raise another problem concerning judgment, namely, whether we are entitled to presuppose "an independent human faculty, unsupported by law and public opinion, that judges anew in full spontaneity every deed and intent whenever the occasion arises" (PRD, 187).

Judgment and the Wind of Thought

Arendt returned to this issue in *The Life of the Mind*, a work which was meant to encompass the three faculties of thinking, willing, and judging. In the introduction to the first volume she declared that the immediate impulse to write it came from attending the Eichmann trial in Jerusalem, while the second, equally important motive, was to provide an account of our mental activities that was missing from her previous work on the *vita activa*. It was Eichmann's absence of thinking, his "thoughtlessness," that struck her most, because it was responsible in her view for his inability to judge in those circumstances where judgment was most needed. "It was this absence of thinking," she wrote, "that awakened my interest. Is evil-doing ... possible in default of not just 'base motives' ... but of any motives whatever ... Might the problem of good and evil, our faculty for telling right from wrong, be connected with our faculty of thought?" (LM, vol. I, 4–5).

Arendt attempted a reply by connecting the activity of thinking to that of judging in a twofold manner. First, thinking — the silent dialogue of me and myself — dissolves our fixed habits of thought and the accepted rules of conduct, and thus prepares the way for the activity of judging particulars without the aid of pre-established universals. It is not that thinking provides judgment with new rules for subsuming the particular under the universal. Rather, it loosens the grip of the universal over the particular, thereby releasing judgment from ossified categories of thought and conventional standards of assessment. It is in times of historical crisis that thinking ceases to be a marginal affair, because by undermining all established criteria and values, it prepares the individual to judge for him or herself instead of being carried away by the actions and opinions of the majority.

The second way in which Arendt connected the activity of thinking with that of judging is by showing that thinking, by actualizing the dialogue of me and myself which is given in consciousness, produces *conscience* as a by-product. This conscience, unlike the voice of God or what later thinkers called *lumen naturale*, gives no positive prescriptions; it only tells us what *not* to do, what to avoid in our actions and dealings with others, as well as what to repent of. Arendt notes in this context that Socrates' dictum "It is better to suffer wrong than to do wrong," and his proposition that "It would be better for me that my lyre or a chorus I directed should be out of tune and loud with discord, and that multitudes of men should disagree with me, rather than that I, *being one*, should be out of harmony with myself and contradict me," derive their validity from the idea that there is a silent partner within ourselves to whom we render account of our actions (TMC, 29–30; 35). What we fear most is the anticipation of the presence of this partner (i.e., our conscience) who awaits us at the end of the day.

Arendt also remarks that thinking, as the actualization of the difference given in consciousness, "is not a prerogative of the few but an ever-present faculty in everybody; by the same token, inability to think is not a failing of the many who lack brain power, but an ever-present possibility for everybody" (LM, vol. I, 191). For those who do engage in thinking, however, conscience emerges as an inevitable by-product. As the side-effect of thinking, conscience has its counterpart in judgment as the by-product of the liberating activity of thought. If conscience represents the inner check by which we evaluate our actions, judgment represents the outer manifestation of our capacity to think critically. Both faculties relate to the question of right and wrong, but while conscience directs attention to the self, judgment directs attention to the world. In this respect, judgment makes possible what Arendt calls "the manifestation of the wind of thought" in the sphere of appearance.

5.4 Judgment and Kant's Aesthetics

The foregoing account has explored the way in which Arendt attempted to connect the activity of thinking to our capacity to judge. To be sure, this connection of thinking and judging seems to operate only in emergencies, in those exceptional moments where individuals, faced with the collapse of traditional standards, must come up with new ones and judge according to their own autonomous values. There is, however, a second, more elaborated view of judgment which does not restrict it to moments of crisis, but which identifies it with the capacity to think representatively, that is, from the standpoint of everyone else. Arendt called this capacity to think representatively an "enlarged mentality," adopting the same terms that Kant employed in his Third Critique to characterize aesthetic judgment. It is to this work that we must now turn our attention, since Arendt based her theory of political judgment on Kant's aesthetics rather than on his moral philosophy.

At first sight this might seem a puzzling choice, since Kant himself based his moral and political philosophy on practical reason and not on our aesthetic faculties. Arendt, however, claimed that the *Critique of Judgment* contained Kant's unwritten political philosophy, and that the first part of it, the "Critique of Aesthetic Judgment," was the most fruitful basis on which to build a theory of political judgment, since it dealt with the world of appearances from the point of view of the judging spectator and took as its starting point the faculty of taste, understood as a faculty of concrete and embodied subjects (BPF, 219–20).

For Arendt the capacity to judge is a specifically political ability insofar as it enables individuals to orient themselves in the public realm and to judge the phenomena that are disclosed within it from a standpoint that is relatively detached and impartial. She credits Kant with having dislodged the prejudice that judgments of taste lie altogether outside the political realm, since they supposedly concern only aesthetic matters. She believes, in fact, that by linking taste to that wider manner of thinking which Kant called an "enlarged mentality" the way was opened to a revaluation of judgment as a specific political ability, namely, as the ability to think in the place of everybody else. It is only in Kant's *Critique of Judgment* that we find a conception of judgment as the ability to deal with particulars in their particularity, that is, without subsuming them under a pre-given universal, but actively searching the universal out of the particular. Kant formulated this distinction as that between *determinant* and *reflective* judgments. For him judgment in general is the faculty of thinking the particular as contained under the universal. If the universal, (the rule, principle, or law) is given, then the judgment which subsumes the particular under it is determinant. If, however, only the particular is given and the universal has to be found for it, then the judgment is reflective. For Kant determinant judgments were cognitive, while reflective judgments were non-cognitive. Reflective judgment is seen as the capacity to ascend from the particular to the universal without the mediation of determinate concepts given in advance; it is reasoning about particulars in their relation to the universal rather than reasoning about universals in their relation to the particular. In the case of aesthetic judgment this means that one can understand and apply the universal predicate of beauty only through experiencing a particular object that exemplifies it. Thus, upon encountering a flower, a unique landscape, or a particular painting, one is able to say that it is an example of beauty, that it possesses "exemplary validity."

For Arendt this notion of exemplary validity is not restricted to aesthetic objects or to individuals who exemplified certain virtues. Rather, she wants to extend this notion to events in the past that carry a meaning beyond their sheer enactment, that is, to events that could be seen as exemplary for those who came after. It is here that aesthetic judgment joins with the retrospective judgment of the historian. The American and French Revolutions, the Paris Commune, the Russian soviets, the German revolutionary councils of 1918–19, the Hungarian uprising of 1956, all these events possess the kind of exemplary validity that makes them of universal significance, while still retaining their own specificity and uniqueness. Thus, by attending to these events in their particularity the historian or judging spectator is able to illuminate their universal import and thereby preserve them as "examples" for posterity.

For Arendt it is the spectators who have the privilege of judging impartially and disinterestedly, and in doing so they exercise two crucial faculties, *imagination* and *common sense*. Imagination is the faculty of representing in one's mind that which has already appeared to one's senses. Through the imagination one can represent objects that are no longer present and thus establish the distance necessary for an impartial judgment. Once this distancing has occurred, one is in a position to reflect upon these representations from a number of different perspectives, and thereby to reach a judgment about the proper value of an object.

The other faculty that spectators have to appeal to is common sense or *sensus communis*, since without it they could not share their judgments or overcome their individual idiosyncrasies. Kant believed that for our judgments to be valid we must transcend our private or subjective conditions in favor of public and intersubjective ones, and we are able to do this by appealing to our community sense, our *sensus communis*.

The criterion for judgment, then, is *communicability*, and the standard for deciding whether our judgments are indeed communicable is to see whether they could fit with the *sensus communis* of others. Arendt points out that the emphasis on the communicability of judgments of taste, and the correlative notion of an enlarged mentality, link up effortlessly with Kant's idea of a united mankind living in eternal peace. She argues that "It is by virtue of this idea of mankind, present in every single man, that men are human, and they can be called civilized or humane to the extent that this idea becomes the principle not only of their judgments but of their actions. It is at this point that *actor* and *spectator* become united; the maxim of the actor and the maxim, the 'standard,' according to which the spectator judges the spectacle of the world, become one" (LKPP, 75).

In her reflections on Kant's Third Critique Arendt acknowledges the links between the standpoint of the actor and that of the spectator. Let us now examine the way in which judgment operates from the standpoint of the actor.

Judgment and the Vita Activa

Arendt presented a model of judgment in the essays "The Crisis in Culture" and "Truth and Politics" which could be characterized as far more 'political' than the one presented so far. In these essays, in fact, she treated judgment as a faculty that enables political actors to decide what courses of action to undertake in the public realm, what kind of objectives are most appropriate or worth pursuing, as well as who to praise or blame for past actions or for the consequences of past decisions. In this model judgment is viewed as a specifically *political* ability, namely, as "the ability to see things not only from one's own point of view but from the perspective of all those who happen to be present," and as being "one of the fundamental abilities of man as a political being insofar as it enables him to orient himself in the public realm, in the common world" (BPF, 221). Arendt claims that "the Greeks called this ability [to judge] *phronesis*, or insight, and they considered it the principal virtue or excellence of the statesman in distinction from the wisdom of the philosopher. The difference between this judging insight and speculative thought lies in that the former has its roots in what we usually call common sense, which the latter constantly transcends. Common sense ... discloses to us the nature of the world insofar as it is a common world; we owe to it the fact that our strictly private and 'subjective' five senses and their sensory data can adjust themselves to a non-subjective and 'objective' world which we have in common and share with others. Judging is one, if not the most, important activity in which this sharing-the-world-with-others comes to pass" (BPF, 221).

Moreover, in discussing the non-coercive character of judgment, the fact that it can only appeal to but never force the agreement of others, she claims that "this 'wooing' or persuading corresponds closely to what the Greeks called *peithein*, the convincing and persuading speech which they regarded as the typically political form of people talking with one another" (BPF, 222). Some commentators have claimed that there is a contradiction in Arendt's employment of the Aristotelian notion of *phronesis* alongside Kant's idea of an "enlarged mentality," since they supposedly pull in opposite directions, the former toward a concern with the particular, the latter toward universality and impartiality. However, this contradiction is more apparent than real, since Kant's theory of aesthetic judgment is a theory of *reflective* judgment, that is, of those judgments where the universal is not given but must be searched out of the particular. In this respect the theory of aesthetic judgment to which Arendt appeals does have close affinities with Aristotle's notion of *phronesis*: both are concerned with the judgment of particulars *qua* particulars, not with their subsumption under universal rules. If a distinction is to be made, it has more to do with the mode of *asserting validity*: In Aristotle *phronesis* is the privilege of a few experienced individuals (the *phronimoi*) who, over time, have shown themselves to be wise in practical matters; the only criterion of validity is their experience and their past record of judiciuos actions. In the case of judgments of taste, on the other hand, individuals have to appeal to the judgments and opinions of others, and thus the validity of their judgments rests on the consent they can elicit from a community of differently situated subjects.

For Arendt the validity of political judgment depends on our ability to think "representatively," that is, from the standpoint of everyone else, so that we are able to look at the world from a number of different perspectives. And this ability, in turn, can only be acquired and tested in a public forum where individuals have the opportunity to exchange their opinions on particular matters and see whether they accord with the opinions of others. In this respect the process of opinion formation is never a solitary activity; rather, it requires a genuine encounter with different opinions so that a particular issue may be examined from every possible standpoint until, as she puts it, "it is flooded and made transparent by the full light of human comprehension" (BPF, 242). Debate and discussion, and the capacity to enlarge one's perspective, are indeed crucial to the formation of opinions that can claim more than subjective validity; individuals may hold personal opinions on many subject matters, but they can form *representative* opinions only by enlarging their standpoint to incorporate those of others. As Arendt says:

Political thought is representative. I form an opinion by considering a given issue from different viewpoints, by making present to my mind the standpoints of those who are absent; that is, I represent them ... The more people's standpoints I have present in my mind while I am pondering a given issue, and the better I can imagine how I would feel and think if I were in their place, the stronger will be my capacity for representative thinking and the more valid my final conclusions, my opinion. (BPF, 241)

Opinions, in fact, are never self-evident. In matters of opinion, but not in matters of truth, "our thinking is truly discursive, running, as it were, from place to place, from one part of the world to another, through all kinds of conflicting views, until it finally ascends from these particularities to some impartial generality" (BPF, 242). In this respect one is never alone while forming an opinion; as Arendt notes, "even if I shun all company or am completely isolated while forming an opinion, I am not simply together only with myself in the solitude of philosophical thought; I remain in this world of universal interdependence, where I can make myself the representative of everybody else" (BPF, 242).

Judgment and Validity

The representative character of judgment and opinion has important implications for the question of validity. Arendt always stressed that the formation of valid opinions requires a public space where individuals can test and purify their views through a process of mutual debate and enlightenment. She was, however, quite opposed to the idea that opinions should be measured by the standard of truth, or that debate should be conducted according to strict scientific standards of validity. In her view, truth belongs to the realm of cognition, the realm of logic, mathematics and the strict sciences, and carries always an element of coercion, since it precludes debate and must be accepted by every individual in possession of her rational faculties. Set against the plurality of opinions, truth has a despotic character: it compels universal assent, leaves the mind little freedom of movement, eliminates the diversity of views and reduces the richness of human discourse. In this respect, truth is anti-political, since by eliminating debate and diversity it eliminates the very principles of political life. As Arendt writes, "The trouble is that factual truth, like all other truth, peremptorily claims to be acknowledged and precludes debate, and debate constitutes the very essence of political life. The modes of thought and communication that deal with truth, if seen from the political perspective, are necessarily domineering; they don't take into account other people's opinions, and taking these into account is the hallmark of all strictly political thinking" (BPF, 241).

Arendt's defense of opinion is motivated not just by her belief that truth leaves no room for debate or dissent, or for the acknowledgment of difference, but also by her conviction that our reasoning faculties can only flourish in a dialogic context. She cites Kant's remark that "the external power that deprives man of the freedom to communicate his thoughts publicly deprives him at the same time of his freedom to think," and underlines the fact that for Kant the only guarantee of the correctness of our thinking is that "we think, as it were, in community with others to whom we communicate our thoughts as they communicate theirs to us" (BPF, 234–5). She also quotes Madison's statement that "the reason of man, like man himself, is timid and cautious when left alone, and acquires firmness and confidence in proportion to the number with which it is associated" (BPF, 234).

The appeal to Kant and Madison is meant to vindicate the power and dignity of opinion against those thinkers, from Plato to Hobbes, who saw it as mere illusion, as a confused or inadequate grasp of the truth. For Arendt opinion is not a defective form of knowledge that should be transcended or left behind as soon as one is in possession of the truth. Rather, it is a distinct form of knowledge which arises out of the collective deliberation of citizens, and which requires the use of the imagination and the capacity to think "representatively." By deliberating in common and engaging in "representative thinking" citizens are in fact able to form opinions that can claim intersubjective validity. It is important to stress that Arendt does not want to dismiss the philosophers' attempt to find universal or absolute standards of knowledge and cognition, but to check their desire to impose those standards upon the sphere of human affairs, since they would eliminate its plurality and essential relativity. The imposition of a single or absolute standard into the domain of *praxis* would do away with the need to persuade others of the relative merits of an opinion, to elicit their consent to a specific proposal, or to obtain their agreement with respect to a particular policy. Indeed, for Arendt the imposition of such a standard would mean that individuals would no longer be required to exercise their judgment, develop their imagination, or cultivate an "enlarged mentality," since they would no longer need to deliberate in common. Strict demonstration, rather than persuasive argumentation, would then become the only legitimate form of discourse.

Now, we must be careful not to impute to Arendt the view that truth has no legitimate role to play in politics or in the sphere of human affairs. She does indeed assert that "All truths — not only the various kinds of rational truth but also factual truth — are opposed to opinion in their mode of asserting validity" (BPF, 239), since they all carry an element of compulsion. However, she is only preoccupied with the negative consequences of rational truth when applied to the sphere of politics and collective deliberation, while she defends the importance of factual truth for the preservation of an accurate account of the past and for the very existence of political communities. Factual truth, she writes, "is always related to other people: it concerns events and circumstances in which many are involved; it is established by witnesses and depends upon testimony ... It is political by nature." It follows, therefore, that "facts and opinions, though they must be kept apart, are not antagonistic to each other; they belong to the same realm. Facts inform opinions, and opinions, inspired by different interests and passions, can differ widely and still be legitimate as long as they respect factual truth. Freedom of opinion is a farce unless factual information is guaranteed and the facts themselves are not in dispute. In other words, factual truth informs political thought just as rational truth informs philosophical speculation" (BPF, 238).

The relationship between facts and opinions is thus one of mutual entailment: if opinions were not based on correct information and the free access to all relevant facts they could scarcely claim any validity. And if they were to be based on fantasy, self-deception, or deliberate falsehood, then no possibility of genuine debate and argumentation could be sustained. Both factual truth and the general habit of truth-telling are therefore basic to the formation of sound opinions and to the flourishing of political debate. Moreover, if the record of the past were to be destroyed by organized lying, or be distorted by an attempt to rewrite history, political life would be deprived of one of its essential and stabilizing elements. In sum, both factual truth and the practice of truth-telling are essential to political life. The antagonism for Arendt is between *rational* truth and well-grounded opinion, since the former does not allow for debate and dissent, while the latter thrives on it. Arendt's defense of opinion must therefore be understood as a defense of political deliberation, and of the role that persuasion and dissuasion play in all matters affecting the political community. Against Plato and

Hobbes, who denigrated the role of opinion in political matters, Arendt reasserts the value and importance of political discourse, of deliberation and persuasion, and thus of a politics that acknowledges difference and the plurality of opinions.

Arendt's Conception of Citizenship

In this last section, we reconstruct Arendt's conception of citizenship around two themes: (1) the public sphere, and (2) political agency and collective identity, and to highlight the contribution of Arendt's conception to a theory of democratic citizenship.

Citizenship and the Public Sphere

For Arendt the public sphere comprises two distinct but interrelated dimensions. The first is the *space of appearance*, a space of political freedom and equality which comes into being whenever citizens act in concert through the medium of speech and persuasion. The second is the *common world*, a shared and public world of human artifacts, institutions and settings which separates us from nature and which provides a relatively permanent and durable context for our activities. Both dimensions are essential to the practice of citizenship, the former providing the spaces where it can flourish, the latter providing the stable background from which public spaces of action and deliberation can arise. For Arendt the reactivation of citizenship in the modern world depends upon both the recovery of a common, shared world and the creation of numerous spaces of appearance in which individuals can disclose their identities and establish relations of reciprocity and solidarity.

There are three features of the public sphere and of the sphere of politics in general that are central to Arendt's conception of citizenship. These are, first, its *artificial* or constructed quality; second, its *spatial* quality; and, third, the distinction between *public* and *private* interests.

As regards the first feature, Arendt always stressed the artificiality of public life and of political activities in general, the fact that they are man-made and constructed rather than natural or given. She regarded this artificiality as something to be celebrated rather than deplored. Politics for her was not the result of some natural predisposition, or the realization of the inherent traits of human nature. Rather, it was a cultural achievement of the first order, enabling individuals to transcend the necessities of life and to fashion a world within which free political action and discourse could flourish.

The stress on the artificiality of politics has a number of important consequences. For example, Arendt emphasized that the principle of political equality does not rest on a theory of natural rights or on some natural condition that precedes the constitution of the political realm. Rather, it is an attribute of citizenship which individuals acquire upon entering the public realm and which can be secured only by democratic political institutions.

Another consequence of Arendt's stress on the artificiality of political life is evident in her rejection of all neo-romantic appeals to the *volk* and to ethnic identity as the basis for political community. She maintained that one's ethnic, religious, or racial identity was irrelevant to one's identity as a citizen, and that it should never be made the basis of membership in a political community.

Arendt's emphasis on the formal qualities of citizenship made her position rather distant from those advocates of participation in the 1960s who saw it in terms of recapturing a sense of intimacy, of warmth and authenticity. For Arendt political participation was important because it permitted the establishment of relations of civility and solidarity among citizens. She claimed that the ties of intimacy and warmth can never become political since they represent psychological substitutes for the loss of the common world. The only truly political ties are those of civic friendship and solidarity, since they make political demands and preserve reference to the world. For Arendt, therefore, the danger of trying to recapture the sense of intimacy and warmth, of authenticity and communal feelings is that one loses the public values of impartiality, civic friendship, and solidarity.

The second feature stressed by Arendt has to do with the *spatial* quality of public life, with the fact that political activities are located in a public space where citizens are able to meet one another, exchange their opinions and debate their differences, and search for some collective solution to their problems. Politics, for Arendt, is a matter of people sharing a common world and a common space of appearance so that public concerns can emerge and be articulated from different perspectives. In her view, it is not enough to have a collection of private individuals voting separately and anonymously according to their private opinions. Rather, these individuals must be able to see and talk to one another in public, to meet in a public-political space, so that their differences as well as their commonalities can emerge and become the subject of democratic debate.

This notion of a common public space helps us to understand how political opinions can be formed which are neither reducible to private, idiosyncratic preferences, on the one hand, nor to a unanimous collective opinion, on the other. Arendt herself distrusted the term "public opinion," since it suggested the mindless unanimity of mass society. In her view representative opinions could arise only when citizens actually confronted one another in a public space, so that they could examine an issue from a number of different perspectives, modify their views, and enlarge their standpoint to incorporate that of others. Political opinions, she claimed, can never be formed in private; rather, they are formed, tested, and enlarged only within a public context of argumentation and debate.

Another implication of Arendt's stress on the spatial quality of politics has to do with the question of how a collection of distinct individuals can be united to form a political community. For Arendt the unity that may be achieved in a political community is neither the result of religious or ethnic affinity, not the expression of some common value system. Rather, the unity in question can be attained by sharing a public space and a set of political institutions, and engaging in the practices and activities which are characteristic of that space and those institutions.

A further implication of Arendt's conception of the spatial quality of politics is that since politics is a public activity, one cannot be part of it without in some sense being present in a public space. To be engaged in politics means actively participating in the various public forums where the decisions affecting one's community are taken. Arendt's insistence on the importance of direct participation in politics is thus based on the idea that, since politics is something that needs a worldly location and can only happen in a public space, then if one is not present in such a space one is simply not engaged in politics.

This public or world-centered conception of politics lies also at the basis of the third feature stressed by Arendt, the distinction between *public* and *private* interests. According to Arendt, political activity is not a means to an end, but an end in itself; one does not engage in political action to promote one's welfare, but to realize the principles intrinsic to political life, such as freedom, equality, justice, and solidarity. In a late essay entitled "Public Rights and Private Interests" (PRPI) Arendt discusses the difference between one's life as an individual and one's life as a citizen, between the life spent on one's own and the life spent in common with others. She argues that our public interest as citizens is quite distinct from our private interest as individuals. The public interest is not the sum of private interests, nor their highest common denominator, nor even the total of enlightened self-interests. In fact, it has little to do with our private interests, since it concerns the world that lies beyond the self, that was there before our birth and that will be there after our death, a world that finds embodiment in activities and institutions with their own intrinsic purposes which might often be at odds with our short-term and private interests. The public interest refers, therefore, to the interests of a public world which we share as citizens and which we can pursue and enjoy only by going beyond our private self-interest.

Citizenship, Agency, and Collective Identity

Arendt's participatory conception of citizenship provides the best starting point for addressing both the question of the constitution of *collective identity* and that concerning the conditions for the exercise of effective *political agency*.

With respect to the first claim, it is important to note that one of the crucial questions at stake in political discourse is the creation of a collective identity, a "we" to which we can appeal when faced with the problem of deciding among alternative courses of action. Since in political discourse there is always disagreement about the possible courses of action, the identity of the "we" that is going to be created through a specific form of action becomes a central question. By engaging in this or that course of action we are, in fact, entering a claim on behalf of a "we," that is, we are creating a specific form of collective identity. Political action and discourse are, in this respect, essential to the constitution of collective identities.

This process of identity-construction, however, is never given once and for all and is never unproblematic. Rather, it is a process of constant renegotiation and struggle, a process in which actors articulate and defend competing conceptions of cultural and political identity. Arendt's participatory conception of citizenship is particularly relevant in this context since it articulates the conditions for the establishment of collective identities. Once citizenship is viewed as the process of active deliberation about competing identities, its value resides in the possibility of establishing forms of collective identity that can be acknowledged, tested, and transformed in a discursive and democratic fashion.

With respect to the second claim, concerning the question of political agency, it is important to stress the connection that Arendt establishes between political action, understood as the active engagement of citizens in the public realm, and the exercise of effective political agency. This connection between action and agency is one of the central contributions of Arendt's participatory conception of citizenship. According to Arendt, the active engagement of citizens in the determination of the affairs of their community provides them not only with the experience of public freedom and public happiness, but also with a sense of political agency and efficacy, the sense, in Thomas Jefferson's words, of being "participators in government." In her view only the sharing of power that comes from civic engagement and common deliberation can provide each citizen with a sense of effective political agency. Arendt's strictures against political representation must be understood in this light. She saw representation as a substitute for the direct involvement of the citizens, and as a means whereby the distinction between rulers and ruled could reassert itself. As an alternative to a system of representation based on bureaucratic parties and state structures, Arendt proposed a federated system of councils through which citizens could effectively determine their own political affairs. For Arendt, it is only by means of direct political participation, that is, by engaging in common action and collective deliberation, that citizenship can be reaffirmed and political agency effectively exercised.

, the sense, in Thomas Jefferson's words, of being "participators in government." In her view only the sharing of power that comes from civic engagement and common deliberation can provide each citizen with a sense of effective political agency. Arendt's strictures against political representation must be understood in this light. She saw representation as a substitute for the direct involvement of the citizens, and as a means whereby the distinction between rulers and ruled could reassert itself.

As an alternative to a system of representation based on bureaucratic parties and state structures, Arendt proposed a federated system of councils through which citizens could effectively determine their own political affairs. For Arendt, it is only by means of direct political participation, that is, by engaging in common action and collective deliberation, that citizenship can be reaffirmed and political agency effectively exercised.

CHAPTER THREE

ALBERT CAMUS

There are various paradoxical elements in Camus's approach to philosophy. In his book-length essay, *The Myth of Sisyphus*, Camus presents a philosophy that contests philosophy itself. This essay belongs squarely in the philosophical tradition of existentialism but Camus denied being an existentialist. Both *The Myth of Sisyphus* and his other philosophical work, *The Rebel*, are systematically skeptical of conclusions about the meaning of life, yet both works assert objectively valid answers to key questions about how to live. Though Camus seemed modest when describing his intellectual ambitions, he was confident enough as a philosopher to articulate not only his own philosophy but also a critique of religion and a fundamental critique of modernity. While rejecting the very idea of a philosophical system, Camus constructed his own original edifice of ideas around the key terms of absurdity and rebellion, aiming to resolve the life-or-death issues that motivated him.

The essential paradox arising in Camus's philosophy concerns his central notion of absurdity. Accepting the Aristotelian idea that philosophy begins in wonder, Camus argues that human beings cannot escape asking the question, “What is the meaning of existence?” Camus, however, denies that there is an answer to this question, and rejects every scientific, teleological, metaphysical, or human-created end that would provide an adequate answer. Thus, while accepting that human beings inevitably seek to understand life’s purpose, Camus takes the skeptical position that the natural world, the universe, and the human enterprise remains silent about any such purpose. Since existence itself has no meaning, we must learn to bear an irresolvable emptiness. This paradoxical situation, then, between our impulse to ask ultimate questions and the impossibility of achieving any adequate answer, is what Camus calls *the absurd*. Camus’s philosophy of the absurd explores the consequences arising from this basic paradox.

Camus’s understanding of absurdity is best captured in an image, not an argument: of Sisyphus straining to push his rock up the mountain, watching it roll down, then descending after the rock to begin all over, in an endless cycle. Like Sisyphus, humans cannot help but continue to ask after the meaning of life, only to see our answers tumble back down. If we accept this thesis about life’s essential absurdity, and Camus’s anti-philosophical approach to philosophical questions, we cannot help but ask: What role is left for rational analysis and argument? Doesn’t Camus the philosopher preside over the death of philosophy in answering the question whether to commit suicide by abandoning the terrain of argument and analysis and turning to metaphor to answer it? If life has no fundamental purpose or meaning that reason can articulate, we cannot help asking about why we continue to live and to reason. Might not Silenus be right in declaring that it would have been better not to have been born, or to die as soon as possible?[1] And, as Francis Jeanson wrote long before his famous criticism of *The Rebel* that precipitated the rupture between Camus and Sartre, isn't absurdist philosophy a contradiction in terms, strictly speaking no philosophy at all but an anti-rational posture that ends in silence (Jeanson 1947)?

Was Camus actually a philosopher? He himself said no, in a famous interview with Jeanine Delpech in *Les Nouvelles Littéraires* in November of 1945, insisting that he did "not believe sufficiently in reason to believe in a system" (Camus 1965, 1427). This was not merely a public posture, since we find the same thought in his notebooks of this period: he describes himself as an artist and not a philosopher because "I think according to words and not according to ideas" (Camus 1995, 113). Still, Jean-Paul Sartre saw immediately that Camus was undertaking important philosophical work, and in his review of *The Stranger* in relation to *Sisyphus*, had no trouble connecting Camus with Pascal, Rousseau, and Nietzsche (Sartre 1962). After they became friends Sartre spoke publicly of his friend's "philosophy of the absurd," which he distinguished from his own thought for which he accepted the "existentialist" label that Camus rejected. In the years since, the apparent unsystematic, indeed, anti-systematic, character of his philosophy, has meant that relatively few scholars have appreciated its full depth and complexity. They have more often praised his towering literary achievements and standing as a political moralist while pointing out his dubious claims and problematic arguments (see Sherman 2008). A significant recent exception to this is Ronald Srigley's *Albert Camus' Critique of Modernity* (Srigley 2011).

This entry will negotiate Camus's deliberate ambivalence as a philosopher while discussing his philosophy. It is not just a matter of giving a philosophical reading of this playwright, journalist, essayist, and novelist but of taking his philosophical writings seriously—exploring their premises, their evolution, their structure, and their coherence. To do so is to see that his writing contains more than a mood and more than images and sweeping, unsupported assertions, although it contains many of both. Camus takes his skepticism as far as possible as a form of methodical doubt—that is, he begins from a presumption of skepticism—until he finds the basis for a non-skeptical conclusion. And he builds a unique philosophical construction, whose premises are often left unstated and which is not always argued clearly, but which develops in distinct stages over the course of his brief lifetime. Camus's philosophy can be thus read as a sustained effort to demonstrate and not just assert what is entailed by the absurdity of human existence. In the process Camus answers the questions posed by *The Myth of Sisyphus*, "Why should I not kill myself?", and by *The Rebel*, "Why should I not kill others?"

Nuptials and Camus's Starting Point

Camus's graduate thesis at the University of Algiers sympathetically explored the relationship between Greek philosophy and Christianity, specifically the relationship of Plotinus to Augustine (Camus 1992). Nevertheless, his philosophy explicitly rejects religion as one of its foundations. Not always taking an openly hostile posture towards religious belief—though he certainly does in the novels *The Stranger* and *The Plague*—Camus centers his work on choosing to live without God. Another way to understand Camus's philosophy is that it is an effort to explore the issues and pitfalls of a post-religious world.

Camus's earliest published writing containing philosophical thinking, *Nuptials*, appeared in Algeria in 1938, and remain the basis of his later work. These lyrical essays and sketches describe a consciousness reveling in the world, a body delighting in nature, and the individual's immersion in sheer physicality. Yet these experiences are presented as the solution to a philosophical problem, namely finding the meaning of life in the face of death. They appear alongside, and reveal themselves to be rooted in, his first extended meditation on ultimate questions.

In these essays, Camus sets two attitudes in opposition. The first is what he regards as religion-based fears. He cites religious warnings about pride, concern for one's immortal soul, hope for an afterlife, resignation about the present and preoccupation with God. Against this conventional Christian perspective Camus asserts what he regards as self-evident facts: that we must die and there is nothing beyond this life. Without mentioning it, Camus draws a conclusion from these facts, namely that the soul is not immortal. Here, as elsewhere in his philosophical writing, he commends to his readers to face a discomforting reality squarely and without flinching, but he does not feel compelled to present reasons or evidence. If not with religion, where then does wisdom lie? His answer is: with the "conscious certainty of a death without hope" and in refusing to hide from the fact that we are going to die. For Camus "there is no superhuman happiness, no eternity outside of the curve of the days.... I can see no point in the happiness of angels" (*N*, 90). There is nothing but *this* world, *this* life, the immediacy of the present.

Camus is sometimes mistakenly called a "pagan" because he rejects Christianity as based on a hope for a life beyond this life. *Hope* is the error Camus wishes to avoid. Rejecting "the delusions of hope" (*N*, 74), *Nuptials* contains an evocation of an alternative. Camus relies for this line of thought on Nietzsche's discussion of Pandora's Box in *Human, All Too Human*: all the evils of humankind, including plagues and disease, have been let loose on the world by Zeus, but the remaining evil, hope, is kept hidden away in the box and treasured. But why, we may ask, is hope an evil? Nietzsche explains that humans have come to see hope as their greatest good, while Zeus, knowing better, has meant it as the greatest source of trouble. It is, after all, the reason why humans let themselves be tormented—because they anticipate an ultimate reward (Nietzsche 1878/1996, 58). For Camus, following this reading of Nietzsche closely, the conventional solution is in fact the problem: hope is disastrous for humans inasmuch as it leads them to minimize the value of this life except as preparation for a life beyond.

If religious hope is based on the mistaken belief that death, in the sense of utter and total extinction body and soul, is not inevitable, it leads us down a blind alley. Worse, because it teaches us to look away from life toward something to come afterwards, such religious hope kills a part of us, for example, the realistic attitude we need to confront the vicissitudes of life. But what then is the appropriate path? The young Camus is neither a skeptic nor a relativist here. His discussion rests on the self-evidence of sensuous experience. He advocates precisely what he takes Christianity to abjure: living a life of the senses, intensely, here and now, in the present. This entails, first, abandoning all hope for an afterlife, indeed rejecting thinking about it. "I do not want to believe that death is the gateway to another life. For me it is a closed door" (*N*, 76).

We might think that facing our total annihilation would be bitter, but for Camus this leads us in a positive direction: "Between this sky and the faces turned toward it there is nothing on which to hang a mythology, a literature, an ethic, or a religion—only stones, flesh, stars, and those truths the hand can touch" (*N*, 90). This insight entails obstinately refusing "all the 'later on's of this world," in order to lay claim to "my present wealth" (*N*, 103), namely the intense here-and-now life of the senses. The "wealth" is precisely what hope cheats us out of by teaching us to look away from it and towards an afterlife. Only by yielding to the fact that our "longing to endure" will be frustrated and accepting our "awareness of death" are we able to open ourselves to the riches of life, which are physical above all.

Camus puts both sides of his argument into a single statement: "The world is beautiful, and outside there is no salvation" (*N*, 103). Only in accepting death and in being "stripped of all hope" does one most intensely appreciate not only the physical side of life, but also, he now suggests, its affective and interpersonal side. Taken together, and contrary to an unverifiable faith in God and afterlife, these are what one *has* and one *knows*: "To feel one's ties to a land, one's love for certain men, to know there is always a place where the heart can find rest—these are already many certainties for one man's life" (*N*, 90).

Only if we accept that Nietzsche is right, that God is dead and there is only nothingness after we die, will we then fully experience—feel, taste, touch, see, and smell—the joys of our bodies and the physical world. Thus the sensuous and lyrical side of these essays, their evocative character, is central to the argument. Or rather, because Camus is promoting intense, joyous, physical experience as opposed to a self-abnegating religious life, rather than developing an argument he asserts that these experiences themselves are the right response. His writing aims to demonstrate what life *means* and *feels like* once we give up hope of an afterlife, so that in reading we will be led to "see" his point. These essays may be taken as containing highly personal thoughts, a young man's musings about his Mediterranean environment, and they scarcely seem to have any system. But they suggest what philosophy is for Camus and how he conceives its relationship to literary expression.

His early philosophy, then, may be conveyed, if not summed up, in this passage from "Nuptials at Tipasa":

In a moment, when I throw myself down among the absinthe plants to bring their scent into my body, I shall know, appearances to the contrary, that I am fulfilling a truth which is the sun's and which will also be my death's. In a sense, it is indeed my life that I am staking here, a life that tastes of warm stone, that is full of the signs of the sea and the rising song of the crickets. The breeze is cool and the sky blue. I love this life with abandon and wish to speak of it boldly: it makes me proud of my human condition. Yet people have often told me: there's nothing to be proud of. Yes, there is: this sun, this sea, my heart leaping with youth, the salt taste of my body and this vast landscape in which tenderness and glory merge in blue and yellow. It is to conquer this that I need my strength and my resources. Everything here leaves me intact, I surrender nothing of myself, and don no mask: learning patiently and arduously how to live is enough for me, well worth all their arts of living. (*N*, 69)

The intense and glistening present tells us that we can fully experience and appreciate life only on the condition that we no longer try to avoid our ultimate and absolute death.

Suicide, Absurdity and Happiness: The Myth of Sisyphus

After completing *Nuptials*, Camus began to work on a planned triptych on the Absurd: a novel, which became *The Stranger*, a philosophical essay, eventually titled *The Myth of Sisyphus*, and a play, *Caligula*. These were completed and sent off from Algeria to the Paris publisher in September 1941. Although Camus would have preferred to see them appear together, even in a single volume, the publisher for both commercial reasons and because of the paper shortage caused by war and occupation, released *The Stranger* in June 1942 and *The Myth of Sisyphus* in October. Camus kept working on the play, which finally appeared in book form two years later (Lottman, 264–67).

Suicide as a Response to Absurdity

"There is only one really serious philosophical problem," Camus says, "and that is suicide. Deciding whether or not life is worth living is to answer the fundamental question in philosophy. All other questions follow from that" (*MS*, 3). One might object that suicide is neither a "problem" nor a "question," but an act. A proper, philosophical question might rather be: "Under what conditions is suicide warranted?" And a philosophical answer might explore the question, "What does it mean to ask whether life is worth living?" as William James did in *The Will to Believe*. For the Camus of *The Myth of Sisyphus*, however, "Should I kill myself?" is *the* essential philosophical question. For him, it seems clear that the primary result of philosophy is action, not comprehension. His concern about "the most urgent of questions" is less a theoretical one than it is the life-and-death problem of whether and how to live.

Camus sees this question of suicide as a natural response to an underlying premise, namely that life is absurd in a variety of ways. As we have seen, both the presence and absence of life (i.e., death) give rise to the condition: it is absurd to continually seek meaning in life when there is none, and it is absurd to hope for some form of continued existence after death given that the latter results in our extinction. But Camus also thinks it absurd to try to know, understand, or explain the world, for he sees the attempt to gain rational knowledge as futile. Here Camus pits himself against science and philosophy, dismissing the claims of all forms of rational analysis: "That universal reason, practical or ethical, that determinism, those categories that explain everything are enough to make a decent man laugh" (*MS*, 21).

These kinds of absurdity are driving Camus's question about suicide, but his way of proceeding evokes another kind of absurdity, one less well-defined, namely, the "absurd sensibility" (MS, 2, tr. changed). This sensibility, vaguely described, seems to be "an intellectual malady" (*MS*, 2) rather than a philosophy. He regards thinking about it as "provisional" and insists that the mood of absurdity, so "widespread in our age" does not arise from, but lies prior to, philosophy. Camus's diagnosis of the essential human problem rests on a series of "truisms" (*MS*, 18) and "obvious themes" (*MS*, 16). But he doesn't argue for life's absurdity or attempt to explain it—he is not interested in either project, nor would such projects engage his strength as a thinker. "I am interested ... not so much in absurd discoveries as in their consequences" (*MS*, 16).

Accepting absurdity as the mood of the times, he asks above all whether and how to live in the face of it. “Does the absurd dictate death” (*MS*, 9)? But he does not argue this question either, and rather chooses to demonstrate the attitude towards life that would deter suicide. In other words, the main concern of the book is to sketch ways of living our lives so as to make them worth living despite their being meaningless.

According to Camus, people commit suicide “because they judge life is not worth living” (*MS*, 4). But if this temptation precedes what is usually considered philosophical reasoning, how to answer it? In order to get to the bottom of things while avoiding *arguing* for the truth of his statements, he depicts, enumerates, and illustrates. As he says in *The Rebel*, “the absurd is an experience that must be lived through, a point of departure, the equivalent, in existence, of Descartes’s methodical doubt” (*R*, 4). *The Myth of Sisyphus* seeks to *describe* “the elusive feeling of absurdity” in our lives, rapidly pointing out themes that “run through all literatures and all philosophies” (*MS*, 12). Appealing to common experience, he tries to render the flavor of the absurd with images, metaphors, and anecdotes that capture the experiential level he regards as lying prior to philosophy.

He begins doing so with an implicit reference to Sartre’s novel, *Nausea*, which echoes the protagonist Antoine Roquentin’s discovery of absurdity. Camus had earlier written that this novel’s theories of absurdity and its images are not in balance. The descriptive and the philosophical aspects of the novel “don’t add up to a work of art: the passage from one to the other is too rapid, too unmotivated, to evoke in the reader the deep conviction that makes art of the novel” (Camus 1968, 200). But in this 1938 review

Camus praises Sartre's descriptions of absurdity, the sense of anguish and nausea that arises as the ordinary structures imposed on existence collapse in Antoine Roquentin's life. As Camus now presents his own version of the experience, "the stage sets collapse. Rising, streetcar, four hours in the office or the factory, meal, streetcar, four hours of work, meal, sleep, and Monday Tuesday Wednesday Thursday Friday Saturday and Sunday according to the same rhythm …" (*MS*, 12–3). As this continues, one slowly becomes fully conscious and senses the absurd.

The Limits of Reason

Camus goes on to sketch other experiences of absurdity, until he arrives at death. But although Camus seeks to avoid arguing for the truth of his claims, he nevertheless concludes this "absurd reasoning" with a series of categorical assertions addressed to "the intelligence" about the inevitable frustration of the human desire to know the world and to be at home in it. Despite his intentions, Camus cannot avoid asserting what he believes to be an objective truth: "We must despair of ever reconstructing the familiar, calm surface which would give us peace of heart" (*MS*, 18). Turning to experiences that are seemingly obvious to large numbers of people who share the absurd sensibility, he declares sweepingly: "This world in itself is not reasonable, that is all that can be said" (*MS*, 21). Our efforts to know are driven by a nostalgia for unity, and there is an inescapable "hiatus between what we fancy we know and what we really know" (*MS*, 18).

"With the exception of professional rationalists, people today despair of true knowledge" (*MS*, 18). Camus asserts that the history of human thought is characterized by "its successive regrets and its impotences" (*MS*, 18), and that "the impossibility of knowledge is established" (*MS*, 25). When writing more carefully, he claims only to be describing a certain "climate," but in any case his bedrock assumptions appear again and again: the world is unknowable and life is without meaning. Our efforts to understand them lead nowhere.

Avi Sagi suggests that in claiming this Camus is not speaking as an irrationalist—which is, after all, how he regards the existentialists—but as someone trying to rationally understand the limits of reason (Sagi 2002, 59–65). For Camus the problem is that by demanding meaning, order, and unity, we seek to go beyond those limits and pursue the impossible. We will never understand, and we will die despite all our efforts. There are two obvious responses to our frustrations: suicide and hope. By hope Camus means just what he described in *Nuptials*, the religion-inspired effort to imagine and live for a life beyond this life. Or, second, as taken up at length in *The Rebel*, bending one's energies to living for a great cause beyond oneself: "Hope of another life one must 'deserve' or trickery of those who live not for life itself but for some great idea that will transcend it, refine it, give it a meaning, and betray it" (*MS*, 8).

What is the Camusean alternative to suicide or hope? The answer is to live without escape and with integrity, in "revolt" and defiance, maintaining the tension intrinsic to human life. Since "the most obvious absurdity" (*MS*, 59) is death, Camus urges us to "die unreconciled and not of one's own free will" (*MS*, 55). In short, he recommends a life without consolation, but instead one characterized by lucidity and by acute consciousness of and rebellion against its mortality and its limits.

Criticism of Existentialists

In his statement of the problem and its solution, Camus's tone, ideas, and style are reminiscent of Nietzsche. "God is dead" is of course their common starting point, as is the determination to confront unpleasant truths and write against received wisdom. At the same time Camus argues against the specific philosophical current with which Nietzsche is often linked as a precursor, and to which he himself is closest—existentialism. *The Myth of Sisyphus* is explicitly written *against* existentialists such as Shestov, Kierkegaard, Jaspers, and Heidegger, as well as against the phenomenology of Husserl. Camus shares their starting point, which he regards as the fact that they all somehow testify to the absurdity of the human condition. But he rejects what he sees as their ultimate escapism and irrationality, claiming that "they deify what crushes them and find reason to hope in what impoverishes them. That forced hope is religious in all of them" (*MS*, 24).

Sartre, too, is subject to Camus's criticisms—and not just politically as will be described in the following section. Although some of the ideas in *The Myth of Sisyphus* drew on Sartre's *Nausea* (as noted above), in 1942 Sartre was not yet regarded as an "existentialist". But as Sartre's philosophy developed, he went on to explore how human activity constitutes a meaningful world from the brute, meaningless existence unveiled in his novel[2] (Aronson 1980, 71–88). In the process, the absurdity of *Nausea* becomes the contingency of *Being and Nothingness*, the fact that humans and things are simply there with no explanation or reason. As Sartre described it, the absurd is "the universal contingency of being which is, but which is not the basis of its being; the absurd is the given, the unjustifiable, primordial quality of existence" (quoted in Sagi 2002, 57). Having rooted human existence in such contingency, Sartre goes on to describe other fundamental structures of existence, core human projects, and characteristic patterns of behavior, including freedom and bad faith, all of which arise on this basis. The original contingency leads to our desire to undo it, to the futile project to "found being," in other words the "useless passion" of the project to become God.

For Sartre absurdity is obviously a fundamental ontological property of existence itself, frustrating us but not restricting our understanding. For Camus, on the other hand, absurdity is not a property of existence as such, but is an essential feature of our *relationship* with the world. It might be argued that Sartre and Camus are really quite similar, and that the core futility of Sartre's philosophy parallels the "despair" Camus describes. After all, if Sisyphus's labor is ultimately futile, so is the project to become God. But Sartre rejects the "classical pessimism" and "disillusionment" he finds in Camus and instead possesses an unCamusean confidence in his ability to understand and explain this project and the rest of the human world. Camus, on the contrary, builds an entire worldview on his central assumption that absurdity is an unsurpassable relationship between humans and their world (Aronson 2013). He postulates an inevitable divorce between human consciousness, with its "wild longing for clarity" (*MS*, 21) and the "unreasonable silence of the world" (*MS*, 28). As discussed above, Camus views the world as irrational, which means that it is not understandable through reason.

According to Camus, each existentialist writer betrayed his initial insight by seeking to appeal to something beyond the limits of the human condition, by turning to the transcendent. And yet even if we avoid what Camus describes as such escapist efforts and continue to live without irrational appeals, the desire to do so is built into our consciousness and thus our humanity. We are unable to free ourselves from "this desire for unity, this longing to solve, this need for clarity and cohesion" (*MS*, 51). But it is urgent to not succumb to these impulses and to instead accept absurdity. In contrast with existentialism, "The absurd is lucid reason noting its limits" (*MS*, 49).

Camus clearly believes that the existentialist philosophers are mistaken but does not argue against them, because he believes that "there is no truth but merely truths" (*MS*, 43). His disagreement rather takes the subtler and less assertive form of an immanent critique, pointing out that each thinker's existentialist philosophy ends up being inconsistent with its own starting point: "starting from a philosophy of the world's lack of meaning, it ends up by finding a meaning and depth in it" (*MS*, 42). These philosophers, he insists, refuse to accept the conclusions that follow from their own premises. Kierkegaard, for example, strongly senses the absurd. But rather than respecting it as the inevitable human ailment, he seeks to be cured of it by making it an attribute of a God who he then embraces.

Camus's most sustained analysis is of Husserl's phenomenology. Along with Sartre, Camus praises the early Husserlian notion of intentionality. Sartre saw this notion as revealing a dynamic consciousness without contents—the basis for his conception of freedom—while Camus is pleased that intentionality follows the absurd spirit in its "apparent modesty of thought that limits itself to describing what it declines to explain" (*MS*, 43). However, Camus criticizes Husserl's later search in *Ideas* for Platonic extra-temporal essences as a quasi-religious leap inconsistent with his original insight.

Happiness in Facing One's Fate

How then to remain consistent with absurd reasoning and avoid falling victim to the "spirit of nostalgia"? *The Myth of Sisyphus* finds the answer by abandoning the terrain of philosophy altogether. Camus describes a number of absurdist fictional characters and activities, including Don Juan and Dostoevsky's Kirolov (*The Possessed*), theater, and literary creation. And then he concludes with the story of Sisyphus, who fully incarnates a sense of life's absurdity, its "futility and hopeless labor" (*MS*, 119). Camus sees Sisyphus's endless effort and intense consciousness of futility as a *triumph*. "His scorn of the gods, his hatred of death, and his passion for life won him that unspeakable penalty in which the whole being is exerted toward accomplishing nothing" (*MS*, 120). After the dense and highly self-conscious earlier chapters, these pages condense the entire line of thought into a vivid image. Sisyphus demonstrates that we can live with "the certainty of a crushing fate, without the resignation that ought to accompany it" (*MS*, 54). For Camus, Sisyphus reminds us that we cannot help seeking to understand the reality that transcends our intelligence, striving to grasp more than our limited and practical scientific understanding allows, and wishing to live without dying. Like Sisyphus, we are our fate, and our frustration is our very life: we can never escape it.

But there is more. After the rock comes tumbling down, confirming the ultimate futility of his project, Sisyphus trudges after it once again. This "is the hour of consciousness. At each of those moments when he leaves the heights and gradually sinks towards the lairs of the gods, he is superior to his fate. He is stronger than his rock" (*MS*, 121). Why use the words "superior" and "stronger" when he has no hope of succeeding the next time? Paradoxically, it is because a sense of tragedy "crowns his victory." "Sisyphus, proletarian of the gods, powerless and rebellious, knows the whole extent of his wretched condition: it is what he thinks of during his descent" (*MS*, 121). Tragic consciousness is the conclusion of "absurd reasoning": living fully aware of the bitterness of our being and consciously facing our fate.

What then is Camus's reply to his question about whether or not to commit suicide? Full consciousness, avoiding false solutions such as religion, refusing to submit, and carrying on with vitality and intensity: these are Camus's answers. This is how a life without ultimate meaning can be made worth living. As he said in *Nuptials*, life's pleasures are inseparable from a keen awareness of these limits. Sisyphus accepts and embraces living with death without the possibility of appealing to God. "All Sisyphus's silent joy is contained therein. His fate belongs to him. His rock is his thing" (*MS*, 123).

Lucidly living the human condition, Sisyphus "knows himself to be the master of his days." By becoming conscious of it, Camus is saying, he takes ownership of it. In this sense Sisyphus reshapes his fate into a condition of "wholly human origin." "Wholly" may be an exaggeration, because after all, death is "inevitable and despicable," but it is the very condition of living. In acknowledging this,

Sisyphus consciously lives out what has been imposed on him, thus making it into his own end. In the same way, Meursault, protagonist of *The Stranger*, comes to consciousness in that book's second part after committing the inexplicable murder that ends the book's first part. He has lived his existence from one moment to the next and without much awareness, but at his trial and while awaiting execution he becomes like Sisyphus, fully conscious of himself and his terrible fate. He will die triumphant as the absurd man.

The Myth of Sisyphus is far from having a skeptical conclusion. In response to the lure of suicide, Camus counsels an intensely conscious and active non-resolution. Rejecting any hope of resolving the strain is also to reject despair. Indeed, it is possible, within and against these limits, to speak of happiness. "Happiness and the absurd are two sons of the same earth. They are inseparable" (*MS*, 122). It is not that discovering the absurd leads necessarily to happiness, but rather that acknowledging the absurd means also accepting human frailty, an awareness of our limitations, and the fact that we cannot help wishing to go beyond what is possible. These are all tokens of being fully alive. "The struggle itself toward the heights is enough to fill a man's heart. One must imagine Sisyphus happy" (*MS*, 123).

Response to Skepticism

We can compare his conclusion with Pyrrho's skepticism and Descartes's methodical doubt. First of all, like Pyrrho, Camus has solved his pressing existential issue, namely, avoiding despair, by a kind of resolution entailed in accepting our mortality and ultimate ignorance. But there are two critical differences with Pyrrho: for Camus we never can abandon the desire to know, and realizing this leads to a quickening of our life-impulses. This last point was already contained in *Nuptials*, but here is expanded to link consciousness with happiness. For Camus, happiness includes living intensely and sensuously in the present coupled with Sisyphus's tragic, lucid, and defiant consciousness, his sense of limits, his bitterness, his determination to keep on, and his refusal of any form of consolation.

Obviously, Camus's sense of happiness is not a conventional one but Sagi argues it may place him closer to Aristotle than to any other thinker insofar as he is championing the full realization of human capacities (Sagi 2002, 79–80) Camus is also similar in this to Nietzsche, who called upon his readers to "say yes to life," and live as completely as possible at every moment. Nietzsche's point was that to be wholly alive means being as aware of the negative as of the positive, feeling pain, not shunning any experience, and embracing life "even in its strangest and hardest problems" (Nietzsche 1888/1954, 562). But how is it possible that, by the end of *The Myth of Sisyphus*, Camus has moved from skepticism (about finding the truth) and nihilism (about whether life has meaning) to advocating an approach to life that is clearly judged to be better than others? How does he justify embracing a normative stance, affirming specific values? This contradiction reveals a certain sleight of hand, as the philosopher gives way to the artist. It is as an artist that Camus now makes his case for acceptance of tragedy, the consciousness of absurdity, and a life of sensuous vitality. He advocates this with the image of Sisyphus straining, fully alive, and happy.

Camus and the World of Violence: The Rebel

This meditation on absurdity and suicide follows closely on the publication of Camus's first novel, *The Stranger*, which also centered on individual experience and revolves around its protagonist's senseless murder of an Arab on a beach in Algiers and concludes with his execution by guillotine. And it is often forgotten that this absurdist novelist and philosopher was also a political activist—he had been a member of the Algerian branch of the French Communist Party in the mid-1930s and was organizer of an Algiers theater company that performed avant-garde and political plays—as well as a crusading journalist. From October 1938 until January 1940 he worked on *Alger républicain* and a sister newspaper. In June 1939 he wrote a series of reports on famine and poverty in the mountainous coastal region of Kabylie, among the first detailed articles ever written by a European Algerian describing the wretched living conditions of the native population.

After the start of World War II, Camus became editor of *Le Soir républicain* and as a pacifist opposed French entry into the war. The spectacle of Camus and his mentor Pascal Pia running their left-wing daily into the ground because they rejected the urgency of fighting Nazism is one of the most striking but least commented-on periods of his life. Misunderstanding Nazism at the beginning of the war, he advocated negotiations with Hitler that would in part reverse the humiliations of the Treaty of Versailles. His pacifism was in keeping with a time-honored French tradition, and Camus nevertheless reported for military service out of solidarity with those young men, like his brother, who had become soldiers. Intending to serve loyally and to advocate a negotiated peace in the barracks, he was angered that his tuberculosis disqualified him (Lottman, 201–31; Aronson 2004, 25–28).

These biographical facts are relevant to Camus's philosophical development after *The Myth of Sisyphus.* Moving to France and eventually becoming engaged in the resistance to the German occupation, in two "Letters to a German Friend" published clandestinely in 1943 and 1944, Camus pondered the question whether violence against the occupiers was justified. He spoke of the "loathing we [French] had for all war," and the need "to find out if we had the right to kill men, if we were allowed to add to the frightful misery of this world" (*RRD*, 8). Despising war, suspicious of heroism, he claimed that the occupied French paid dearly for this detour "with prison sentences and executions at dawn, with desertions and separations, with daily pangs of hunger, with emaciated children, and above all, with humiliation of our human dignity" (*RRD*, 8). Only when we were "at death's door," and "far behind" the Germans, did we understand the reasons for fighting, so that henceforth we would struggle with a clear conscience and "clean hands." In other words killing was morally permissible only within strict limits and after great provocation. Our moral strength was rooted in the fact that we were fighting for justice and national survival. The subsequent letters continued to contrast the French with the Germans on moral grounds drawn directly from Camus's evolving philosophy, and suggested the transition from *The Myth of Sisyphus* to *The Rebel*: if both adversaries began with a sense of the world's absurdity, Camus claimed that the French acknowledged and lived within this awareness, while the Germans sought to overcome it by dominating the world.

Camus's anti-Nazi commitment and newspaper experience led to him succeeding Pia in March 1944 as editor of *Combat*, the main underground newspaper of the non-Communist left. During this period Camus worked on *The Plague* which, as he later said, "has as its obvious content the struggle of the European resistance movements against Nazism" (*LCE*, 339). The novel, begun during the war, describes an epidemic of the bubonic plague in the small Algerian city of Oran, which transforms every aspect of daily life and shuts off the city from the surrounding world. The only possible response besides quarantine is refusing to passively accept disease and death and to actively organize "sanitary squads" to combat it. *The Plague* philosophically anticipates *The Rebel*: despite individuals' most ambitious goals, for example of Tarrou who seeks to end the death penalty and Father Paneloux, who demands that the people of Oran embrace their guilt and God's love, the actual situation calls for a very limited and specific activity. Individuals must act without fanfare or heroics and above all, in solidarity with each other in seeking to limit the effects of the plague. Like Sisyphus, they act in full consciousness of their limits, except now as a we. The Plague depicts a collective and nonviolent resistance to an unexplained pestilence, and thus quite deliberately does not raise the tactical, strategic, and moral issues built into the struggle of the Resistance against human occupiers (*LCE*, 340–1). If readers did not see this as an issue in 1947, it became contentious as the political climate changed, and the novel was attacked by Roland Barthes and later by Sartre (Aronson 2004, 228–9). In point of fact, after the Liberation the question of violence continued to occupy Camus both politically and philosophically. In 1945 his was one of the few voices raised in protest against the American use of nuclear weapons to defeat Japan (Aronson 2004, 61–63). After the Liberation he opposed the death penalty for collaborators, then turned against Marxism and Communism for embracing revolution, while rejecting the looming cold war and its threatening violence. And then in *The Rebel*, Camus began to spell out his deeper understanding of violence.

Absurdity, Rebellion, and Murder

At the beginning of *The Rebel*, Camus picks up where he left off in *The Myth of Sisyphus*. Writing as a philosopher again, he returns to the terrain of argument by explaining what absurdist reasoning entails. Its "final conclusion" is "the repudiation of suicide and the acceptance of the desperate encounter between human inquiry and the silence of the universe" (*R*, 6). Since to conclude otherwise would negate its very premise, namely the existence of the questioner, absurdism must logically accept life as the one necessary good. "To say that life is absurd, consciousness must be alive" (*R*, 6, tr. changed). Living and eating "are themselves value judgments" (*LCE*, 160). "To breathe is to judge" (*R*, 8). As in his criticism of the existentialists, Camus advocates a single standpoint from which to argue for objective validity, that of consistency.

At first blush, however, the book's subject seems to have more of a historical theme than a philosophical one. "The purpose of this essay is ... to face the reality of the present, which is logical crime, and to examine meticulously the arguments by which it is justified; it is an attempt to understand the times in which we live. One might think that a period which, in a space of fifty years, uproots, enslaves, or kills seventy million human beings should be condemned out of hand. But its culpability must still be understood" (*R*, 3).

Do such questions represent an entirely new philosophy or are they continuous with *The Myth of Sisyphus*? The issue is not resolved by the explanations that Camus gives for his shift in the first pages of *The Rebel*—by referring to the mass murders of the middle third of the twentieth century. "The age of negation," he says, once fostered a concern for suicide, but now in "the age of ideologies, we must examine our position in relation to murder" (*R*, 4). Have the "ages" changed in the less than ten years between the two books? He may be right to say that whether murder has rational foundations is "the question implicit in the blood and strife of this century," but in changing his focus from suicide to murder, it is also clear that Camus is shifting his philosophical optic from the individual to our social belonging.

In so doing Camus applies the philosophy of the absurd in new, social directions, and seeks to answer new, historical questions. But as we see him setting this up at the beginning of *The Rebel* the continuity with a philosophical reading of *The Stranger* is also strikingly clear. Novelist Kamel Daoud, retelling The *Stranger* from the point of view of the victim, correctly calls the murder of his Arab "kinsman" a "philosophical crime" (Daoud 19). At the beginning of *The Rebel* Camus explains:

> Awareness of the absurd, when we first claim to deduce a rule of behavior from it, makes murder seem a matter of indifference, to say the least, and hence possible. ... There is no pro or con: the murderer is neither right nor wrong. We are free to stoke the crematory fires or to devote ourselves to the care of lepers. Evil and virtue are mere chance or caprice. (*R*, 5)

If historically "murder is the problem today" (*R*, 5), the encounter with absurdity tells us that the same is true philosophically. Having ruled out suicide, what is there to say about murder?

Starting from the absence of God, the key theme of *Nuptials*, and the inevitability of absurdity, the key theme of *The Myth of Sisyphus*, Camus incorporates both of these into *The Rebel*, but alongside them he now stresses revolt. The act of rebellion assumes the status of a primary datum of human experience, like the Cartesian cogito taken by Sartre as his point of departure. Camus first expressed this directly under the inspiration of his encounter with *Being and Nothingness*. But in calling it "revolt" he takes it in a direction sharply different from Sartre, who built from the cogito an "essay in phenomenological ontology." Ignoring completely the ontological dimension, Camus is now concerned with immediate issues of human social experience. Revolt, to be sure, still includes the rebellion against absurdity that Camus described in *The Myth of Sisyphus*, and once again he will speak of rebelling against our own mortality and the universe's meaninglessness and incoherence. But *The Rebel* begins with the kind of revolt that rejects oppression and slavery, and protests against the world's injustice.

It is at first, like *The Myth of Sisyphus*, a single individual's rebellion, but now Camus stresses that revolt creates values, dignity, and solidarity. "I revolt, therefore we are" (*R*, 22) is his paradoxical statement. But how can an *I* lead to a *we*? How does "we are" follow from "I revolt"? How can the individual's experience of absurdity, and the rebellion against it, stem from, produce, imply, or entail the wider social sense of injustice and solidarity? The *we* in fact is the subject of *The Rebel*, although the title *L'Homme revolté* suggests that one's original motivation may be individual. Acting against oppression entails having recourse to social values, and at the same time joining with others in struggle. On both levels solidarity is our common condition.

In *The Rebel* Camus takes the further step, which occupies most of the book, of developing his notion of metaphysical and historical rebellion in opposition to the concept of revolution. Applying his philosophical themes directly to politics in the years immediately after the Liberation of France in 1944, Camus had already concluded that Marxists, and especially the Communists, were guilty of evading life's absurdity by aiming at a wholesale transformation of society, which must necessarily be violent. And now, in *The Rebel*, he describes this as a major trend of modern history, using similar terms to those he had used in *The Myth of Sisyphus* to describe the religious and philosophical evasions.

What sort of work is this? In a book so charged with political meaning, Camus makes no explicitly political arguments or revelations, and presents little in the way of actual social analysis or concrete historical study. *The Rebel* is, rather, a historically framed philosophical essay about underlying ideas and attitudes of civilization. David Sprintzen suggests these taken-for-granted attitudes operate implicitly and in the background of human projects and very rarely become conscious (Sprintzen 1988, 123).

Camus felt that it was urgent to critically examine these attitudes in a world in which calculated murder had become common. Applying his absurdist ideas and insights to politics, in *The Rebel* Camus explains what he regards as the modern world's increasingly organized and catastrophic refusal to face, accept, and live with absurdity. The book provides a unique perspective—presenting a coherent and original structure of premise, mood, description, philosophy, history, and even prejudice.

Against Communism

Camus's hostility to Communism had its personal, political, and philosophical reasons. These certainly reached back to his expulsion from the Communist Party in the mid-1930s for refusing to adhere to its Popular Front strategy of playing down French colonialism in Algeria in order to win support from the white working class. Then, making no mention of Marxism, *The Myth of Sisyphus* is eloquently silent on its claims to present a coherent understanding of human history and a meaningful path to the future. His mutually respectful relations with Communists during the Resistance and the immediate postwar period turned bitter after he was attacked in the Communist press and repaid the attack in a series of newspaper articles in 1946 entitled "Neither Victims nor Executioners" (Aronson, 2004, 66–93).

In *The Rebel* Camus insisted that both Communism's appeal and its negative features sprang from the same irrepressible human impulse: faced with absurdity and injustice, humans refuse to accept their existence and instead seek to remake the world. Validating revolt as a necessary starting point, Camus criticizes politics aimed at building a utopian future, affirming once more that life should be lived in the present and in the sensuous world. He explores the history of post-religious and nihilistic intellectual and literary movements; he attacks political violence with his views on limits and solidarity; and he ends by articulating the metaphysical role of art as well as a self-limiting radical politics. In place of striving to transform the world, he speaks of *mésure*—"measure", in the sense of proportion or balance—and of living in the tension of the human condition. He labels this outlook "Mediterranean" in an attempt to anchor his views to the place he grew up and to evoke in his readers its sense of harmony and appreciation of physical life. There is no substantive argument for the label, nor is one possible given his method of simply selecting who and what counts as representative of the "Mediterranean" view while excluding others—e.g., some Greek writers, not many Romans. In place of argument, he paints a concluding vision of Mediterranean harmony that he hopes will be stirring and lyrical, binding the reader to his insights.

As a political tract *The Rebel* asserts that Communism leads inexorably to murder, and then explains how revolutions arise from certain ideas and states of spirit. But he makes no close analysis of movements or events, gives no role to material needs or oppression, and regards the quest for social justice as a metaphysically inspired attempt to replace "the reign of grace by the reign of justice" (*R*, 56).

Furthermore, Camus insists that these attitudes are built into Marxism. In "Neither Victims nor Executioners" he declared himself a socialist but not a Marxist. He rejected the Marxist acceptance of violent revolution and the consequentialist maxim that "the end justifies the means."[3] "In the Marxian perspective," he wrote sweepingly, "a hundred thousand deaths is a small price to pay for the happiness of hundreds of millions" (Camus 1991, 130). Marxists think this, Camus asserted, because they believe that history has a necessary logic leading to human happiness, and thus they accept violence to bring it about.

In *The Rebel* Camus takes this assertion a further step: Marxism is not primarily about social change but is rather a revolt that "attempts to annex all creation." Revolution emerges when revolt seeks to ignore the limits built into human life. By an "inevitable logic of nihilism" Communism climaxes the modern trend to deify man and to transform and unify the world. Today's revolutions yield to the blind impulse, originally described in *The Myth of Sisyphus*, "to demand order in the midst of chaos, and unity in the very heart of the ephemeral" (*MS*, 10). As does the rebel who becomes a revolutionary who kills and then justifies murder as legitimate.

According to Camus, the execution of King Louis XVI during the French Revolution was the decisive step demonstrating the pursuit of justice without regard to limits. It contradicted the original life-affirming, self-affirming, and unifying purpose of revolt. This discussion belongs to Camus's "history of European pride," which is prefaced by certain ideas from the Greeks and certain aspects of early Christianity, but begins in earnest with the advent of modernity. Camus focuses on a variety of major figures, movements, and literary works: the Marquis de Sade, romanticism, dandyism, *The Brothers Karamazov*, Hegel, Marx, Nietzsche, surrealism, the Nazis, and above all the Bolsheviks. Camus describes revolt as increasing its force over time and turning into an ever more desperate nihilism, overthrowing God and putting man in his place, wielding power more and more brutally. Historical revolt, rooted in metaphysical revolt, leads to revolutions seeking to eliminate absurdity by using murder as their central tool to take total control over the world. Communism is the contemporary expression of this Western sickness.

In the twentieth century, Camus claims, murder has become "reasonable," "theoretically defensible," and justified by doctrine. People have grown accustomed to "logical crimes"—that is, mass death either planned or foreseen, and rationally justified. Thus Camus calls "logical crime" the central issue of the time, seeks to "examine meticulously the arguments by which it is justified" (*R*, 3), and sets out to explore how the twentieth century became a century of slaughter.

We might justly expect an analysis of the arguments he speaks of, but *The Rebel* changes focus. Human reason is confused by "slave camps under the flag of freedom, massacres justified by philanthropy or by a taste for the superhuman" (*R*, 4)—the first two refer to Communism, the third to Nazism. In the body of the text, Nazism virtually drops out (it was, he says, a system of "irrational terror"—not at all what interested Camus), sharply narrowing the inquiry. His shift is revealed by his question: How can murder be committed with premeditation and be justified by philosophy? It turns out that the "rational murder" Camus was concerned with is not committed by capitalists or democrats, colonialists or imperialists, or by Nazis—but only by Communists.

He does not address the Holocaust, and although his had been a lone voice of protest against Hiroshima in 1945, he does not now ask how it happened. As a journalist he had been one of the few to indict French colonialism, but he does not mention it, except in a footnote. How was it possible for Camus to focus solely on the violence of Communism, given the history he had lived, in the age of nuclear weapons, in the very midst of the French colonial war in Vietnam, and when he knew that a bitter struggle over Algeria lay ahead? It seems he became blinded by ideology, separating Communism from the other evils of the century and directing his animus there. Camus's ideas, of course, had developed and matured over the years since he first began writing about revolt. But something else had happened: his agenda had changed. Absurdity and revolt, his original themes, had been harnessed as an alternative to Communism, which had become the archenemy. Even as he rejected its violent confrontations, the philosophy of revolt became Cold-War ideology.

Because *The Rebel* claimed to describe the attitude that lay behind the evil features of contemporary revolutionary politics, it became a major political event. Readers could hardly miss his description of how the impulse for emancipation turned into organized, rational murder as the rebel-become-revolutionary attempted to order an absurd universe. In presenting this message, Camus sought not so much to critique Stalinism as its apologists. His specific targets were intellectuals attracted to Communism—as he himself had been in the 1930s.

One of these targets was Jean-Paul Sartre, and toward the end of *The Rebel* Camus now took aim at his friend's evolving politics. Camus focuses on "the cult of history" against which the entire book is directed and his belief that "the existentialists," led by Sartre, had fallen victim to the idea that revolt should lead to revolution. Within Camus's framework, Sartre is challenged as trying, like the predecessors criticized in *The Myth of Sisyphus*, to escape the absurdity with which his own thinking began by turning to "history," that is to Marxism. This is a bit of a stretch because Sartre was still several years from declaring himself a Marxist, and it shows Camus's tendency towards sweeping generalization rather than close analysis. But it also reflects his awareness that his friend was determined to find a meaning in the world even as he himself foreswore doing so. And it shows his capacity for interpreting a specific disagreement in the broadest possible terms—as a fundamental conflict of philosophies.

Violence: Inevitable and Impossible

The concluding chapters of *The Rebel* are punctuated with emphatic words of conclusion (*alors*, *donc*, *ainsi*, *c'est pourquoi*), which are rarely followed by consequences of what comes before and often introduce further assertions, without any evidence or analysis. They are studded with carefully composed topic sentences for major ideas—which one expects to be followed by paragraphs, pages, and chapters of development but, instead, merely follow one another and wait until the next equally well-wrought topic sentence.

As often in the book, the reader must be prepared to follow an abstract dance of concepts, as "rebellion," "revolution," "history," "nihilism," and other substantives stand on their own, without reference to human agents. The going gets even muddier as we near the end and the text verges on incoherence. How then is it possible that Foley judges *The Rebel* philosophically as Camus's "most important book" (Foley 55)?

In these pages Camus is going back over familiar ground, contrasting the implicit religiosity of a future-oriented outlook that claims to understand and promote the logic of history, and justifying violence to implement it, with his more tentative "philosophy of limits," with its sense of risk, "calculated ignorance," and living in the present. However the strain stems from the fact that he is doing so much more. As he tries to bring the book to a conclusion he is wrestling with its most difficult theme—that the resort to violence is both inevitable and "impossible." The rebel lives in contradiction. He or she cannot abandon the possibility of lying, injustice, and violence, for they are part of the rebel's condition, and will of necessity enter into the struggle against oppression. "He cannot, therefore, absolutely claim not to kill or lie, without renouncing his rebellion and accepting, once and for all, evil and murder." In other words, to not rebel is to become an accomplice of oppression. Rebellion, Camus has insisted, will entail murder. Yet rebellion, "in principle," is a protest against death, just as it is a source of the solidarity that binds the human community. He has said that death is the most fundamental of absurdities, and that at root rebellion is a protest against absurdity. Thus to kill any other human being, even an oppressor, is to disrupt our solidarity, in a sense to contradict our very being. It is impossible, then, to embrace rebellion while rejecting violence.

There are those, however, who ignore the dilemma: these are the believers in history, heirs of Hegel and Marx who imagine a time when inequality and oppression will cease and humans will finally be happy. For Camus such a hope resembles the paradise beyond this life promised by religions. Living for, and sacrificing humans to, a supposedly better future is, very simply, another religion. Moreover, his sharpest hostility is reserved for intellectuals who theorize and justify such movements. Accepting the dilemma, Camus is unable to spell out how a successful revolution can remain committed to the solidaristic and life-affirming principle of rebellion with which it began. He does however suggest two actions which, if implemented, would be signs of a revolution's commitment to remain rebellious: it would abolish the death penalty and it would encourage rather than restrict freedom of speech.

In *The Rebel* Camus extends the ideas he asserted in *Nuptials*, developed in *The Myth of Sisyphus*, and then foreshadowed in *The Plague*: the human condition is inherently frustrating, indeed absurd, but we betray ourselves and solicit catastrophe by seeking solutions beyond our capacity. "The rebel obstinately confronts a world condemned to death and the impenetrable obscurity of the human condition with his demand for life and absolute clarity. He is seeking, without knowing it, a moral philosophy or a religion" (*R*, 101). The book sets out the alternative: to accept the fact that we are living in a Godless universe and rebel against this within limits as do most of the members of the "sanitary squads" in *The Plague* – or to become a revolutionary, who, like the religious believer committed to the abstract and total triumph of justice, refuses to accept living in the present.

Having critiqued religion in *Nuptials* and *The Plague*, Camus is self-consciously exploring the starting points, projects, weaknesses, illusions, and political temptations of a post-religious universe. He describes how traditional religion has lost its force, and how younger generations have been growing up amid an increasing emptiness and a sense that anything is possible. He further claims that modern secularism stumbles into a nihilistic state of mind because it does not really free itself from religion. "Then the only kingdom that is opposed to the kingdom of grace must be founded-namely, the kingdom of justice-and the human community must be reunited among the debris of the fallen City of God. To kill God and to build a church are the constant and contradictory purpose of rebellion" (*R*, 103). If rebellion spills over its limits and is given free rein, our modern need to create kingdoms and our continuing search for salvation is the path of catastrophe. "When the throne of God is overturned, the rebel realizes that it is now his own responsibility to create the justice, the order, and the unity that he sought in vain within his own condition, and in this way to justify the fall of God. Then begins the desperate effort to create, at the price of crime and murder if necessary, the dominion of man" (*R*, 25). But to restrain oneself from this effort is to feel bereft of justice, order, and unity. Camus recognizes that hope and the revolutionary drive are essential directions of the post-classical Western spirit, stemming from its entire world of culture, thought, and feeling. This is the path of the metaphysical rebel, who does not see that "human insurrection, in its exalted and tragic forms, is only, and can only be, a prolonged protest against death" (*R*, 100).

The Fall

We have been exploring one of the most interesting and perplexing aspects of Camus's thought: his determination to criticize attitudes that he finds to be natural and inevitable. For one, the possibility of suicide haunts humans, and so does the desire for an impossible order and an unachievable permanence. Existentialist writers had similar insights, but Camus criticizes their inability to remain consistent with their initial insight. Similarly, he insists throughout *The Rebel* that the metaphysical need he sees leading to Communism's terror is universal: he describes it and its consequences so that we can better resist it in ourselves as well as others. His reflexive anti-Communism notwithstanding, an underlying sympathy unites Camus to those revolutionaries he opposes, because he freely acknowledges that he and they share the same starting points, outlook, stresses, temptations, and pitfalls. Although in political argument he frequently took refuge in a tone of moral superiority, Camus makes clear through his skepticism that those he disagrees with are no less and no more than fellow creatures who give in to the same fundamental drive to escape the absurdity that we all share. This sense of moral complexity is most eloquent in his short novel *The Fall*, whose single character, Clamence, has been variously identified as everyman, a Camus-character, and a Sartre-character. He was all of these. Clamence is clearly evil, guilty of standing by as a young woman commits suicide. In him Camus seeks to describe and indict his generation, including both his enemies and himself. Clamence's life is filled with good works, but he is a hypocrite and knows it. His monologue is filled with self-justification as well as the confession of someone torn apart by his guilt but unable to fully acknowledge it. Sitting at a bar in Amsterdam, he descends into his own personal hell, inviting the reader to follow him. In telling Clamence's story, Camus was clearly seeking to empathize as well as describe, to understand as well as condemn. Clamence is a monster, but Clamence is also just another human being (Aronson 2004, 192–200). Beyond the character and actions of Clamence, *The Fall* demonstrates a unique message at the heart of Camus's writing. Life is no one single, simple thing, but a series of tensions and dilemmas. The most seemingly straightforward features of life are in fact ambiguous and even contradictory. Camus recommends that we avoid trying to resolve them. We need to face the fact that we can never successfully purge ourselves of the impulses that threaten to wreak havoc with our lives. Camus's philosophy, if it has a single meaning, is that we should learn to tolerate, indeed embrace the frustration and ambivalence that humans cannot escape.

Philosopher of the Present

Well into the twenty-first century, the career of Camus's thought, like that of his onetime friend Jean-Paul Sartre, has been remarkable. Two generations after his death, his complex and profound philosophical project, as discussed by Srigley, is very much with us because it seeks not only to critique modernity but reaches back to the ancient world to lay the basis for alternative ways of thinking and living in the present. Thus, if in some respects he anticipated the postmodernists, he retained a central metaphysical concern with such ideas as absurdity and revolt. Unlike postmodernism, Camus was, as Jeffrey C. Isaac says, a "chastened humanist" who remained deeply attached, as was Hannah Arendt, to "the language of right, freedom, and truth" (Isaac 244).

Camus's ideas and name have come up again and again during the twenty-first century, not only among philosophers and literary scholars, among specialists in a wide variety of fields, in the press and among political writers, and in conversations among the general public who read his books or have heard about his ideas. First, his exploration of living in a Godless universe has led to his name being mentioned often in discussions about religious nonbelief (Aronson 2011). Yet unlike the "new atheists" the great nonbeliever Camus was never assured enough to declare that God does not exist and was not militantly opposed to religious belief and practice (Carlson 2014). Even as Camus presents in *The Plague* a profoundly critical picture of Father Paneloux's sermons describing the plague first as a punishment for human sin and then as a call to embrace the divine mystery, for a time the priest nevertheless humbly joins the collective project of the "sanitary squads."

Second, after the 9/11 attack and during the "war on terror," Camus's writings on violence became much discussed. For example *The Rebel* was explored anew for hints about the motivations behind twenty-first century terrorism. Paul Berman deployed Camus in his justification for the "war on terror" against Islamic "pathological mass movements" (Berman 2003, 27–33). Foley, on the other hand, devoted attention to the actual relevance of Camus's attempts to think through the question of political violence on a small-group and individual level. He shows how, both in *The Rebel* and in his plays *Caligula* and *The Just Assassins*, Camus brings his philosophy to bear directly on the question of the exceptional conditions under which an act of political murder can considered legitimate: (1) The target must be a tyrant; (2) the killing must not involve innocent civilians; (3) the killer must be in direct physical proximity to the victim; and (4) there must be no alternative to killing (Foley 2008, 93). Furthermore, because the killer has violated the moral order on which human society is based, Camus makes the demand that he or she must be prepared to sacrifice his or her own life in return. But if he accepts killing in certain circumstances, Foley stresses that Camus rules out mass killing, indirect murder, killing civilians, and killing without an urgent need to remove murderous and tyrannical individuals. These demands rest on the core idea of *The Rebel*, that to rebel is to assert and respect a moral order, and this must be sustained both by clear limits and by the murderer's willingness to die.

During the beginning of the Covid-19 pandemic in 2020, sales of *The Plague* exploded and interest was so great that the *New York Times* republished its original 1948 review by Stephen Spender. Hundreds of articles were written about it in all languages – by bloggers, artists, cartoonists, journalists, Camus specialists, medical practitioners, scholars from every conceivable discipline – and philosophers. Camus's work was being mined for what it had to teach about living in and coping with the pandemic, including such topics as: functioning amidst the absurdity of a disease that appeared for seemingly no reason at all (de Botton 2021); the similarities and differences between his plague and ours (Aronson, 2020); living and working within the paralyzing existential fear imposed by the pandemic (Farr 2021); retaining hope amidst catastrophe (Kabel & Phillipson 2020); and the solidarity among members of the "sanitary squads" doing so (Illing 2020). In the face of absurdity and mass death many writers extolled the modest and self-limiting philosophy behind *The Plague*, rooted in *The Myth of Sisyphus* and further developed in *The Rebel*: one must act, with others, wherever one happens to be, by simply doing one's job. As Rieux says: "there's no question of heroism in all this. It's a matter of common decency. That's an idea which may make some people smile, but the only means of fighting a plague is – common decency"

CHAPTER FOUR

Simone de Beauvoir

Some have found Beauvoir's exclusion from the domain of philosophy more than a matter of taking Beauvoir at her word. They attribute it to an exclusively systematic view of philosophy which, deaf to the philosophical methodology of the metaphysical novel, ignored the ways that Beauvoir embedded phenomenological-existential arguments in her literary works. Between those who did not challenge Beauvoir's self-portrait, those who did not accept her understanding of the relationship between literature and philosophy, and those who missed the unique signature of her philosophical essays, Beauvoir the philosopher remained a lady-in-waiting.

Some have argued that the belated admission of Beauvoir into the ranks of philosophers is a matter of sexism on two counts. The first concerns the fact that Beauvoir was a woman. Her philosophical writings were read as echoes of Sartre rather than explored for their own contributions because it was only "natural" to think of a woman as a disciple of her male companion. The second concerns the fact that she wrote about women. *The Second*

Sex, recognized as one of the hundred most important works of the twentieth century, would not be counted as philosophy because it dealt with sex, hardly a burning philosophical issue (so it was said). This encyclopedia entry shows how much things have changed. Long overdue, Beauvoir's recognition as a philosopher is now secure.

Situating Beauvoir

Simone de Beauvoir was born on January 9, 1908. She died seventy-eight years later, on April 14, 1986. At the time of her death she was honored as a crucial figure in the struggle for women's rights, and as an eminent writer, having won the Prix Goncourt, the prestigious French literary award, for her novel *The Mandarins* (1954). She was also famous for being the life-long companion of Jean Paul Sartre. Active in the French intellectual scene all of her life, and a central player in the philosophical debates of the times both in her role as an author of philosophical essays, novels, plays, memoirs, travel diaries, and newspaper articles, and as an editor of *Les Temps Modernes*, Beauvoir was not considered a philosopher in her own right at the time of her death.

Beauvoir would have appreciated the fact that her current philosophical status reflects our changed understanding of the domain of philosophy and the changed situation of women, for it confirms her idea of situated freedom—that our capacity for agency and meaning-making, that whether or not we are identified as agents and meaning-makers, is constrained, though never determined, by our situation. She would also have appreciated the fact that while her works were instrumental in effecting these changes, their lasting effect is a tribute to the ways that others have taken up her philosophical and feminist legacies; for one of her crucial contributions to our ethical and political vocabularies is the concept of the appeal—that the success of our projects depends on the extent to which they are adopted by others

Beauvoir detailed her phenomenological and existential critique of the philosophical *status quo* in her 1946 essay *Literature and the Metaphysical Essay*, and her 1965 and 1966 essays *Que Peut la Littérature?* and *Mon Expérience d'écrivain*. This critique, influenced by both Husserl and Heidegger, focused on the significance of lived experience and on the ways that the meanings of the world are revealed in language. Heidegger turned to the language of poetry for this revelation. Beauvoir, Camus and Sartre turned to the language of the novel and the theater. They looked to Husserl to theorize their turn to these discourses by insisting on grounding their theoretical analyses in the concrete particulars of lived experience. They looked to Heidegger to challenge the privileged position of abstract discourses. For Beauvoir, however, the turn to literature carried ethical and political as well as philosophical implications. It allowed her to explore the limits of the appeal (the activity of calling on others to take up one's political projects); to portray the temptations of violence; to enact her existential ethics of freedom, responsibility, joy and generosity, and to examine the intimacies and complexities of our relationships with others.

Beauvoir's challenge to the philosophical tradition was part of the existential-phenomenological project. Her challenge to the patriarchal *status quo* was more dramatic. It was an event. Not at first, however, for at its publication *The Second Sex* was regarded more as an affront to sexual decency than a political indictment of patriarchy or a phenomenological account of the meaning of "woman". The women who came to be known as second-wave feminists understood what Beauvoir's first readers missed. It was not sexual decency that was being attacked but patriarchal indecency that was on trial. *The Second Sex* expressed their sense of injustice, focused their demands for social, political, and personal change and alerted them to the connections between private practices and public policies. *The Second Sex* remains a contentious book. No longer considered sexually scandalous, its analysis of patriarchy and its proposed antidotes to women's domination are still debated. What is not contested, however, is the fact that feminism as we know it remains in its debt.

As *The Second Sex* became a catalyst for challenging women's situations, Beauvoir's political and intellectual place was also reset. With regard to feminism, she herself was responsible for the change. After repeatedly refusing to align herself with the feminist movement, Beauvoir declared herself a feminist in a 1972 interview in *Le Nouvel observateur* and joined other Marxist feminists in founding the journal *Questions féministes.* With regard to the philosophical field it took the efforts of others to get her a seat at the table; for though Beauvoir belatedly identified herself as a feminist, she never called herself a philosopher. Her philosophical voice, she insisted, was merely an elaboration of Sartre's. Those denials coupled with the fact of her life-long intimate relationship with Sartre positioned her in the public and philosophical eye as his alter ego. Decoupling Beauvoir from Sartre became the first priority of those interested in establishing her independent philosophical credentials. Sometimes the issue concerned Sartre's originality: Were the ideas of his *Being and*

Nothingness (1943) stolen from Beauvoir's *She Came to Stay* (1943)? Sometimes they concerned matters of influence: What happened in their discussions and critiques of each other's work? Eventually these arguments abated and scholars turned from exclusive attention to the matter of Sartre's influence to the more fruitful question of influence in the broader sense. They began to trace the ways that she, like her existential-phenomenological contemporaries, took up and reconfigured their philosophical heritage to reflect their shared methodology and unique insights. We now understand that to fully appreciate the rich complexities of Beauvoir's thought, we need to attend to the fact that her graduate thesis was on Leibniz; that her reading of Hegel was influenced by the interpretations of Kojève; that she was introduced to Husserl and Heidegger by her teacher Baruzi; that Marx and Descartes were familiar figures in her philosophical vocabulary; and that Bergson was an early influence on her thinking.

She Came to Stay: Freedom and Violence

Though Beauvoir's first philosophical essay was *Pyrrhus and Cinéas* (1944) many of her interpreters identify *She Came to Stay* (1943) as her inaugural philosophical foray. It is a clear example of what Beauvoir calls the metaphysical novel. The letters between Sartre and Beauvoir and Beauvoir's diaries of that period (published in the 1980s), show that both Beauvoir and Sartre were concerned with the question of the other, the issue of bad faith and the dynamics of desire. They were also examining the relationship and tensions between our singular existential status and the social conditions within which our singularity is lived. *She Came to Stay* is packed with philosophical reflections—reflections on our relationship to time, to each other, to ourselves. These reflections are never, however, presented in systematic arguments or brought to closure. They are lived in the concrete, ambiguously triangulated lives of Pierre, Xavière and Françoise. Opening with a quote from Hegel, "Each conscience seeks the death of the other", and ending with Françoise's murder of Xavière, which Beauvoir narrates as an act in which Françoise confronts her solitude and announces her freedom, the novel does not necessarily confirm Hegel's claim; for the point of the murder was not to eliminate the other *per se* but to destroy a particular other, Xavière, the other who threatened to leave Françoise without the other she loved, Pierre. Existential ambiguity trumps Hegelian clarity. The issues raised in this first novel, however, the ambiguity regarding the responsibilities and limits of freedom, the legitimacy of violence, the tension between our experience of ourselves as simultaneously solitary and intertwined with others, the temptations of bad faith and the examination of the existentially faithful relationship to time will pervade Beauvoir's subsequent reflections.

Radical Freedom and the Other

Pyrrhus and Cinéas (1944), published one year after *She Came To Stay*, is Beauvoir's first philosophical essay. It addresses such fundamental ethical and political issues as: What are the criteria of ethical action? How can I distinguish ethical from unethical political projects? What are the principles of ethical relationships? Can violence ever be justified? It examines these questions from an existential-phenomenological perspective. Taking the situation of the concrete existing individual as its point of departure, it provides an analysis of the ways that as particular subjects we are necessarily embedded in the world, and inescapably related to others. Though not feminist in any identifiable sense, *Pyrrhus and Cinéas* raises such compelling feminist questions as: Under what conditions, if any, may I speak for/ in the name of another?

After opening *Pyrrhus and Cinéas* with Plutarch's account of a conversation between Pyrrhus and Cinéas, where the justification of action is questioned, Beauvoir, finding the recommendation to be passive inconsistent with the realities of human nature and desire, asks three questions: What is the measure of a person? What goals can one set for oneself? What hopes are permitted to us? She then divides the text into two parts. Part one moves from the ontological truth—that I am a finite freedom whose endings are always and necessarily new beginnings—to the existential questions: How can I desire to be what I am? How can I live my finitude with passion? These existential questions lead to moral and political ones: What actions express the truth and passion of our condition? How can I act in such a way as to create the conditions that sustain and support the humanity of human beings? Part I concludes with the observation that: "A man alone in the world would be paralyzed by ... the vanity of all of his goals. But man is not alone in the world" (PhilW 115, cf. P&C 42). Beauvoir opens Part II with the properly ethical question: What is my relation to the other? Here the analysis is dominated by the problem created by Beauvoir's insistence on the radical nature of freedom. According to Beauvoir, the other, as free, is immune to my power. Whatever I do—if as master I exploit slaves, or as executioner I hang murderers—I cannot violate their inner subjective freedom. Substituting the inner-outer difference for the Cartesian mind-body distinction, Beauvoir argues that we can never directly touch the freedom of others. Our relationships are either superficial, engaging only the outer surface of each other's being, or mediated through our common commitment to a shared goal or value. As free, I am saved from the dangers of intimacy and the threat of dehumanization.

This line of argument would seem to lead either to benign Stoic conclusions of mutual indifference, or to the finding that tyrants and terrorists pose no threat to individual freedom. Beauvoir does not, however, let it drift in these directions. Instead she uses the inner-outer distinction and the idea that I need others to take up my projects if they are to have a future, to introduce the ideas of the appeal and risk. She develops the concept of freedom as transcendence (the movement toward an open future and indeterminate possibilities) to argue that we cannot be determined by the present. The essence of freedom as transcendence aligns freedom with uncertainty and risk. To be free is to be radically contingent. Though I find myself in a world of value and meaning, these values and meanings were brought into the world by others. I am free to reject, alter or endorse them for the meaning of the world is determined by human choices. Whatever choice I make, however, I cannot support it without the help of others. My values will find a home in the world only if others embrace them; only if I persuade others to make my values theirs.

As radically free I need the other. I need to be able to appeal to others to join me in my projects. The knot of the ethical problem lies here: How can I, a radically free being who is existentially severed from all other human freedoms, transcend the isolations of freedom to create a community of allies? Given the necessity of appealing to the other's freedom, under what conditions is such an appeal possible?

In answering these questions Beauvoir turns the inner-outer distinction to her advantage as she develops the concept of situated freedom. Though I can neither act for another nor directly influence their freedom, I must, Beauvoir argues, accept responsibility for the fact that my actions produce the conditions within which the other acts. However irrelevant my conduct may be for the other's inner freedom, it concerns mine. "I am", Beauvoir writes, "the face of the other's misery... I am the facticity of their situation" (PhilW 126, cf. P&C 58). Pursuing this difference between my power to effect the other's freedom and my responsibility for their situation, and exploring the conditions under which my appeal to the other can/will be heard, Beauvoir determines that there are two conditions of the appeal. First, I must be allowed to call to the other and must struggle against those who try to silence me. Second, there must be others who can respond to my call. The first condition may be purely political. The second is political and material. Only equals, Beauvoir argues, can hear or respond to my call. Only those who are not consumed by the struggle for survival, only those who exist in the material conditions of freedom, health, leisure and security can become my allies in the struggle against injustice. The first rule of justice, therefore, is to work for a world where the material and political conditions of the appeal are secured.

Violence is not ruled out. Given that Beauvoir has argued that we can never reach the other in the depths of their freedom, she cannot call it evil. She does not, however, endorse it. Neither does she envision a future without conflict. The fact that we are differently situated and engage in the work of transcendence from different historical, economic, sexed and racial positions ensures that some of us will always be an obstacle to another's freedom. "We are", Beauvoir writes, "condemned to violence" (PhilW 138, cf. P&C 77). As neither evil nor avoidable, violence, she argues, is "the mark of a failure which nothing can offset" (PhilW 138, cf. P&C 77). It is the tragedy of the human condition.

The argument of *Pyrrhus and Cinéas* ends on an uneasy note. As ethical, we are obliged to work for the conditions of material and political equality. In calling on others to take up our projects and give these projects a future, we are precluded from forcing others to become our allies. We are enjoined to appeal to their freedom. Where persuasion fails, however, we are permitted the recourse to violence. The ambiguity of our being as subjects for ourselves and objects for others in the world is lived in this dilemma of violence and justice. Becoming lucid about the meaning of freedom, we learn to live our freedom by accepting its finitude and contingency, its risks and its failures.

The Ethics of Ambiguity: Bad Faith, the Appeal, the Artist

It is impossible to know where Simone de Beauvoir's thinking would have gone had she been spared the cold, the hunger and the fear of living in Nazi occupied Paris. What we do know is that coming face to face with forces of injustice beyond her control, the questions of evil and the Other took on new urgency. Beauvoir speaks of the war as creating an existential rupture in time. She speaks of herself as having undergone a conversion. She can no longer afford the luxury of focusing on her own happiness and pleasure. The question of evil becomes a pressing concern. One cannot refuse to take a stand. One is either a collaborator or not. In writing *The Ethics of Ambiguity*, Beauvoir takes her stand. She identifies herself as an existentialist and identifies existentialism as the philosophy of our (her) times because it is the only philosophy that takes the question of evil seriously. It is the only philosophy prepared to counter Dostoevsky's claim that without God everything is permissible. That we are alone in the world and that we exist without guarantees, are not, however, the only truths of the human condition. There is also the truth of our freedom and this truth, as detailed in *The Ethics of Ambiguity*, entails a logic of reciprocity and responsibility that contests the terrors of a world ruled only by the authority of power.

The Ethics of Ambiguity, published in 1947, reconsiders the *Pyrrhus and Cinéas* idea of invulnerable freedom. Dropping the distinction between the inner and outer domains of freedom and deploying a unique understanding of consciousness as an intentional activity, Beauvoir now finds that I can be alienated from my freedom. Similar to *She Came To Stay*, which bears the imprint of Hegel's account of the fight to the death that sets the stage for the master-slave dialectic, and *Pyrrhus and Cinéas*, which works through the Cartesian implications of our existential situation, *The Ethics of Ambiguity* redeploys concepts of canonical philosophical figures. Here Beauvoir takes up the phenomenologies of Husserl and Hegel to provide an analysis of intersubjectivity that accepts the singularity of the existing individual without allowing that singularity to justify an epistemological solipsism, an existential isolationism or an ethical egoism. The Hegel drawn on here is the Hegel who resolves the inequalities of the master-slave relationship through the justice of mutual recognition. The Husserl appealed to is the Husserl who introduced Beauvoir to the thesis of intentionality.

The Ethics of Ambiguity opens with an account of intentionality which designates the meaning-disclosing, meaning-making and meaning-desiring activities of consciousness as both insistent and ambiguous—insistent in that they are spontaneous and unstoppable; ambiguous in that they preclude any possibility of self-unification or closure. Beauvoir describes the intentionality of consciousness as operating in two ways. First there is the activity of wanting to disclose the meaning of being. Second there is the activity of bringing meaning to the world. In the first mode of activity consciousness expresses its freedom to discover meaning. In the second, it uses its freedom to become the author of the meaning of the world. Beauvoir identifies each of these intentionalities with a mood: the first with the mood of joy, the second with the dual moods of hope and domination. Whether the second moment of intentionality becomes the ground of projects of liberation or exploitation depends on whether the mood of hope or domination prevails.

Describing consciousness as ambiguous, Beauvoir identifies our ambiguity with the idea of failure. We can never fulfill our passion for meaning in either of its intentional expressions; that is, we will never succeed in fully revealing the meaning of the world, and never become God, the author of the meaning of the world. These truths of intentionality set the criteria of Beauvoir's ethics. Finding that ethical systems and absolutes, insofar as they claim to give final answers to our ethical dilemmas and authoritarian justifications for our actions, offer dangerous consolations for our failure to be the absolute source of the world's meaning or being, Beauvoir rejects these systems of absolutes in favor of ethical projects that acknowledge our limits and recognize the future as open. From this perspective her ethics of ambiguity might be characterized as an ethics of existential hope.

Beauvoir's *Ethics of Ambiguity* is a secularism that rejects the ideas of God and Humanity. Their apparent differences conceal a common core: both claim to have identified an absolute source for, and justifications of our beliefs and actions. They allow us to evade responsibility for creating the conditions of our existence and to flee the anxieties of ambiguity. Whether it is called the age of the Messiah or the classless society, these appeals to a utopian destiny encourage us to think in terms of ends which justify means. They invite us to sacrifice the present for the future. They are the stuff of inquisitions, imperialisms, gulags and Auschwitz. Privileging the future over the present they pervert our relationship to time, each other and ourselves. Insisting that the future is undecided and that its form will be shaped by our present decisions Beauvoir argues that it is only by insisting on the dignity of today's human beings that the dignity of those to come can be secured.

Beauvoir rejects the familiar charge against secularism made famous by Dostoevsky's Grand Inquisitor: "If God is dead everything is permitted". As she sees it, without God to pardon us for our "sins" we are totally and inexcusably responsible for our actions. Dostoevsky was mistaken. The problem of secularism is not that of license, it is the problem of the "we". Can separate existing individuals be bound to each other? Can they forge laws binding for all? *The Ethics of Ambiguity* insists that they can. It does this by arguing that evil resides in the denial of freedom (mine and others), that we are responsible for ensuring the existence of the conditions of freedom (the material conditions of a minimal standard of living and the political conditions of uncensored discourse and association), and that I can neither affirm nor live my freedom without also affirming the freedom of others.

Beauvoir's argument for ethical freedom begins by noting a fundamental fact of the human condition. We begin our lives as children who are dependent on others and embedded in a world already endowed with meaning. We are born into the condition that Beauvoir calls the "serious world". This is a world of ready made values and established authorities. This is a world where obedience is demanded. For children, this world is neither alienating nor stifling for they are too young to assume the responsibilities of freedom. As children who create imaginary worlds, we are in effect learning the lessons of freedom—that we are creators of the meaning and value of the world. Free to play, children develop their creative capacities and their meaning-making abilities without, however, being held accountable for the worlds they bring into being. Considering these two dimensions of children's lives, their imaginative freedom and their freedom from responsibility, Beauvoir determines that the child lives a metaphysically privileged existence. Children, she says, experience the joys but not the anxieties of freedom. Beauvoir also, however, describes children as mystified. By this she means that they believe that the foundations of the world are secure and that their place in the world is naturally given and unchangeable. Beauvoir marks adolescence as the end of this idyllic era. It is the time of moral decision. Emerging into the world of adults, we are now called upon to renounce the serious world, to reject the mystification of childhood and to take responsibility for our choices.

All of us pass through the age of adolescence; not all of us take up its ethical demands. The fact of our initial dependency has moral implications, for it predisposes us to the temptations of bad faith, strategies by which we deny our existential freedom and our moral responsibility. It sets our desire in the direction of a nostalgia for those lost Halcyon days. Looking to return to the security of that metaphysically privileged time, some of us evade the responsibilities of freedom by choosing to remain children, that is, to submit to the authority of others.

Beauvoir does not object to the mystification of childhood. She acknowledges that parental authority is necessary for the child's survival. To treat adults as children, however, is immoral and evil. To choose to remain a child is an act of bad faith. If we are exploited, enslaved or terrorized, however, our submission to authority of the other cannot be counted as an act of bad faith. Absent these conditions, Beauvoir holds us accountable for our response to the experience of freedom. We cannot use the anxieties of freedom either as an excuse for our active participation in, or our passive acceptance of the exploitation of others. Hiding behind the authority of others or establishing ourselves as authorities over others are culpable offenses.

Beauvoir portrays the complexity of the ways that we either avoid or accept the responsibilities of freedom in the imaginary and (sometimes) historical figures of the sub-man, the serious man, the nihilist, the adventurer, the passionate man, the critical thinker and the artist-writer. The point of delineating these human types is several fold. It is a way of distinguishing between two kinds of unethical positions. One, portrayed in the portraits of the sub-man and the serious man, refuses to recognize the experience of freedom. The other, depicted in the pictures of the nihilist, the adventurer and the maniacally passionate man, misreads the meanings of freedom. The ethical person, as portrayed by Beauvoir, is driven by passion. Unlike the egoistic, maniacal passion of the tyrant, however, the ethical passion of the artist-writer is defined by its generosity—specifically the generosity of recognizing the other's singularity and protecting the other in their difference from becoming an object of another's will.

In describing the different ways that freedom is evaded or misused, Beauvoir distinguishes ontological from ethical freedom. She shows us that acknowledging our freedom is a necessary but not a sufficient condition for ethical action. To meet the conditions of the ethical, freedom must be used properly. It must, according to Beauvoir, embrace the ties that bind me to others, and take up the appeal—an act whereby I call on others, in their freedom, to join me in bringing certain values, projects, conditions into being. Artists and writers embody the ethical ideal in several respects. Their work expresses the subjective passion that grounds the ethical life. They describe the ways that the material and political complexities of our situations can either alienate us from our freedom or open us to it. By envisioning the future as open and contingent, artists and writers challenge the mystifications that validate sacrificing the present for the future. They establish the essential relationship between my freedom and the freedom of others.

The Ethics of Ambiguity does not avoid the question of violence. Determining that violence is sometimes necessary, Beauvoir uses the example of the young Nazi soldier to argue that to liberate the oppressed we may have to destroy their oppressors. She distances herself from the argument of *Pyrrhus and Cinéas*; now she identifies violence as an assault on the other's freedom (however misused) and as such this violence marks our failure to respect the "we" of our humanity. Thus, *The Ethics of Ambiguity* provides an analysis of our existential-ethical situation that joins a hard-headed realism (violence is an unavoidable fact of our condition) with demanding requirements. It is unique, however, in aligning this realism and these requirements with the passion of generosity and a mood of joy.

The Second Sex: Woman As Other

In her memoir *The Force of Circumstance* (1963), Beauvoir looks back at *The Ethics of Ambiguity* and criticizes it for being too abstract. She does not repudiate the arguments of her text, but finds that it erred in trying to define morality independent of a social context. *The Second Sex* may be read as correcting this error—as reworking and materially situating the analyses of *The Ethics of Ambiguity*. Imaginary caricatures will be replaced by phenomenological descriptions of the situations of real women.

Where Beauvoir's earlier works blurred the borders separating philosophy and literature, her later writings disrupt the boundaries between the personal, the political and the philosophical. Now, Beauvoir takes herself, her situation, her embodiment and the situations and embodiments of other women, as the subjects of her philosophical reflections. Where *The Ethics of Ambiguity* conjured up images of ethical and unethical figures to make its arguments tangible, the analyses of *The Second Sex* are materialized in Beauvoir's experiences as a woman and in women's lived realities. Where *The Ethics of Ambiguity* speaks of mystification in a general sense, *The Second Sex* speaks of the specific ways that the natural and social sciences and the European literary, social, political and religious traditions have created a world where impossible and conflicting ideals of femininity produce an ideology of women's "natural" inferiority to justify patriarchal domination.

Beauvoir's self criticism suggests that her later works mark a break with her earlier writings. We should, however, resist the temptation to take this notion of discontinuity too far. Rather than thinking in terms of breaks it is more fruitful to see *The Second Sex* in terms of a more radical commitment to the phenomenological insight that it is as embodied beings that we engage the world. Our access to, awareness of, and possibilities for world engagement cannot be considered absent a consideration of the body.

Before *The Second Sex*, the sexed/gendered body was not an object of phenomenological investigation. Beauvoir changed that. Her argument for sexual equality takes two directions. First, it exposes the ways that masculine ideology exploits the sexual difference to create systems of inequality. Second, it identifies the ways that arguments for equality erase the sexual difference in order to establish the masculine subject as the absolute human type. Here Plato is her target. Plato, beginning with the premise that sex is an accidental quality, concludes that women and men are equally qualified to become members of the guardian class. The price of women's admission to this privileged class, however, is that they must train and live like men. Thus the discriminatory sexual difference remains in play. Only men or those who emulate them may rule. Beauvoir's argument for equality does not fall into this trap. She insists that women and men treat each other as equals and that such treatment requires that their sexual differences be validated. Equality is not a synonym for sameness.

The Second Sex argues against the either/or frame of the woman question (either women and men are equal or they are different). It argues for women's equality, while insisting on the reality of the sexual difference. Beauvoir finds it unjust and immoral to use the sexual difference as an argument for women's subordination. She finds it un-phenomenological, however, to ignore it. As a phenomenologist she is obliged to examine women's unique experiences of their bodies and to determine how these experiences are co-determined by what phenomenology calls the everyday attitude (the common-sense assumptions that we unreflectively bring to our experience). As a feminist phenomenologist assessing the meanings of the lived female body, Beauvoir explores the ways that cultural assumptions frame women's experience of their bodies and alienate them from their body's possibilities. For example, it is assumed that women are the weaker sex. What, she directs us to ask, is the ground of this assumption? What criteria of strength are used? Upper body power? Average body size? Is there a reason not to consider longevity a sign of strength? Using this criterion, would women still be considered the weaker sex? A bit of reflection exposes the biases of the criteria used to support the supposedly obvious fact of women's weakness and transforms it from an unassailable reality to an unreliable assumption. Once we begin this questioning, it is not long before other so-called facts fall to the side of "common sense" in the phenomenological sense.

What is perhaps the most famous line of *The Second Sex*, "On ne naît pas femme: on le devient" (1949, 13), translated in 1953 as "One is not born but becomes a woman" (1953, 267) and in 2010 as "One is not born but becomes woman", is credited by many as alerting us to the sex-gender distinction. Whether or not Beauvoir understood herself to be inaugurating this distinction, whether or not she followed this distinction to its logical/ radical conclusions, or whether or not radical conclusions are justified are currently matters of feminist debate. What is not a matter of dispute is that *The Second Sex* gave us the vocabulary for analyzing the social constructions of femininity and a method for critiquing these constructions. By not accepting the common sense idea that to be born with female genitalia is to be born a woman this most famous line of *The Second Sex* pursues the first rule of phenomenology: identify your assumptions, treat them as prejudices and put them aside; do not bring them back into play until and unless they have been validated by experience.

Taken within the context of its contemporary philosophical scene, *The Second Sex* was a phenomenological analysis waiting to happen. Whether or not it required a woman phenomenologist to discover the effects of sex/gender on the lived body's experience cannot be said. That it was a woman who taught us to bracket the assumption that the lived body's sex/gender was accidental to its lived relations, positions, engagements, etc. is a matter of history. What was a phenomenological breakthrough became in *The Second Sex* a liberatory tool: by attending to the ways that patriarchal structures used the sexual difference to deprive women of their "can do" bodies, Beauvoir made the case for declaring this deprivation oppressive. Taken within the context of the feminist movement, this declaration of oppression was an event. It opened the way for the consciousness-raising that characterized second-wave feminism; it validated women's experiences of injustice. What from an existential-phenomenological perspective, was a detailed analysis of the lived body, and an ethical and political indictment of the ways that patriarchy alienated women from their embodied capacities, was, from a feminist perspective, an appeal that called on women to take up the politics of liberation.

Several concepts are crucial to the argument of *The Second Sex*. The concept of the Other is introduced early in the text and drives the entire analysis. It has also become a critical concept in theories that analyze the oppressions of colonized, enslaved and other exploited people. Beauvoir will use it again in her last major work, *The Coming of Age* (1970), to structure her critique of the ways that the elderly are "othered" by society.

Beauvoir bases her idea of the Other on Hegel's account of the master-slave dialectic. Instead of the terms "master" and "slave", however, she uses the terms "Subject" and "Other". The Subject is the absolute. The Other is the inessential. Unlike Hegel who universalized this dialectic, Beauvoir distinguishes the dialectic of exploitation between historically constituted Subjects and Others from the exploitation that ensues when the Subject is Man and the Other is Woman. In the first case those marked as Other experience their oppression as a communal reality. They see themselves as part of an oppressed group. Here, oppressed Others may call on the resources of a common history and a shared abusive situation to assert their subjectivity and demand recognition and reciprocity.

The situation of women is comparable to the condition of the Hegelian Other in that men, like the Hegelian Master, identify themselves as the Subject, the absolute human type, and, measuring women by this standard of the human, identify them as inferior. Women's so-called inadequacies are then used as justification for seeing them as the Other and for treating them accordingly. Unlike the Hegelian Other, however, women are unable to identify the origin of their otherness. They cannot call on the bond of a shared history to reestablish their lost status as Subjects. Further, dispersed among the world of men, they identify themselves in terms of the differences of their oppressors (e.g., as white or black women, as working-class or middle-class women, as Muslim, Christian, Jewish, Buddhist or Hindu women) rather than with each other. They lack the solidarity and resources of the Hegelian Other for organizing themselves into a "we" that demands recognition. Finally, their conflict with men is ambiguous. According to Beauvoir, women and men exist in a "primordial *Mitsein*" (SS: 2010, 9, cf. 1949, 22): there is a unique bond between this Subject and its Other. In contesting their status as inessential, women must discover their "we" and take account of the *Mitsein*. Beauvoir uses the category of the Inessential Other to designate the unique situation of women as the ambiguous Other of men. Unlike the Other of the master-slave dialectic, women are not positioned to rebel. As Inessential Others, women's routes to subjectivity and recognition cannot follow the Hegelian script (SS: 2010, 6–9, cf. 1949, 18–22).

This attention to what Beauvoir, borrowing from Heidegger, calls a "primordial *Mitsein*" may be why she does not repeat her earlier argument that violence is sometimes necessary for the pursuit of justice in *The Second Sex*. Often criticized as one mark of Beauvoir's heterosexism, this reference to the *Mitsein* is not made in ignorance of lesbian sexuality and is not a rejection of non-heterosexual sexualities. It is a recognition of the present state of affairs where the heterosexual norm prevails. If patriarchy is to be dismantled we will have to understand how heteronormative sexuality serves it. We will have to denaturalize it. To Beauvoir's way of thinking, however, the institutional alienations of heterosexuality ought not be confused with the erotics of heterosexual desire. The realities of this desire and the bond of the "primordial *Mitsein*" that it forges must be taken into account: not only is it used to enforce women's isolation and to support their inability to identify a common history, it is also responsible for the value and relationship that Beauvoir calls the "bond", a situation-specific articulation of the appeal found in in *The Ethics of Ambiguity*.

A brief but packed sentence that appears early in the *The Second Sex* alerts us to the ways that Beauvoir used existential and Marxist categories to analyze the unique complexities of women's situation. It reads,

Hence woman makes no claim for herself as subject because she lacks the concrete means, because she senses the necessary link connecting her to man without positing its reciprocity, and because she often derives satisfaction from her role as *the Other*. (SS: 2010, 10, cf. 1949, 24)

This statement needs to be read in the context of Beauvoir's ethical-political question, "How can a human being in a woman's situation attain fulfillment?"

Between the statement and the question we discover that the ethical-political issue of fulfillment does not concern a woman's happiness. Happiness may be chosen or accepted in exchange for the deprivations of freedom. Recalling the argument of *The Ethics of Ambiguity* we know why. As Others, women are returned to the metaphysically privileged world of the child. They experience the happiness brought about by bad faith—a happiness of not being responsible for themselves, of not having to make consequential choices. From this existential perspective women may be said to be complicitious in their subjugation. But this is not the whole story. If women are happy as the other, it may be because this is the only avenue of happiness open to them given the material and ideological realities of their situation. Beauvoir's existential charge of bad faith must be understood within her Marxist analysis of the social, economic and cultural structures that frame women's lives. Though Beauvoir will not argue that these structures deprive women of their freedom, neither will she ignore the situations that make the exercise of that freedom extremely difficult. Her assertion that woman feels a necessary bond with man regardless of a lack of reciprocity, however, escapes existential and Marxist categories. It is crucial to Beauvoir's analysis of women's condition and draws on the notion of the appeal developed in *The Ethics of Ambiguity*. In making an appeal to others to join me in my pursuit of justice I validate myself and my values. Given that my appeal must be an appeal to the other in their freedom, I must allow for the fact that the other may reject it. When this happens, I must (assuming that the rejection is not a threat to the ground value of freedom) recognize the other's freedom and affirm the bond of humanity that ties us to each other. In the case of women, Beauvoir notes, this aspect of the appeal (the affirmation of the bond between us) dominates. She does not approve of the way that women allow it to eclipse the requirement that they be recognized as free subjects, but she does alert us to the fact that recognition in itself is not the full story of the ethical relationship. To demand recognition without regard for the bond of humanity is unethical. It is the position of the Subject as master.

Moving between the statement that women are pleased with their alienated status as the Other and the question, "How can women achieve human fulfillment?", Beauvoir argues that women's exploitation is historical, and therefore amenable to change. As an existential situation, however, women are responsible for changing it. Liberation must be women's work. It is not a matter of appealing to men to give women their freedom, but a matter of women discovering their solidarity, rejecting the bad faith temptations of happiness and discovering the pleasures of freedom. Further, though Beauvoir alerts us to the tensions and conflicts that this will create between men and women, she does not envision a permanent war of the sexes. Here her Hegelian-Marxist optimism prevails. Men will (ultimately) recognize women as free subjects.

The last chapters of *The Second Sex*, "The Independent Woman" and the "Conclusion", speak of the current (1947) status of women's situation—what has changed and what remains to be done. Without ignoring the importance of women's gaining the right to vote and without dismissing the necessity of women attaining economic independence, Beauvoir finds these liberal and Marxist solutions to women's situation inadequate. They ignore the effects of women's socialization (the subject of volume two of *The Second Sex*) and they are inattentive to the ways that the norm of masculinity remains the standard of the human. The liberated woman must free herself from two shackles: first, the idea that to be independent she must be like men, and second, the socialization through which she becomes feminized. The first alienates her from her sexuality. The second makes her adverse to risking herself for her ideas/

ideals. Attentive to this current state of affairs, and to the phenomenology of the body, Beauvoir sets two prerequisites for liberation. First, women must be socialized to engage the world. Second, they must be allowed to discover the unique ways that their embodiment engages the world. In short, the myth of woman must be dismantled. So long as it prevails, economic and political advances will fall short of the goal of liberation. Speaking in reference to sexual difference, Beauvoir notes that disabling the myth of woman is not a recipe for an androgynous future. Given the realities of embodiment, there will be sexual differences. Unlike today, however, these differences will not be used to justify the difference between a Subject and his inessential Other.

The goal of liberation, according to Beauvoir, is our mutual recognition of each other as free and as other. She finds one situation in which this mutual recognition (sometimes) exists today, the intimate heterosexual erotic encounter. Speaking of this intimacy she writes, "the dimension of the *other* remains; but the fact is that alterity no longer has a hostile character" (SS: 2010, 415, cf. 1949, 189). Why? Because lovers experience themselves and each other ambiguously, that is as both subjects and objects of erotic desire rather than as delineated according to institutionalized positions of man and woman. In Beauvoir's words,

The erotic experience is one that most poignantly reveals to human beings their ambiguous condition; they experience it as flesh and as spirit, as the other and as subject.(SS: 2010, 416, cf. 1949, 190)

The concept of ambiguity, developed abstractly in *The Ethics of Ambiguity*, is erotically embodied in *The Second Sex* and is identified as a crucial piece of the prescription for transcending the oppressions of patriarchy. This description of the liberating possibilities of the erotic encounter is also one of those places where Beauvoir reworks Merleau-Ponty's phenomenology of embodiment. For in drawing on Merleau-Ponty's descriptions of the ways that we are world-making and world-embedded subject-objects, she reveals the ways that it is as subject-objects "for the world", "to the world", and "in the world" that we are passionately drawn to each other.

"Must We Burn Sade?" Freedom and the Flesh

We are a long way away from *Pyrrhus and Cinéas*, where Beauvoir declared our freedom immune from assault. In that early work, our freedom insulated us from the risks of intimacy. In *The Second Sex*, avoiding these risks remains possible, but now this avoidance is identified as a mark of our moral failure to live the ambiguity of our condition. Beauvoir's essay, "Must We Burn Sade?" (1951–52), written in response to a request to write an introduction to Sade's *Justine*, details the effects Beauvoir's changed position on the relationship between freedom and intimacy has on her ethical reflections. The central ethical question, "the problem of the true relation between man and man", remains unchanged (Bergoffen 2012a, 41, cf. 2012b, 95). Indeed what interests Beauvoir about Sade is that, "[he] posed the problem of the *other* in its most extreme terms"(1965[1963], 243, cf. 1963, 333). What has changed is Beauvoir's understanding of the drama of intersubjectivity. Marking this change, this essay also marks a return to the question of the responsibility of the artist raised in *The Ethics of Ambiguity*.

"Must we Burn Sade?" identifies the Marquis's decision to write as an existential project, an authentic ethics and a politics of rebellion. Beauvoir credits Sade with uncovering the despotic secrets of the patriarchal political machine. She is sympathetic to his utopian appeal to freedom. She finds, however, that Sade perverted the meaning of freedom. Thus Beauvoir identifies Sade as a great moralist who endorsed an unsatisfactory ethics.

Sade is Beauvoir's Janus-faced ally. She does not refute his claim that cruelty establishes a relationship between the self and the other. Sade is correct. Cruelty reveals us to each other in the particularities and ambiguities of our conscious and fleshed existence. The tyrant and victim, Beauvoir tells us, are a genuine couple. They are united by the bonds of the flesh and freedom.

Sade is the epitome of maniacal passion dedicated to the project of cruelty. Because he takes full responsibility for his choices, he must be credited with choosing freedom and accepted as being authentically ethical. This does not, however, make him either an ethical or moral figure; for his choices destroy the intersubjective bonds of humanity. Though his account of the power of cruelty provides a convincing critique of our social, political and personal hypocrisies, it does not critique the ways that cruelty is a perversion of freedom and an exploitation of the vulnerability of the flesh. Thus his descriptions of the powers of cruelty and the meaning of torture are incomplete and inadequate. The case of the Marquis de Sade makes it clear that authenticity, assuming responsibility for one's choices, is a necessary, but not sufficient, condition of an existential ethics of freedom.

In the end, Beauvoir finds that Sade was misled (which does not mean that he was innocent). He mistook power for freedom and misunderstood the meanings of the erotic. In his fascination with the conflict between consciousness and the flesh, Sade exposed the failure of the sadistic enterprise; for in attempting to lose himself in the pleasures of the flesh and in this way to experience both the ambiguity of his being as consciousness made flesh (or flesh made consciousness) and the reality of his being for and with others, Sade substitutes the spectacle for the lived experience and accepts counterfeit transactions of domination and assimilation/incorporation for genuine relationships of reciprocity and gratuitous generosity. He never reaches the other.

Centering his life in the erotic, Sade missed the truth of the erotic. This truth, Beauvoir tells us, can only be found by those who abandon themselves to the risks of emotional intoxication. Living this intoxication we discover the ways that the body turned flesh dissolves all arguments against the immediacy of our bonds with each other and grounds an ethic of the appeal, risk and mutual vulnerability.

Between the early *Pyrrhus and Cinéas* and the later "Must We Burn Sade?" we discern the impact of what might be called Beauvoir's phenomenological turn to the body. Once she abandons the idea that our freedom, as absolutely internal, is immune from an assault by the other, and accepts the radical vulnerability of our lived embodiment, questions of violence and desire cannot be severed from the question of our shared humanity or questions of ethics and justice. In condemning Sade for his perversion of the erotic, Beauvoir also faults him as an artist. Though she accuses him of being a technically poor writer, the heart of her criticism is ethical not aesthetic. Sade, according to Beauvoir, violated his obligations as an author. Instead of revealing the world to us in its promise and possibilities, and instead of appealing to us to work for justice, he took refuge in the imaginary and developed metaphysical justifications for suffering and cruelty. In the end, Beauvoir accuses Sade of being the serious man described in her *Ethics of Ambiguity*.

The Concrete Appeal

In 1962, Beauvoir and Gisile Halimi co-authored the story of Djamila Boupacha, an Algerian girl accused of being a terrorist and tortured by the French during the French-Algerian War. This book may be read as an extension of Beauvoir's critique of the Marquis de Sade. Instead of fleeing from the horrors of the real into the safety of the imaginary, Beauvoir takes up her responsibility as an author to expose and confront realities that the state would rather hide. Her purpose in writing is concrete and political. The book is both a protest and an appeal. Countering Sade, Beauvoir and Halimi show that the truth of torture lies in the unjustifiable politics of abusive power.

Finitude, Passion and the Body

The ways that the phenomenological turn to the body becomes increasingly important in Beauvoir's work, and the ways that this turn heightens Beauvoir's sensitivity to the materialities of our situated freedom and to the power of the category of the Other, may be traced in Beauvoir's attention to the question of human finitude. This question is raised early in her 1946 novel, *All Men Are Mortal*, the story of Fosca, a man who chooses to cheat death. His desire for immortality, however, is driven by his desire to realize the abstract ideal of humanism. Fosca does not embrace immortality to escape the ambiguities of the flesh and embodiment. His decision is motivated by his desire to save the world. He believes that time is his enemy so long as his time is limited. He believes that with sufficient time he can take the humanist a project, bring it to closure and secure it from failure.

Fosca learns, however, that contrary to his initial belief, time becomes his enemy when it stretches endlessly before him. It is not time that he needs to secure his vision, but the commitment of others. No amount of time can secure that. As immortal, Fosca confronts the inevitability of failure that haunts humanity. Unlike mortals, however, who, confronted with the constraints of time, take up their failures with passion, Fosca becomes immobilized. Indifference to life replaces the passion for life. In the end, he discovers the crucial truth of ethical action from his many-generations-removed grandson, Armand. Understanding that the future belongs to others who may or may not take up his projects, Armand commits himself to the concrete possibilities of the present. His passion is embodied in the appeal to others, not in an abstract goal that, however just it might seem, would deny future generations the right to determine their own destiny.

In *All Men Are Mortal* the givenness of finitude and death concerns our relationship to time. Eighteen years later, writing about the dying and death of her mother in *A Very Easy Death* (1964); six years after that, analyzing the situation of the aged in *Coming of Age* (1970), and eleven years subsequent to that, chronicling Sartre's last days in *Adieux: A Farewell to Sartre* (1981), it is not so much our relationship to time but more a matter of our embodiment that concerns Beauvoir. In *A Very Easy Death* and *Adieux*, Beauvoir assumes the position of the phenomenological witness. The bodies of her mother and Sartre are given to us in all their disturbing breakdowns and deteriorations. Some have found these works cold, insensitive and even cruel. They miss Beauvoir's point. She is showing us who we are. The "I can" body revealed by other phenomenologists as a crucial mark of embodiment is the limited condition of the mature healthy body. It is but one phase of the life of the body. In its early days the body is still learning its "I can's". As we age, the body begins losing them. It is one thing, as with the myth of woman, to alienate an "I can" from its capacities. It is quite another to refuse to attend to the full range of embodied life and to assess the value of that life in terms of its I can possibilities.

The Other Again

We need to read *A Very Easy Death* and *Adieux* within the context of the analyses of *The Coming of Age* to fully appreciate Beauvoir's role as witness. The project of *The Coming of Age* is similar to that of *The Second Sex*. Like *The Second Sex*, it focuses on a group of people designated as Other; like *The Second Sex* it exposes the mythical status of the "facts" about aging and the aged; and like *The Second Sex* it indicts society for its dehumanization of those it designates as Other. *The Coming of Age* also emulates *The Second Sex* in its method and scope. It trains a phenomenological lens on biological, psychological and sociological factors in order to understand the phenomenon of marginalized otherness. In many ways, however, *The Coming of Age* corrects what Beauvoir sees as the flaw of *The Second Sex*.

In reflecting on *The Second Sex*, Beauvoir says that were she to write it again she would pay less attention to the abstract issue of consciousness and more attention to the material conditions of scarcity. Though it is impossible to say what a revised version of *The Second Sex* would look like, *The Coming of Age* gives us some idea of how it might read. There is no talk here of the aged. Reminding us that old age is our universal destiny, Beauvoir tells us that its lived meaning is specific to our historical, class and cultural situations. Where *The Second Sex* identifies the ways that the myth of woman hides the diversity of women and does not seem to see that the single category of the inessential Other may not capture the diverse meanings of women's situations, *The Coming of Age* keeps making the point that if we speak of old age as a universal category we will miss the crucial differences among the aged that the myths and images of aging hide.

Comparing the status of the aged to that of women as woman, Beauvoir notes that both occupy the position of the Other and that as Other both are subject to the powers of mythical, exploitive biologies. Though *The Coming of Age* pays closer attention to the diversity behind the unifying myths and works with a somewhat different conception of otherness, it sounds remarkably similar to *The Second Sex* as it traces the sources of the marginal status of the aged. While *The Second Sex* accused patriarchy of depriving women of their subject status by barring them from the project and devaluating the fleshed experience of the erotic, *The Coming of Age* argues that the non-subject status of the aged can be traced to the fact that they are barred from their projects and their erotic possibilities. "The old man", Beauvoir writes, "looks to active members of the community like one of a 'different species'" because he is not engaged in a project (1972[1970], 217, cf. 1970, 231).

Like *The Second Sex*, which attended to the givens of biology without allowing them to determine the meaning of the subject, *The Coming of Age* also gives biology its due. The lack of engagement of the aged, Beauvoir notes, is in part imposed from without and in part comes from within; for as we age, the body is transformed from an instrument that engages the world into a hindrance that makes our access to the world difficult. The point of *The Coming of Age*, however, is that it is unjust to use these difficulties to justify reducing the aged to the status of the Other. *Adieux*'s witnessing makes this point clearly. However diminished Sartre's body became, it never severed him from his projects. He could not have sustained his work by himself, but he was in a situation where others refused to marginalize him. They did not equate his diminished bodily capacities with a diminished humanity. *The Coming of Age* argues that the situation of a privileged Sartre ought to be our common destiny.

In a world which recognized the phenomenological truth of the body, the existential truth of freedom, the Marxist truth of exploitation and the human truth of the bond, the derogatory category of the Other would be eradicated. Neither the aged nor women, nor anyone by virtue of their race, class, ethnicity or religion would find themselves rendered inessential. Beauvoir knows that it is too much to hope for such a world. She understands the lures of domination and violence. Throughout her career, however, she used philosophical and literary tools to reveal the possibilities of such a world and appealed to us to work for it.

CHAPTER FIVE

JEAN-PAUL SARTRE

Sartre's life has been examined by many biographies, starting with Simone de Beauvoir's *Adieux* (and, subsequently, Cohen-Solal 1985; Levy 2003; Flynn 2014; Cox 2019). Sartre's own literary "life" exemplifies trends he thematized in both *Words* and *Being and Nothingness*, summed up by his claim that "to be dead is to be prey for the living" (Sartre 1943 [1956: 543]). Sartre himself was one of the first to undertake such an autobiographical effort, via the evocation of his own childhood in *Words* (1964a)—in which Sartre applies to himself his method of existential psychoanalysis, thereby complicating this life/death binary.

Like many of his generation, Sartre lived through a series of major cultural and historical events that his existential philosophy responded to and attempted to shape. He was born in 1905 and died in 1980, spanning most of the twentieth century and the trajectory that the Marxist historian Eric Hobsbawm refers to as the "age of extremes", a period that was also well-described in the middle of that century in Albert Camus' *The Rebel*, notwithstanding that the reception of Camus' book in *Les Temps Modernes* in 1951–2 caused Sartre and Camus to very publicly fall out.

The major events of Sartre's life seem relatively clear, at least viewed from an external perspective. A child throughout World War 1, he was a young man during the Great Depression but born into relative affluence, brought up by his grandmother. At least as presented in *Words*, Sartre's childhood was filled with books, the dream of posterity and immortality in those books, and in which he grappled with his loss of the use of one eye and encountered the realities of his own appearance revealed through his mother's look after a haircut—suffice to say, he was not classically beautiful.

Sartre's education, by contrast, was classical—the École Normale Supérieure. His education at the ENS was oriented around the history of philosophy, and the influential bifurcation of that time between the neo-Kantianism of Brunschvicg and the vitalism of Bergson. While Sartre failed his first attempt at the aggregation, apparently by virtue of being overly ambitious, on repeating the year he topped the class (de Beauvoir was second, at her first attempt and at the age of 21, then the youngest to complete). Sartre then taught philosophy at various schools, notably at Le Havre from 1931–36 and while he was composing his early philosophy and his great philosophical novel, *Nausea*. He never entered a classical university position.

Although Sartre's philosophical encounter with phenomenology had already occurred (around 1933), which de Beauvoir described as causing him to turn pale with emotion (de Beauvoir 1960 [1962: 112]), with the onset of World War 2 Sartre merged those philosophical concerns with more obviously existential themes like freedom, authenticity, responsibility, and anguish, as translated into English from the French *angoisse* by both Hazel Barnes and Sarah Richmond. He was a Meteorologist in Alsace in the war and was captured by the German Army in 1940 and imprisoned for just under a year (see *War Diaries*). During this socio-political turmoil, Sartre remained remarkably prolific. Notable publications include his play, *No Exit* (1947), *Being and Nothingness* (1943), and then completing *Existentialism is a Humanism* (1946), *Anti-semite and Jew* (1946), and founding and coediting *Les Temps Modernes*, commencing from 1943 (Sartre's major contributions are collected in his series *Situations*, especially volume V).

Sartre continued to lead various social and political protests after that period, especially concerning French colonialism. By the time of the student revolutions in May 1968 he was no longer quite the dominant cultural and intellectual force he had been, but he did not retreat from public life and engagement and died in 1980. Estimates of the numbers of those attending his funeral procession in Paris range from 50–100,000 people. Sartre had been in the midst of a collaboration with Benny Levy regarding ethics, the so-called "Hope Now" interviews, whose status remain somewhat controversial in Sartrean scholarship, given the interviews were produced in the midst of Sartre's illness and shortly before he died, and the fact that the relevant audio-recordings are not publicly available.

Transcendence of the Ego: The Discovery of Intentionality

One of the most famous foundational moments of existentialism concerns Sartre's discovery of phenomenology around the turn of 1932/3, when in a Parisian bar listening to his friend Raymond Aron's description of an apricot cocktail (de Beauvoir 1960 [1962: 135]). From this moment, Sartre was fascinated by the originality and novelty of Husserl's method, which he identified straight away as a means to fulfil his own philosophical expectations: overcoming the opposition between idealism and realism; getting a view on the world that would allow him "to describe objects just as he saw and touched them, and extract philosophy from the process". Sartre became immediately acquainted with Emmanuel Levinas's early translation of Husserl's *Cartesian Meditations* and his introductory book on Husserl's theory of intuition. He spent the following year in Berlin, so as to study more closely Husserl's method and to familiarise himself with the works of his students, Heidegger and Scheler. With Levinas, and then later with Merleau-Ponty, Ricœur, and Tran Duc Thao, Sartre became one of the first serious interpreters and proponent of Husserl's phenomenology in France.

While he was studying in Berlin, Sartre tried to convert his study of Husserl into an article that documents his enthusiastic discovery of intentionality. It was published a few years later under the title "Intentionality: a fundamental idea of Husserl's phenomenology". This article, which had considerable influence over the early French reception of phenomenology, makes explicit the reasons Sartre had to be fascinated by Husserl's descriptive approach to consciousness, and how he managed to merge it with his previous philosophical concerns. Purposefully leaving aside the idealist aspects of Husserl's transcendental phenomenology, Sartre proposes a radicalisation of intentionality that stresses its anti-idealistic potential. Against the French contemporary versions of neo-Kantianism (Brochard, Lachelier), and more particularly against the kind of idealism advocated by Léon Brunschvicg, Sartre famously claims that intentionality allows us to discard the metaphysical oppositions between the inner and outer and to renounce to the very notion of the interiority of consciousness. If it is true, as Husserl states, that every consciousness is consciousness *of* something, and if intentionality accounts for this fundamental direction that orients consciousness towards its object and beyond itself, then, Sartre concludes, the phenomenological description of intentionality does away with the illusion that makes us responsible for the way the world appears to us. According to Sartre's radicalised reading of Husserl's thesis, intentionality is intrinsically realistic: it lets the world appear to consciousness *as it really is*, and not as a mere correlate of an intellectual act. This realistic interpretation, being perfectly in tune with Sartre's lifelong ambition to provide a philosophical account of the contingency of being—its non-negotiable lack of necessity—convinced him to adopt Husserl's method of phenomenological description.

While he was still in Berlin, Sartre also began to work on a more personal essay, which a few years later resulted in his first significant philosophical contribution, *Transcendence of the Ego*. With this influential essay Sartre engages in a much more critical way with the conception of the "transcendental ego" presented in Husserl's *Ideas* and defends his realistic interpretation of intentionality against the idealistic tendencies of Husserl's own phenomenology after the publication of *Logical Investigations*. Stressing the irreducible transparency of intentional experience—its fundamental orientation beyond itself towards its object, whatever this object may be—Sartre distinguishes between the dimensions of our subjective experiences that are pre-reflectively lived through, and the reflective stance thanks to which one can always make their experience the intentional object towards which consciousness is oriented. One of Sartre's most fundamental claims in *Transcendence of the Ego* is that these two forms of consciousness cannot and must not be mistaken with one another: reflexive consciousness is a form of intentional consciousness that takes one's own lived-experiences as its specific object, whereas pre-reflexive consciousness need not involve the intentional distance to the object that the act of reflection entails. In regard to self-consciousness, Sartre argues there is an immediate and non-cognitive form of self-awareness, as well as reflective forms of self-consciousness. The latter is unable to give access to oneself as the *subject* of unreflected consciousness, but only as the intentional *object* of the act of reflection, i.e., the Ego in Sartre's terminology. The Ego is the specific object that intentional consciousness is directed upon when performing reflection—an object that consciousness "posits and grasps [...] in the same act" (Sartre 1936a [1957: 41; 2004: 5]), and that is constituted in and by the act of reflection (Sartre 1936a [1957: 80–1; 2004: 20]). Instead of a transcendental subject, the Ego must consequently be understood as a transcendent object similar to any other object, with the only difference that it is given to us through a particular kind of experience, i.e., reflection. The Ego, Sartre argues, "is outside, *in the world*. It is a being of the world, like the Ego of another" (Sartre 1936a [1957: 31; 2004: 1]).

This critique of the transcendental Ego is less opposed to Husserl than it may seem, notwithstanding Sartre's reservations about the transcendental radicalisation of Husserl's phenomenology. The neo-Humean claim that the "I" or Ego is nowhere to be found "within" ourselves remains faithful to the 5th *Logical Investigation*, in which Husserl had initially followed the very same line of reasoning (see Husserl 1901 [2001: vol. 2, 91–93]), before developing a transcendental methodology that substantially modified his approach to subjectivity (as exposed in particular in Husserl 1913 [1983]). However, for the Husserl of the *Ideas Pertaining to a Phenomenology* (published in 1913), the sense in which a perceptual object, which is necessarily seen from one side but also presented to us as a unified object (involving other unseen sides), requires that there be a unifying structure within consciousness itself: the transcendental ego. Sartre argues that such an account would entail that the perception of an object would always also involve an intermediary perception—such as some kind of perception or consciousness of the transcendental ego—thus threatening to disrupt the "transparency" or "translucidity" of consciousness. All forms of perception and consciousness would involve (at least) these two components, and there would be an opaqueness to consciousness that is not phenomenologically apparent. In addition, it appears that Husserl's transcendental ego would have to pre-exist all of our particular actions and perceptions, which is something that the existentialist dictum "existence precedes essence", which we will explicate shortly, seems committed to denying. Without considering here the extent to which Husserl can be defended against these charges, Sartre's general claim is that the notion of a self or ego is not given in experience. Rather, it is something that is not immanent but transcendent to pre-reflective experience. The Ego is the transcendent *object* of one's reflexive experience, and not the subject of the pre-reflective experience that was initially lived (but not known).

Sartre devotes a great deal of effort to establishing the impersonal (or "pre-personal") character of consciousness, which stems from its non-egological structure and results directly from the absence of the *I* in the transcendental field. According to him, intentional (positional) consciousness typically involves an anonymous and "impersonal" relation to a transcendent object:

When I run after a streetcar, when I look at the time, when I am absorbed in contemplating a portrait, there is no *I*. [...] In fact I am plunged in the world of objects; it is they which constitute the unity of my consciousness; [...] but *me*, I have disappeared; I have annihilated myself. There is no place for *me* on this level. (Sartre 1936a [1957: 49; 2004: 8])

The tram appears to me *in a specific way* (as "having-to-be-overtaken", in this case) that is experienced as its *own* mode of phenomenalization, and not as a mere relational aspect of its appearing to *me*. The object presents itself as carrying a set of objective properties that are strictly independent from one's personal relation to it. The streetcar is experienced as a transcendent object, in a way that obliterates and *overrides*, so to speak, the subjective features of conscious experience; its "having-to-be-overtaken-ness" does not belong to my *subjective* experience of the world but to the *objective* description of the way the world is (see also Sartre 1936a [1957: 56; 2004: 10–11]). When I run after the streetcar, my consciousness is absorbed in the relation to its intentional object, "*the streetcar-having-to-be-overtaken*", and there is no trace of the "I" in such lived-experience. I do not need to be aware of my intention to take the streetcar, since the object itself appears as having-to-be-overtaken, and the subjective properties of my experience disappear in the intentional relation to the object. They are lived-through without any reference to the experiencing subject (or to the fact that this experience has to be experienced *by someone*). This particular feature derives from the diaphanousness of lived-experiences. In a different example of this, Sartre argues that when I perceive Pierre as loathsome, say, I do not perceive my feeling of hatred; rather, Pierre repulses me and I experience *him* as repulsive (Sartre 1936a [1957: 63–4; 2004: 13]). Repulsiveness constitutes an essential feature of *his* distinctive mode of appearing, rather than a trait of *my* feelings towards him. Sartre concludes that reflective statements about one's Ego cannot be logically derived from non-reflective ("*irréfléchies*") lived-experiences:

Thus to say "I hate" or "I love" on the occasion of a singular consciousness of attraction or repulsion, is to carry out a veritable passage to the infinite [...] Nothing more is needed for the rights of reflection to be singularly limited: it is certain that Pierre repulses me, yet it is and will remain forever doubtful that I hate him. Indeed, this affirmation infinitely exceeds the power of reflection. (Sartre 1936a [1957: 63–4; 2004: 13])

This critique of the powers of reflection forms one important part of Sartre's argument for the primacy of pre-reflective consciousness over reflective consciousness, which is central to many of the pivotal arguments of *Being and Nothingness*, as we indicate in the relevant sections below.

Imagination, Phenomenology and Literature

For many of his readers, the book on the *Imaginary* that Sartre published in 1940 constitutes one of the most rigorous and fruitful developments of his Husserl-inspired phenomenological investigations. Along with the *The Emotions: Outline of a Theory* which was published one year before (Sartre 1939b), Sartre presented this study of imagination as an essay in phenomenological psychology, which drew on his lifetime interest in psychological studies and brought to completion the research on imagination he had undertaken since the very beginning of his philosophical career. With this new essay, Sartre continues to explore the relationship between intentional consciousness and reality by focusing upon the specific case of the intentional relations to the unreal and the fictional, so as to produce an in-depth analysis of "the great 'irrealizing' function of consciousness". Engaging in a detailed discussion with recent psychological research that Sartre juxtaposes with (and against) fine-grained phenomenological descriptions of the structures of imagination, his essay proposes his own theory of the imaginary as the corollary of a specific intentional attitude that orients consciousness towards the unreal.

In a similar fashion to his analysis of the world-shaping powers of emotions (Sartre 1939b), Sartre describes and highlights how imagination presents us with a coherent world, although made of objects that do not precede but *result* from the imaging capacities of consciousness. "The object as imaged, Sartre claims, is never anything more than the consciousness one has of it" (Sartre 1940 [2004:

15]). Contrary to other modes of consciousness such as perception or memory, which connect us to a world that is essentially one and the same, the objects to which imaginative consciousness connects us belong to imaginary worlds, which may not only be extremely diverse, but also follow their own rules, having their own spatiality and temporality. The island of Thrinacia where Odysseus lands on his way back to Ithaca needs not be located anywhere on our maps nor have existed at a specific time: its mode of existence is that of a fictional object, which possesses its own spatiality and temporality within the imaginary world it belongs to.

Sartre stresses that the intentional dimension of imaging consciousness is essentially characterised by its *negativity*. The negative act, Sartre writes, is "constitutive of the image" (Sartre 1940 [2004: 183]): an image consciousness is a consciousness of something that *is not*, whether its object is absent, non-existing, or fictional. When we picture Odysseus sailing back to his native island, Odysseus is given to us "as absent to intuition". In this sense, Sartre concludes,

> one can say that the image has wrapped within it a certain nothingness. [...] However lively, appealing, strong the image, it gives its object as not being. (Sartre 1940 [2004: 14])

The irrealizing function of imagination results from this immediate consciousness of the nothingness of its object. Sartre's essay investigates how imaging consciousness allows us to operate with its objects as if they were present, even though these very objects are given to us as non-existing or absent. This is for instance what happens when we go to the theatre or read a novel:

To be present at a play is to apprehend the characters on the actors, the forest of *As You Like It* on the cardboard trees. To read is to realize contact with the irreal world on the signs. In this world there are plants, animals, fields, towns, people: initially those mentioned in the book and then a host of others that are not named but are in the background and give this world its depth. (Sartre 1940 [2004: 64])

The irreality of imaginary worlds does not prevent the spectator or reader from projecting herself into this world *as if it was real*. The acts of imagination can consequently be described as "magical acts" (Sartre 1940 [2004: 125]), similar to incantations with respect to the way they operate, since they are designed to make the object of one's thought or desire appear in such a way that one can take possession of it.

In the conclusion of his essay, Sartre stresses the philosophical significance of the relationship between imagination and freedom, which are both necessarily involved in our relationship to the world. Imagination, Sartre writes, "is the whole of consciousness as it realizes its freedom" (Sartre 1940 [2004: 186]). Imaging consciousness posits its object as "out of reach" in relation to the world understood as the synthetic totality within which consciousness situates itself. For Sartre, the imaginary creation is only possible if consciousness is not placed "in-the-midst-of-the-world" as one existent among others.

For consciousness to be able to imagine, it must be able to escape from the world by its very nature, it must be able to stand back from the world by its own efforts. In a word, it must be free. (Sartre 1940 [2004: 184])

In that respect, the irrealizing function of imagination allows consciousness to "surpass the real" so as to constitute it as a proper *world*: "the nihilation of the real is always implied by its constitution as a world". This capacity of surpassing the real to make it a proper world defines the very notion of "situation" that becomes central in Sartre's philosophical thought after the publication of the *Imaginary*. Situations are nothing but "the different immediate modes of apprehension of the real as a world" (Sartre 1940 [2004: 185]). Consciousness' situation-in-the-world is precisely that which motivates the constitution of any irreal object and accounts for the creation of imaginary worlds—for instance, and perhaps above all, in art:

> Every apprehension of the real as a world tends of its own accord to end up with the production of irreal objects since it is always, in a sense, free nihilation of the world and this always from a particular point of view. (Sartre 1940 [2004: 185])

With this conclusion, which prioritises the question of the world over that of reality, Sartre begins to move away from the realist perspective he was initially aiming at when he first discovered phenomenology, so as to make the phenomenological investigation of our "being-in-the-world" (influenced by his careful rereading of Heidegger in the late 30s) his new priority.

Although Sartre never stated it explicitly, his interest in the question of the unreal and imaging consciousness appears to be intimately connected with his general conception of literature and his self-understanding of his own literary production. The concluding remarks of the *Imaginary* extend the scope of Sartre's phenomenological analyses of the irrealizing powers of imagination, by applying them to the domain of aesthetics so as to answer the question about the ontological status of works of art. For Sartre, any product of artistic creation—a novel, a painting, a piece of music, or a theatre play—is just as irreal an object as the imaginary world it gives rise to. The irreality of the work of art allows us to experience—though only imaginatively—the world it gives flesh to as an "analogon" of reality. Even a cubist painting, which might not depict nor represent anything, still functions as an analogon, which manifests

> an irreal ensemble of *new things*, of objects that I have never seen nor will ever see but that are nonetheless irreal objects. (Sartre 1940 [2004: 191])

Likewise, the novelist, the poet, the dramatist, constitute irreal objects through verbal analogons.

This original conception of the nature of the work of art dominates Sartre's critical approach to literature in the many essays he dedicates to the art of the novel. This includes his critical analyses of recent writers' novels in the 30s—Faulkner, Dos Passos, Hemingway, Mauriac, etc.—and the publication in the late 40s of his own summative view, *What is literature?* (Sartre 1948a [1988]). In a series of articles gathered in the first volume of his *Situations* (1947, *Sit. I*), Sartre defends a strong version of literary realism that can, somewhat paradoxically, be read as a consequence of his theory of the irreality of the work of art. If imagination projects the spectator within the imaginary world created by the artist, then the success of the artistic process is proportional to the capacity of the artwork to let the spectator experience it as a reality of its own, giving rise to a full-fledged world. Sartre applies in particular this analysis to novels, which must aim, according to him, at immersing the reader within the fictional world they depict so as to make her experience the events and adventures of the characters *as if* she was living them in first person. The complete absorption of the reader within the imaginary world created by the novelist must ultimately recreate the particular feel of reality that defines Sartre's *phenomenological* kind of literary realism (Renaudie 2017), which became highly influential over the following decades in French literature. The reader must be able to experience the actions of the characters of the novel as if they did not result from the imagination of the novelist, but proceeded from the character's own freedom—and Sartre goes as far as to claim that this radical "spellbinding" ("envoûtante", Sartre 1940 [2004: 175])) quality of literary fiction defines the touchstone of the art of the novel (See "François Mauriac and Freedom", in Sartre *Sit. I*).

This original version of literary realism is intrinsically tied to the question of freedom, and opposed to the idea according to which realist literature is expected to provide a mere description of reality *as it is*. In *What is Literature?*, Sartre describes the task of the novelist as that of disclosing the world as if it arose from human freedom—rather than from a deterministic chain of causes and consequences. The author's art consists in obliging her reader "to *create* what [she] *discloses*", and so to share with the writer the responsibility and freedom involved in the act of literary creation (Sartre 1948a [1988: 61]). In order for the world of the novel to offer its maximum density,

> the disclosure-creation by which the reader discovers it must also be an imaginary engagement in the action; in other words, the more disposed one is to change it, the more alive it will be.

The conception of the writer's engagement that resulted from these analyses constitutes probably the most well-known aspect of Sartre's relation to literature. The writer only has one topic: freedom.

This analysis of the role of imaginative creations of art can also help us to understand the role of philosophy within his own novels, particularly in *Nausea*, a novel which Sartre began as he was studying Husserl in Berlin. In this novel Sartre's pre-phenomenological interest for the irreducibility of contingency intersects with his newly-acquired competences in phenomenological analyses, making *Nausea* a beautifully illustrated expression of the metaphysical register Sartre gave to Husserl's conception of intentionality. The feeling of nausea that Roquentin, the main character of Sartre's novel, famously experienced in a public garden while obsessively watching a chestnut tree, accounts for his sensitivity to the absolute lack of necessity of whatever exists. Sartre understands this radical absence of necessity as the expression of the fundamental contingency of being. Roquentin's traumatic moment of realisation that there is absolutely no reason for the existence of all that exists illustrates the intuition that motivated Sartre's philosophical thinking since the very beginning of his intellectual career as a student at the Ecole Normale Supérieure, as Simone de Beauvoir recalls (1981 [1986]). It constitutes the metaphysical background of his interpretation of intentionality, which he would come to develop and systematise in the early dense parts of *Being and Nothingness*. While the experience of nausea when confronting the contingency of the chestnut tree does not give us conceptual knowledge, it involves a form of non-conceptual ontological awareness that is of a fundamentally different order to, and cannot be derived from, our conceptual understanding and knowledge of brute existence.

Negation and freedom

Being and Nothingness (1943) remains the defining treatise of the existentialist "movement", along with works from de Beauvoir from this period (e.g., *The Ethics of Ambiguity*). We cannot do justice to the entirety of the book here, but we can indicate the broad outlines of the position. In brief, Sartre provides a series of arguments for the necessary freedom of "human reality" (his gloss on Heidegger's conception of Dasein), based upon an ontological distinction between what he calls being-for-itself (*pour soi*) and being-in-itself (*en soi*), roughly between that which negates and transcends (consciousness) and the "pure plenitude" of objects. That kind of metaphysical position might seem to "beg the question" by assuming what it purports to establish (i.e., radical human freedom). However, Sartre argues that realism and idealism cannot sufficiently account for a wide range of phenomena associated with negation. He also draws on the direct evidence of phenomenological experience (i.e., the experience of anguish). But the argument for his metaphysical picture and human freedom is, on balance, an inference to the best explanation. He contends that his complex metaphysical vision best captures and explains central aspects of human reality.

As the title of the book suggests, nothingness plays a significant role. While Sartre's concern with nothingness might be a deal-breaker for some, following Rudolph Carnap's trenchant criticisms of Heidegger's idea that the "nothing noths/nothings" (depending on translation from the German), Sartre's account of negation and nothingness (the latter of which is the ostensible ground of the former) is nevertheless philosophically interesting. Sartre does not say much about the genesis of consciousness or the for-itself, other than that it is contingent and arises from "the effort of an in-itself to found itself" (Sartre 1943 [1956: 84]). He describes the appearance of the for-itself as the absolute event, which occurs through being's attempt "to remove contingency from its being". Accordingly, the for-itself is radically and inescapably distinct from the in-itself. In particular, it functions primarily through negation, whether in relation to objects, values, meaning, or social facts. According to Sartre this negation is not about any reflective judgement or cognition, but an ontological relation to the world. This ontological interpretation of negation minimises the subjectivist interpretations of his philosophy. The most vivid example he provides to illustrate this pre-reflective negation is the apprehension of Pierre's absence from a café. Sartre describes Pierre's absence as pervading the whole café. The café is cast in the metaphorical "shade" of Pierre not being there at the time he had been expected. This experience depends on human expectations, of course. But Sartre argues that if, by contrast, we imagine or reflect that someone else is not present (say the Duke of Wellington, an elephant, etc.), these abstract negative facts are not existentially given in the same manner as our pre-reflective encounter with Pierre's absence. They are not given as an "objective fact", as a "component of the real".

Sartre provides numerous other examples of pre-reflective negation throughout *Being and Nothingness*. He argues that the apprehension of fragility and destruction are likewise premised on negativity, and any effort to adequately describe these phenomena requires negative concepts, but also that they presuppose more than just negative thoughts and judgements. In regard to destruction,

Sartre suggests that there is not *less* after the storm, just something else (Sartre 1943 [1956: 8]). Generally, we do not need to reflectively judge that a building has been destroyed, but directly see it in terms of that which it is *not*—the building, say, in its former glory before being wrecked by the storm. Humans introduce the possibility of destruction and fragility into the world, since objectively there is just a change. Sartre's basic question is: how could we accomplish this unless we are a being by whom nothingness comes into the world, i.e., free? He poses similar arguments in regard to a range of phenomena that present as basic to our modes of inhabiting the world, from bad faith through to anguish. In all of these cases Sartre argues that while we can expressly pose negative judgements, or deliberately ask questions that admit of the possibility of negative reply, or consciously individuate and distinguish objects by reference to the objects which they are not, there is a pre-comprehension of non-being that is the condition of such negative judgements.

Although the for-itself and the in-itself are initially defined very abstractly, the book ultimately comes to say a lot more about the for-itself, even if not much more about the in-itself. The picture of the for-itself and its freedom gradually becomes more "concrete", reflecting the architectonic of the text, which has more sustained treatments of the body, others, and action, in the second half. Throughout, Sartre gives a series of paradoxical glosses on the nature of the for-itself—i.e., a "being which is what it is not and is not what it is" (Sartre 1943 [1956: 79]). Although this might appear to be a contradiction, Sartre's claim is that it is the fundamental mode of existence of the for-itself that is future-oriented and does not have a stable identity in the manner of a chair, say, or a penknife. Rather, "existence precedes essence", as he famously remarks in both *Being and Nothingness* and *Existentialism is a Humanism*.

In later chapters he develops the basic ontological position in regard to free action. His point is not, of course, to say we are free to do or achieve anything (freedom as power), or even to claim that we are free to "project" anything at all. The for-itself is always in a factical situation. Nonetheless, he asserts that the combination of the motives and ends we aspire to in relation to that facticity depend on an act of negation in relation to the given. As he puts it: "Action necessarily implies as its condition the recognition of a "desideratum"; that is, of an objective lack or again of a negatité" (Sartre 1943 [1956: 433]). Even suffering in-itself is not a sufficient motive to determine particular acts. Rather, it is the apprehension of the revolution as possible (and as desired) which gives to the worker's suffering its value as motive (Sartre 1943 [1956: 437]). A factual state, even poverty, does not determine consciousness to apprehend it as a lack. No factual state, whatever it may be, can cause consciousness to respond to it in any one way. Rather, we make a choice (usually pre-reflective) about the significance of that factual state for us, and the ends and motives that we adopt in relation to it. We are "condemned" to freedom of this ontological sort, with resulting anguish and responsibility for our individual situation, as well as for more collective situations of racism, oppression, and colonialism. These are the themes for which Sartre became famous, especially after World War 2 and *Existentialism is a Humanism*.

In *Being and Nothingness* he provides various examples that are designed to make this quite radical philosophy of freedom plausible, including the hiker who gives in to their fatigue and collapses to the ground. Sartre says that a necessary condition for the hiker to give in to their fatigue—short of fainting—is that their fatigue goes from being experienced as simply part of the background to their activity, with their direct conscious attention focusing on something else (e.g., the scenery, the challenge, competing with a friend, philosophising, etc.), to being the direct focus of their attention and thus becoming a motive for direct recognition of one's exhaustion and the potential action of collapsing to the ground. Although we are not necessarily reflectively aware of having made such a decision, things could have been otherwise and thus Sartre contends we have made a choice. Despite appearances, however, Sartre insists that his view is not a voluntarist or capricious account of freedom, but one that necessarily involves a situation and a context. His account of situated freedom in the chapter "Freedom and Action" affirms the inability to extricate intentions, ends, motives, and reasons, from the embodied context of the actor. As a synthetic whole, it is not merely freedom of intention or motive (and hence even consciousness) that Sartre affirms. Rather, our freedom is realised only in its projections and actions, and is nothing without such action.

Bad faith and the critique of Freudian psychoanalysis

Sartre's account of bad faith (*mauvaise foi*) is of major interest. It is said to be a phenomenon distinctive of the for-itself, thus warranting ontological treatment. It also feeds into questions to do with self-knowledge (see Moran 2001), as well as serving as the basis for some of his criticisms of racism and colonialism in his later work. His account of bad faith juxtaposes a critique of Freud with its own "depth" interpretive account, "existential psychoanalysis", which is itself indebted to Freud, as Sartre admits.

We will start with Sartre's critique of Freud, which is both simple and complex, and features in the early parts of the chapter on bad faith in *Being and Nothingness*. In short, Freud's differing meta-psychological pictures (Conscious, Preconscious, Unconscious, or Id, Ego, Superego) are charged with splitting the subject in two (or more) in attempting to provide a mechanistic explanation of bad faith: that is, how there can be a "liar" and a "lied to" duality within a single consciousness. But Sartre accuses Freud of reifying this structure, and rather than adequately explaining the problem of bad faith, he argues that Freud simply transfers the problem to another level where it remains unsolved, thus consisting in a pseudo-explanation (which today might be called a "homuncular fallacy"). Rather than the problem being something that pertains to an embodied subject, and how they might both be aware of something and yet also repress it at the same time, Sartre argues that the early Freudian meta-psychological model transfers the seat of this paradox to the censor: that is, to a functional part of the brain/mind that both knows and does not know. It must know enough in order to efficiently repress, but it also must not know too much or nothing is hidden and the problematic truth is manifest directly to consciousness. Freud's "explanation" is hence accused of recapitulating the problem of bad faith in an ostensible mechanism that is itself "conscious" in some paradoxical sense. Sartre even provocatively suggests that the practice of psychoanalysis is itself in bad faith, since it treats a part of ourselves as "Id"-like and thereby denies responsibility for it. That is not the end of Sartre's story, however, because he ultimately wants to revive a version of psychoanalysis that does not pivot around the "unconscious" and these compartmentalised models of the mind. We will come back to that, but it is first necessary to introduce Sartre's own positive account of bad faith.

While bad faith is inevitable in Sartre's view, it is also important to recognise that the "germ of its destruction" lies within. This is because bad faith always remains at least partly available to us in our own lived-experience, albeit not in a manner that might be given propositional form in the same way as knowledge of an external object. In short, when I existentially comprehend that my life is dissatisfying, or even reflect on this basis that I have lived an inauthentic life, while I am grasping something about myself (it is given differently to the recognition that others have lived a lie and more likely to induce anxiety), I am nonetheless not strictly equivalent or identical with the "I" that is claimed to be in bad faith (cf. Moran 2001). There is a distanciation involved in coming to this recognition and the potential for self-transformation of a more practical kind, even if this is under-thematised in *Being and Nothingness*.

Sartre gives many examples of bad faith that remain of interest. His most famous example of bad faith is the café waiter who plays at being a café waiter, and who attempts to institutionalise themselves as this object. While Sartre's implied criticisms of their manner of inhabiting the world might seem to disparage social roles and affirm an individualism, arguably this is not a fair reading of the details of the text. For Sartre we do have a factical situation, but the claim is that we cannot be wholly reduced to it. As Sartre puts it:

There is no doubt I am in a sense a café waiter—otherwise could I not just as well call myself a diplomat or reporter? But if I am one, this cannot be in the mode of being-in-itself. I am a waiter in the mode of *being what I am not*. (Sartre 1943 [1956: 60])

In subsequent work, racism becomes emblematic of bad faith, when we reduce the other to some ostensible identity (e.g., *Anti-semite and the Jew*).

It is important to recognise that no project of "sincerity", if that is understood as strictly being what one is, is possible for Sartre given his view of the for-itself. Likewise, in regard to any substantive self-knowledge that might be achieved through direct self-consciousness, our options are limited. On Sartre's view we cannot look inwards and discover the truth about our identity or our own bad faith through simple introspection (there is literally no-thing to observe). Moreover, when we have a lived experience, and then reflect on ourselves from outside (e.g., third-personally), we are not strictly reducible to that Ego that is so posited. We transcend it. Or, to be more precise, we both are that Ego (just as we are what the Other perceives) and yet are also not reducible to it. This is due to the structure of consciousness and the arguments from *Transcendence of the Ego* examined in section 2. In *Being and Nothingness*, the temporal aspects of this non-coincidence are also emphasised. We are not just our past and our objective attributes in accord with some sort of principle of identity, because we are also our "projects", and these are intrinsically future oriented.

Nonetheless, Sartre argues that it would be false to conclude that all modes of inhabiting the world are thereby equivalent in terms of "faith" and "bad faith". Rather, there are what he calls "patterns of bad faith" and he says these are "objective". Any conduct can be seen from two perspectives—transcendence and facticity, being-for-itself and being-for-others. But it is the exclusive affirmation of one or the others of these (or a motivated and selective oscillation between them) which constitutes bad faith. There is no direct account of good faith in *Being and Nothingness*, other than the enigmatic footnote at the end of the book that promises an ethics. There are more sustained treatments of authenticity in his *Notebooks for an Ethics* and in *Anti-semite and Jew* (see also the entry on authenticity).

The Look, shame and intersubjectivity

Sartre's work on inter-subjectivity is often the subject of premature dismissal. The hyperbolic dimension of his writings on the Look of the Other and the pessimism of his chapter on "concrete relations with others", which is essentially a restatement of the "master-slave" stage of Hegel's struggle for recognition without the possibility of its overcoming, are sometimes treated as if they were nothing but the product of a certain sort of mind—a kind of adolescent paranoia or hysteria about the Other (see, e.g., Marcuse 1948). What this has meant, however, is that the significance of Sartre's work on inter-subjectivity, both within phenomenological circles and more broadly in regard to philosophy of mind and social cognition, has been downplayed. Building on the insights of Hegel, Husserl and Heidegger, Sartre proposes a set of necessary and sufficient conditions for any theory of the other, which are far from trivial. In *Being and Nothingness*, Sartre suggests that various philosophical positions—realism and idealism, and beyond—have been shipwrecked, often unawares, on what he calls the "reef of solipsism". His own solution to the problem of other minds consists, first and foremost, in his descriptions of being subject to the look of another, and the way in which in such an experience we become a "transcendence transcended". On his famous description, we are asked to imagine that we are peeping through a keyhole, pre-reflectively immersed and absorbed in the scene on the other side of the door. Maybe we would be nervous engaging in such activities given the socio-cultural associations of being a "Peeping Tom", but after a period of time we would be given over to the scene with self-reflection and self-awareness limited to merely the minimal (tacit or "non-thetic" in Sartre's language) understanding that we are not what we are perceiving. Suddenly, though, we hear footsteps, and we have an involuntary apprehension of ourselves as an object in the eyes of another; a "pre-moral" experience of shame; a shudder of recognition that we are the object that the other sees, without room for any sort of inferential theorising or cognising (at least that is manifest to our own consciousness). This ontological shift, Sartre says, has another person as its condition, notwithstanding whether or not one is in error on a particular occasion of such an experience (i.e., the floor creaks but there is no-one actually literally present). While many other phenomenological accounts emphasise empathy or direct perception of mental states (for example, Scheler and Merleau-Ponty), Sartre thereby adds something significant and distinctive to these accounts that focus on our experience of the other person as an object (albeit of a special kind) rather than as a subject. In common with other phenomenologists like Merleau-Ponty and Scheler, Sartre also maintains that it is a mistake to view our relations with the other as one characterised by a radical separation that we can only bridge with inferential reasoning. Any argument by analogy, either to establish the existence of others in general or to particular mental states like anger, is problematic, begging the question and having insufficient warrant.

For Sartre, at least in his early work, our experience of being what he calls a "we subject"—as a co-spectator in a lecture or concert for example, which involves no objectification of the other people we are with—is said to be merely a subjective and psychological phenomenon that does not ground our understanding and knowledge of others ontologically (Sartre 1943 [1956: 413–5]). Originally, human relations are typified by dyadic mode of conflict best captured in the look of the other, and the sort of scenario concerning the key-hole we just considered above. Given that we also do not grasp a plural look, for Sartre, this means that social life is fundamentally an attempt to control the impact of the look upon us, either by anticipating it in advance and attempting to invalidate that perspective (sadism) or by anticipating it and attempting to embrace that solicited perspective when it comes (masochism). In Sartre's words:

It is useless for human reality to seek to escape this dilemma: one must either transcend the Other or allow oneself to be transcended by him. The essence of the relations between consciousness is not the *Mitsein* (being-with); it is conflict. (Sartre 1943 [1956: 429])

Existential Psychoanalysis and the Fundamental Project

Sartre's radical criticism of Freud's theory of the unconscious is not his last word on psychoanalysis. In the last chapters of *Being and Nothingness*, Sartre presents his own conception of an existential psychoanalysis, drawing on some insights from his attempt to account for Emperor Wilhelm II as a "human-reality" in the 14th notebook from his *War Diaries* (Sartre 1983b [1984]). This existential version of psychoanalysis is claimed to be compatible with Sartre's rejection of the unconscious, and is expected to achieve a "psychoanalysis of consciousness" (Moati 2020: 219), allowing us to understand one's existence in light of their fundamental free choice of themselves.

The very idea of a psychoanalysis oriented towards the study of consciousness rather than the unconscious seems paradoxical—a paradox increased by Sartre's efforts to highlight the fundamental differences that oppose his own version of psychoanalysis to Freud's. Sartre contends that Freud's "empirical" psychoanalysis

> is based on the hypothesis of the existence of an unconscious psyche, which on principle escapes the intuition of the subject.

By contrast, Sartre's own existential psychoanalysis aims to remain faithful to one of the earliest claims of Husserl's phenomenology: that all psychic acts are "coextensive with consciousness" (Sartre 1943 [1956: 570]). For Sartre, however, the basic motivation for rejecting Freud's hypothesis is less an inheritance of Brentano's descriptive psychology (as was the case for Husserl) than a consequence of Sartre's fundamental critique of determinism, applied to the naturalist presuppositions of empirical psychoanalysis and the particular kind of determinism that it involves. In agreement with Freud, Sartre holds that psychic life remains inevitably "opaque" and at least somewhat impenetrable to us. He also stresses that the philosophical understanding of human reality requires a method for investigating the *meaning* of psychic facts. But Sartre denies that the methods and causal laws of the natural sciences are of any help in that respect. The human *psyche* cannot be fully analysed and explained as a mere *result* of external constraints acting like physical forces or natural causes. The for-itself, being always what it is not and not what it is, remains free whatever the external and social constraints. Sartre is consequently bound to reject any emphasis on the causal impact of the past upon the present, which he argues is the basic methodological framework of empirical psychoanalysis. That does not mean that past psychic or physical facts have no impact on one's existence whatsoever. Rather, Sartre contends that the impact of past events is determined in relation to one's present choice, and understood as the consequence of the power invested in this free choice. As he puts it:

Since the force of compulsion in my past is borrowed from my free, reflecting choice and from the very power which this choice has given itself, it is impossible to determine a priori the compelling power of a past. (Sartre 1943 [1956: 503])

Past events bear no other meaning than the one given by a subject, in agreement with the free project that orients his or her existence towards the future. Conversely, determinist explanations that construe one's present as a mere consequence of the past proceed from a kind of self-delusion that operates by concealing one's free project, and thus contributes to the obliteration of responsibility. Sartre hence seeks to redefine the scope of psychoanalysis: rather than a proper explanation of human behaviour that relies on the identification of the laws of its causation, psychoanalysis consists in understanding the meaning of our conducts in light of one's project of existence and free choice. One might wonder, then, why we need any such psychoanalysis, if the existential project that constitutes its object is freely chosen by the subject. Sartre addresses this objection in *Being and Nothingness*, claiming that

> if the fundamental project is fully experienced by the subject and hence wholly conscious, that certainly does not mean that it must by the same token be known by him; quite the contrary. (Sartre 1943 [1956: 570])

What Freud calls the unconscious must be redescribed as the paradoxical entanglement of a "total absence of knowledge" combined with a "true understanding" (*réelle comprehension*) of oneself (1972, *Sit. IX*: 111). The legitimacy of Sartre's existential psychoanalysis of consciousness lies in its ability to unveil the original project according to which one chooses (more or less obscurely) to develop the fundamental orientations of their existence. According to Sartre, analysing a human subject and understanding the meaning that orients their existence as a whole requires that we grasp the specific kind of unity that lies behind their various attitudes and conducts. This unity can only appear once we discover the synthetic principle of unification or "totalization" (*totalisation*) that commands the whole of their behaviours. Sartre understands this totalization as an an-going process that covers the entire course of one's existence, a process which is constantly reassumed so as to integrate the new developments of this existence. For this reason, this never ending process of totalization cannot be fully self-conscious or the object of reflective self-knowledge. The synthetic principle that makes this totalization possible is identified by Sartre in terms of fundamental choice: existential psychoanalysis describes human subjects as synthetic totalities in which every attitude, conduct, or behaviour finds its meaning in relation to the unity of a primary choice, which all of the subject's behaviour expresses in its own way.

All human behaviour can thus be described as a secondary particularisation of a fundamental project which expresses the subject's free choice, and conditions the intelligibility of their actions. On the basis of his diagnosis of Baudelaire's existential project, for instance, Sartre goes as far as to claim that he is "prepared to wager that he preferred meats cooked in sauces to grills, preserves to fresh vegetables" (Sartre 1947a [1967: 113]). Sartre legitimates such a daring statement by showing its logical connection to Baudelaire's irresistible hatred for nature, from which his gastronomic preferences must derive, and which Sartre identifies as the expression of the initial free choice of himself that commands the whole of the French *poète maudit*'s existence. In Sartre's words:

He chose to exist for himself as he was for others. He wanted his freedom to appear to himself like a "nature"; and he wanted this "nature" which others discovered in him to appear to them like the very emanation of his freedom. From that point everything becomes clear. [...] We should look in vain for a single circumstance for which he was not fully and consciously responsible. Every event was a reflection of that indecomposable totality which he was from the first to the last day of his life (Sartre 1947a [1967: 191–192]).

Baudelaire's choice of himself both accounts for the subject's freedom (insofar as it has been freely accepted as the subject's own project of existence) and exerts a constraint on particular behaviours and attitudes towards the world, so that he is bound to act and behave in a way that must be compatible with that choice. Although absolutely free, such an initial choice takes the shape and the meaning of an inescapable and relentless *destiny*—a destiny in which one's sense of freedom and their inability to act in any other way than they actually did come to merge perfectly: "the free choice which a man makes of himself is completely identified with what is called his destiny" (Sartre 1947a [1967: 192]).

In the years following the publication of *Being and Nothingness*, Sartre refines this original conception of existential psychoanalysis. He applies it methodically to the biographical analysis of a series of major French writers (Baudelaire first, then Mallarmé, Jean Genêt, Flaubert, and himself in *Words*), warning against the dangers of all kinds of determinist interpretations, from the constitution of psychological types to materialist explanations inherited from Marxian historical analyses. Sartre's analyses become more subtle over time, as he substitutes fine-grained descriptions of the concrete constraints that frame and shape the limits of human lives to the strongly metaphysical theses on freedom that he was first tempted to apply indistinctly to each of these writers. Accordingly, existential psychoanalysis plays a central role in the development of Sartre's thought from the early 40s up to his last published work on Flaubert. It allows him to unify and articulate two fundamental threads of his philosophical thinking: his ontological analysis of the absolute freedom of the for-itself in *Being and Nothingness*; and his later attempt to take into consideration the social, historical and political factors that are inevitably involved in the determination of one's free choice of their own existence. Already in his *War Diaries* from 1940, the method of analysis of "human reality" arises from Sartre's attempt to *understand* rather than explain (according to Dilthey's famous distinction) Emperor Wilhelm II's historical situation and its relation to the aspects of his personal life that express his specific way of being-in-the-world (Sartre 1983b [1984: 308–309]). The application of his method to the specific cases of these French writers allowed him to refine the ahistorical descriptions of his earlier work, by bringing the analysis of the subject's freedom back to the material/historical conditions (both internal and external) of constitution of their particular modes of existing.

Sartre's inquiries into existential psychoanalysis also anticipate and intersect with his philosophical investigations on historical anthropology. The progressive-regressive method presented in *Search for a Method* and *Critique of Dialectical Reason* (Sartre 1960a [1976]) was first sketched and experimented through Sartre's essays in existential psychoanalysis. Sartre's detailed analyses of Flaubert's biography in *The Family Idiot* can be read as synthesising the hermeneutical methodology theorised in *Search for A Method* and the conception of the freedom involved in one's initial choice of themselves that arose from *Being and Nothingness*. Moving discretely away from an all-too metaphysical doctrine of absolute freedom, Sartre goes back to the most concrete details of Flaubert's material conditions of existence in order to account for the specific way in which Flaubert made himself able, through the writing of his novels, to overcome his painful situation as a "frustrated and jealous younger brother" and "unloved child" thanks to a totalizing project that made him "the author of *Madame Bovary*" (Sartre 1971–72 [1987, vol. 2: 7]). If Flaubert's novel and masterpiece is consequently understood and described as the final objectivation of

Gustave's fundamental project, Sartre is now careful to point out the economic, historic and social conditions within which this project only finds its full intelligibility. Sartre's psychoanalytic method is then expected to reveal, beyond what society has made of Flaubert, what he himself could make of what society has made of him. In order to fly away from the painful reality of his unbearable familial situation, the young Gustave chooses irreality over reality, and chooses it freely, though achingly. From that moment on, his dedication to literature commits him to a fictional world that he couldn't but choose to elect as the realm of his genius.

Existentialist Marxism: Critique of Dialectical Reason

While *Search for a Method* (1957) had been published earlier, it is not until 1960 that Sartre completed the first volume—"Theory of Practical Ensembles"—of what is his final systematic work of philosophy, *Critique of Dialectical Reason*. The second volume, "The Intelligibility of History", was published posthumously in French in 1985. It would be 1991 before both volumes were to be available in English, which goes some of the way towards explaining their subsequent neglect. It is also a book that rivals *Being and Nothingness* for difficulty, even if some of its goals and ambitions can be expressed straightforwardly enough. Never a member of the French Communist Party, Sartre nonetheless begins by laying his Marxist cards on the table:

> we were convinced at one and the same time that historical materialism furnished the only valid interpretation of history and that existentialism remained the only concrete approach to reality. (Sartre 1957 [1963:

21])

Critique offers a systematic attempt to justify these two perspectives and render them compatible. In broad terms, some of the main steps needed to effect such a synthesis are clear, most notably to deny or limit strong structuralist and determinist versions of Marxism. Borrowing some themes from Merleau-Ponty's *Humanism and Terror*, Sartre maintained that any genuinely dialectical method refuses to reduce; it refuses scientific and economic determinism that treats humans as things, contrary to reductive versions of Marxism. He pithily puts his objection to such explanations in terms of what we might today call the genetic fallacy. Sartre says,

Valery is a petit bourgeois intellectual, no doubt about it. But not every petit bourgeois intellectual is Valery. The heuristic inadequacy of contemporary Marxism is contained in these two sentences. (Sartre 1957 [1963: 56])

Moreover, for Sartre, class struggle is not the only factor that determines and orients history and the field of possibilities. There is human choice and commitment in class formation that is equally fundamental. The way in which this plays out in *Critique* is through an emphasis on praxis rather than consciousness, which we have seen is also characteristic of his existential psychoanalytic work of the prior decade.

Without being able to adequately summarise the vast *Critique* here (see Flynn 1984), one of the book's core conceptual innovations is the idea of the practico-inert. Sartre defines this as "the activity of others insofar as it is sustained and diverted by inorganic inertia" (Sartre 1960a [1976: 556]). The concept is intended to capture the forms of social and historical sedimentation that had only minimally featured in *Being and Nothingness*. It is the reign of necessity,

> the domain ... in which inorganic materiality envelops human multiplicity and transforms the producer into its product. (Sartre 1960a [1976: 339])

For Sartre, the practico-inert is the negation of humanity. Any reaffirmation of humanity, in which genuine freedom resides, must take the form of the negation of this negation (negation is productive here, as it also was in *Being and Nothingness*). For Sartre, then, there are two fundamental kinds of social reality: a positive one in which an active group constitutes the common field; and a negative one in which individuals are effectively separated from each other (even though they appear united) in a practico-inert field. In the practico-inert field, relations are typified by what Sartre calls seriality, like a number, or a worker in a factory who is allocated to a place within a given system that is indifferent to the individual. Sartre's prime example of this is of waiting for a bus, or street-car, on the way to work. If the people involved do not know each other reasonably well there is likely to be a kind of anonymity to such experiences in which individuals are substitutable for each other in relation to this imminent bus, and their relations are organised around functional need. If the bus is late, or if there are too many people on it, however, those who are waiting go from being indifferent and anonymous (something akin to what Heidegger calls *das Man* in *Being and Time*) to becoming competitors and rivals. In a related spirit Sartre also discusses the serial unity of the TV watching public, of the popular music charts, bourgeois property, and petty racism and stereotyping as well. These collective objects keep serial individuals apart from one another under the pretext of unifying them. Sartre thus appears to accept a version of the Marxian theses concerning commodity fetishism. This competitive or antagonistic dimension of the practico-inert is amplified in situations of material scarcity. This kind of seriality is argued to be the basic type of sociality, thus transforming the focus on dyadic consciousnesses of *Being and Nothingness*. In the *Critique*, otherness becomes produced not simply through the look that Sartre had previously described as the original meaning of being-for-others, but through the sedimentation of social processes and through practico-inert mediation. Society produces in us serial behaviour, serial feelings, serial thoughts, and "passive activity" (Sartre 1960a [1976: 266]), where events and history are conceived as external occurrences that befall us, and we feel compelled by the force of circumstance, or "monstrous forces" as Sartre puts it. It is the practico-inert, modified by material and economic scarcity, which turns us into conflictual competitors and alienates us from each other and ourselves. Only an end to both material scarcity and the alienating mediation of the practico-inert will allow for the actualisation of socialism.

While Sartre is pessimistic about the prospects for any sort of permanent revolution of society, he maintains that we get a fleeting glimpse of this unalienated condition in the experience of the "group in fusion". This occurs when the members of a group relate to each other through praxis and in a particular way. The group in fusion is not a collective *à la* the practico-inert, but a social whole that spontaneously forms as a plurality of serial individuals respond to some danger, pressing situation, or to the likelihood of a collective reaction to their stance (Flynn 1984: 114). We could consider what happens when an individual acts so as to make manifest this serial otherness, like Rosa Parkes when she refused to give up her seat and thus drew attention to the specific nature of the colonialist seriality at the heart of many states in the USA. This sometimes creates a rupture and others might follow. Sartre's own prime example is of a crowd of workers who were fleeing during the French Revolution in 1789. At some point the workers stopped fleeing, turned around and reversed direction, suddenly energised alongside each other by their practical awareness that they were doing something together. For this kind of "fusion" to happen it must fulfil the following four key conditions for genuine reciprocity that Flynn summarises as follows:

1. That the other be a means to the exact degree that I am a means myself, i.e., that he be the means towards a transcendent goal and not my means;
2. That I recognize the other as praxis at the same time as I integrate him into my totalizing project;
3. That I recognize his movement towards his own ends in the very movement by which I project myself towards mine;
4. That I discover myself as an object and instrument of his own ends by the same act that makes him an object and instrument of mine. (Flynn 1984: 115, also see previous version of this entry [Flynn 2004 [2013]] and cf. Sartre 1960a [1976: 112–3]).

Sartre calls the resurrection of this freedom an "apocalypse", indicating that it is an unforeseen and (potentially) revolutionary event that happens when serial abuse and exploitation can no longer be tolerated. The group in fusion has a maximum of praxis and a minimum of inertia, but serial sociality has the reverse.

Unfortunately, Sartre insists that this group in fusion is destined to meet with what he calls an "ontological check" in the form of the institution, which cannot be escaped as some versions of anarchism and Marxism might hope. The group relapses into seriality when groups are formalised into hierarchical institutional structures. Serial otherness comes to implicate itself in interpersonal relations in at least three ways in the institution: sovereignty; authority; and bureaucracy (see Book 2, Chapter 6, "The Institution"). From the co-sovereignty of the group in fusion, someone inevitably becomes sovereign in any new social order. Similarly, a command-obedience relation comes about in institutions, to greater and lesser extents, and there will be exhortations to company loyalty, to do one's duty, etc. (Flynn 1984: 120). Bureaucratic rules and regulation also inevitably follow, partly as a reaction to fear of sovereignty, and this installs what Sartre calls vertical otherness—top-down hierarchies, as opposed to the horizontal and immanent organisation of the group in fusion (Sartre 1960a [1976: 655–663]). As such, the revolutionary force of the group in fusion is necessarily subject to mediation by the practico-inert, as well as the problems associated with institutionality just described. Although is it still structured through a series of oppositions, the *Critique* delivers a sophisticated social ontology that both addresses some weaknesses in Sartre's earlier work and unifies the social and political reflections of much of his later work.

Politics and Anti-Colonialism

Although it is not possible to address all of Sartre's rich and varied contributions to ethics and politics here, we will introduce some of the key ideas about race and anti-colonialism that were important themes in his post *Being and Nothingness* work and are currently significant issues in our times. Sartre was generally stridently anti-colonialist, perhaps even advocating a multiculturalism *avant la lettre*, as Michael Walzer has argued in his Preface to *Anti-semite and Jew* (Walzer 1995: xiv). His books and more journalistic writings typically call out what he saw as the bad faith of many French and European citizens.

The issue of race was part of Sartre's French intellectual scene, and Sartre himself played a major role in facilitating that in the pages of *Les Temps Modernes*, *L'Express*, and elsewhere. Debates about the intersection of philosophy and race, and colonialism and multiculturalism, were all being had. These concerned not only the French Algerian and African "colonies" but also Vietnam via Tran Duc Thao, who had challenged Sartre's efforts to bring phenomenological existentialism together with Marxism. Initially at least, Sartre's arguments here typically drew on and extended some of the categories deployed in *Being and Nothingness*. There is an obvious sense in which a critique of racism automatically ensues from Sartrean existentialism. Racism is a form of bad faith, for Sartre, since it typically (perhaps necessarily) involves believing in essences or types, and indeed constructing essences and types. His *Notebooks* suggest that all oppression rests on bad faith. In racism, in particular, there is an "infernal circle of irresponsible responsibility, of culpable ignorance and ignorance which is knowledge" (Sartre 1943 [1956: 49]), as well as what Sartre calls passive complicity. Many of us (or Sartre's own French society) may not obviously be bigots, but we sustain a system that is objectively unjust through our choices and sometimes wilful ignorance. In relation to colonialism, Sartre likewise contends that we have all profited from colonialist exploitation and sustained its systems, even if we are not ourselves a "settler".

This is also the key argument of *Anti-semite and the Jew*, composed very quickly in 1944 and without much detailed knowledge of Judaism but with more direct knowledge of the sort of passive anti-semitism of many French citizens. The text was written following the Dreyfus affair and before all of the horrors of the holocaust were widely known. Sartre was aiming to understand (and critique) the situation he observed around him, in which the imminent return of the French Jews exiled by the Nazis was not unambiguously welcomed by all. The book is perceptive about its prime targets, the explicit or implicit anti-semite, who defines the real Frenchmen by excluding others, notably the Jew. Now, of course, few of his contemporaries would admit to being anti-semites, just as few would admit to being racist. But there are patterns of bad faith that Sartre thinks are clear: we participate in social systems that force the dilemma of authenticity or inauthenticity upon the Jew, asking them to choose between their concrete practical identities (religious and cultural) and more universal ascriptions (liberty, etc.) in a way that cannot be readily navigated within the terms of the debate. Sartre consistently ascribes responsibility to collectives here, even if those collectives are ultimately sustained by individual decisions and choices. For him, it is not just the assassin say, nor just Eichmann and the Nazi regime, who are held responsible. Rather, these more obviously egregious activities were sustained by their society and the individuals in it, through culpable ignorance and patterns of bad faith.

Sartre also addressed the negritude movement in his Preface to *Black Orpheus* (1948), an anthology of negritude poetry. He called for an anti-racist racism and saw himself as resolutely on the side of the negritude movement, but he also envisaged such interventions as a step towards ultimately revealing the category of race itself as an example of bad faith. Here the reception from Frantz Fanon and others was mixed. In *Black Skin, White Masks* (1952), Fanon argues this effectively undermined his own lived-experience and its power (see entries on negritude and Fanon; cf. also Gordon 1995). Sartre continued to address colonialism and racism in subsequent work, effecting a rapprochement of sorts with Fanon that culminated in his "Introduction" to Fanon's *The Wretched of the Earth* (1961), where also Sartre appears to endorse a counter-violence.

Although we have not given much attention to Sartre's literary and artistic productions since section 3 above, he continued to produce artistic work of political significance throughout his career. Continuous with insights from his *What is Literature?*, Sartre argues that in a society that remains unjust and dominated by oppression, the prose-writer (if not the poet) must combat this violence by jolting the reader and audience from their complacency, rather than simply be concerned with art for its own sake. His literary works hence are typically both philosophical and political. Although the number of these works diminished over time, there is still a powerful literary exploration of the philosophical and political themes of the *Critique* in the play, *The Condemned of Altona* (1960).

We cannot neatly sum up a public intellectual and man of letters, like Sartre, to conclude. We do think, however, that it is arguable, with the benefit of hindsight, that some of Sartre's interventions are prescient rather than outmoded remnants of the nineteenth century. They certainly presage issues that are in the foreground today, concerning class, race, and gender. That doesn't mean that Sartre got it all correct, of course, whatever that might mean in regard to the complex realities of socio-political life. Indeed, if one is to take a stand on so many of the major socio-political issues of one's time, as Sartre did, it is inevitable that history will not look kindly on them all. Sartre's life and writings hence present a complex and difficult interpretive task, but they remain a powerful provocation for thought and action today.

CHAPTER SIX

MICHEL FOUCAULT

Foucault was born in Poitiers, France, on October 15, 1926. As a student he was brilliant but psychologically tormented. He became academically established during the 1960s, holding a series of positions at French universities, before his election in 1969 to the ultra-prestigious Collège de France, where he was Professor of the History of Systems of Thought until his death. From the 1970s on, Foucault was very active politically. He was a founder of the *Groupe d'information sur les prisons* and often protested on behalf of marginalized groups. He frequently lectured outside France, particularly in the United States, and in 1983 had agreed to teach annually at the University of California at Berkeley. An early victim of AIDS, Foucault died in Paris on June 25, 1984. In addition to works published during his lifetime, his lectures at the Collège de France, published posthumously, contain important elucidations and extensions of his ideas.

One might question whether Foucault is in fact a philosopher. His academic formation was in psychology and its history as well as in philosophy, his books were mostly histories of medical and social sciences, his passions were literary and political. Nonetheless, almost all of Foucault's works can be fruitfully read as philosophical in either or both of two ways: as carrying out philosophy's traditional critical project in a new (historical) manner; and as a critical engagement with the thought of traditional philosophers. This article will present him as a philosopher in these two dimensions.

Intellectual Background

We begin, however, with a sketch of the philosophical environment in which Foucault was educated. He entered the École Normale Supérieure (the standard launching pad for major French philosophers) in 1946, during the heyday of existential phenomenology. Merleau-Ponty, whose lectures he attended, and Heidegger were particularly important. Hegel and Marx were also major interests, Hegel through the interpretation of his work offered by Jean Hyppolite and Marx through the structuralist reading of Louis Althusser—both teachers who had a strong impact on Foucault at the École Normale. It is not surprising that Foucault's earliest works (his long "Introduction" to Jacqueline Verdeaux' French translation of *Traum und Existenz* by Ludwig Binswanger, a Heideggerian psychiatrist, and *Maladie mentale et personnalité*, a short book on mental illness) were written in the grip of, respectively, existentialism and Marxism. But he soon turned away from both.

Jean-Paul Sartre, working outside the University system, had no personal influence on Foucault. But, as the French master-thinker of the previous generation, he is always in the background. Like Sartre, Foucault began from a relentless hatred of bourgeois society and culture and with a spontaneous sympathy for marginal groups such as the mad, homosexuals, and prisoners. They both also had strong interests in literature and psychology as well as philosophy, and both, after an early relative lack of political interest, became committed activists. But in the end, Foucault seemed to insist on defining himself in contradiction to Sartre. Philosophically, he rejected what he saw as Sartre's privileging of the subject (which he mocked as "transcendental narcissism"). Personally and politically, he rejected Sartre's role as what Foucault called a "universal intellectual", judging society by appeals to universal moral principles, such as the inviolability of individual freedom. There is, however, more than a hint of protesting too much in Foucault's rejection of Sartre, and the question of the relation of their work remains a fertile one.

Three other factors were of much more positive significance for the young Foucault. First, there was the French tradition of history and philosophy of science, particularly as represented by Georges Canguilhem, a powerful figure in the French University establishment, whose work in the history and philosophy of biology provided a model for much of Foucault's work in the history of the human sciences. Canguilhem sponsored Foucault's doctoral thesis on the history of madness and, throughout Foucault's career, remained one of his most important and effective supporters. Canguilhem's approach to the history of science (an approach developed from the work of Gaston Bachelard), provided Foucault with a strong sense (in some ways Kuhnian *avant la lettre*, see entry on scientific revolutions, section 5.3) of the discontinuities in scientific history, along with a "rationalist" understanding of the historical role of concepts that made them independent of the phenomenologists' transcendental consciousness. Foucault found this understanding reinforced in the structuralist linguistics and psychology developed, respectively, by Ferdinand de Saussure and Jacques Lacan, as well as in Georges Dumézil's proto-structuralist work on comparative religion. These anti-subjective standpoints provide the context for Foucault's marginalization of the subject in his "structuralist histories", *The Birth of the Clinic* (on the origins of modern medicine) and *The Order of Things* (on the origins of the modern human sciences).

In a quite different vein, Foucault was enthralled by French avant-garde literature, especially the writings of Georges Bataille and Maurice Blanchot, where he found the experiential concreteness of existential phenomenology without what he came to see as dubious philosophical assumptions about subjectivity. Of particular interest was this literature's evocation of "limit-experiences", which push us to extremes where conventional categories of intelligibility begin to break down.

This philosophical milieu provided materials for the critique of subjectivity and the corresponding "archaeological" and "genealogical" methods of writing history that inform Foucault's projects of historical critique, to which we now turn.

Major Works

Since its beginnings with Socrates, philosophy has typically involved the project of questioning the accepted knowledge of the day. Later, Locke, Hume, and especially, Kant developed a distinctively modern idea of philosophy as the critique of knowledge. Kant's great epistemological innovation was to maintain that the same critique that revealed the limits of our knowing powers could also reveal necessary conditions for their exercise. What might have seemed just contingent features of human cognition (for example, the spatial and temporal character of its perceptual objects) turn out to be necessary truths. Foucault, however, suggests the need to invert this Kantian move. Rather than asking what, in the apparently contingent, is actually necessary, he suggests asking what, in the apparently necessary, might be contingent. The focus of his questioning is the modern human sciences (biological, psychological, social). These purport to offer universal scientific truths about human nature that are, in fact, often mere expressions of ethical and political commitments of a particular society. Foucault's "critical philosophy" undermines such claims by exhibiting how they are the outcome of contingent historical forces, not scientifically grounded truths. Each of his major books is a critique of historical reason.

Histories of Madness and Medicine

Foucault's *History of Madness in the Classical Age* (1961) originated in his academic study of psychology (a *licence de psychologie* in 1949 and a *diplome de psycho-pathologie* in 1952), his work in a Parisian mental hospital, and his own personal psychological problems. It was mainly written during his post-graduate *Wanderjahren* (1955–59) through a succession of diplomatic/educational posts in Sweden, Germany, and Poland. A study of the emergence of the modern concept of "mental illness" in Europe, *History of Madness* is formed from both Foucault's extensive archival work and his intense anger at what he saw as the moral hypocrisy of modern psychiatry. Standard histories saw the nineteenth-century medical treatment of madness (developed from the reforms of Pinel in France and the Tuke brothers in England) as an enlightened liberation of the mad from the ignorance and brutality of preceding ages. But, according to Foucault, the new idea that the mad were merely sick ("mentally" ill) and in need of medical treatment was not at all a clear improvement on earlier conceptions (e.g., the Renaissance idea that the mad were in contact with the mysterious forces of cosmic tragedy or the seventeenth-eighteenth-century view of madness as a renouncing of reason). Moreover, he argued that the alleged scientific neutrality of modern medical treatments of insanity are in fact covers for controlling challenges to conventional bourgeois morality. In short, Foucault argued that what was presented as an objective, incontrovertible scientific discovery (that madness is mental illness) was in fact the product of eminently questionable social and ethical commitments.

Foucault's next history, *The Birth of the Clinic* (1963) also presents a critique of modern clinical medicine. But the socio-ethical critique is muted (except for a few vehement passages), presumably because there is a substantial core of objective truth in medicine (as opposed to psychiatry) and so less basis for criticism. As a result *The Birth of the Clinic* is much closer to a standard history of science, in the tradition of Canguilhem's history of concepts.

The Order of Things

The book that made Foucault famous, *Les mots et les choses* (translated into English under the title *The Order of Things*), is in many ways an odd interpolation into the development of his thought. Its subtitle, "An Archaeology of the Human Sciences", suggests an expansion of the earlier critical histories of psychiatry and clinical medicine into other modern disciplines such as economics, biology, and philology. And indeed there is an extensive account of the various "empirical disciplines" of the Renaissance and the Classical Age that precede these modern human sciences. But there is little or nothing of the implicit social critique found in the *History of Madness* or even *The Birth of the Clinic*. Instead, Foucault offers an analysis of what knowledge meant—and how this meaning changed—in Western thought from the Renaissance to the present. At the heart of his account is the notion of representation. Here we focus on his treatment of representation in philosophical thought, where we find Foucault's most direct engagement with traditional philosophical questions.

Foucault argues that from Descartes up to Kant (during what he calls the Classical Age) representation was simply assimilated to thought: to think just was to employ ideas to represent the object of thought. But, he says, we need to be clear about what it meant for an idea to represent an object. This was not, first of all, any sort of relation of resemblance: there were no features (properties) of the idea that themselves constituted the representation of the object. (Saying this, however, does not require that the idea itself have no properties or even that these properties are not relevant to the idea's representation of the object.) By contrast, during the Renaissance, knowledge was understood as a matter of resemblance between things.

The map is a useful model of Classical representation. It consists, for example, of a set of lines of varying widths, lengths, and colors, and thereby represents the roads in and around a city. This is not because the roads have the properties of the map (the widths, lengths, and colors of the lines) but because the abstract structure given in the map (the relations among the lines) duplicates the abstract structure of the roads. At the heart of Classical thought is the principle that we know in virtue of having ideas that, in this sense, represent what we know. Of course, in contrast to the map, we do not need to know what the actual features of our ideas are in virtue of which they are able to represent. (In Descartes' scholastic terminology, we do not need to know their "formal reality".) We need to know only the abstract structure that they share with the things they represent (the structure of what Descartes calls their "objective reality"). We do, however, have direct (introspective) access to the abstract structures of our ideas: we can "see" what representational structure they have. Further, we can alter an idea's structure to make it a better representation of an object, as we can alter a map to improve it.

How, on the Classical view, do we know that an idea is a representation of an object—and an adequate representation? Not, Foucault argues, by comparing the idea with the object as it is apart from its representation. This is impossible, since it would require knowing the object without a representation (when, for Classical thought, to know *is* to represent). The only possibility is that the idea itself must make it apparent that it is a representation. The idea represents the very fact that it is a representation. As to the question of whether an idea is a representation, this "self-referential" feature is all there is to it. As to adequacy, it must be that some subset of ideas likewise bear witness to their own adequacy—as, for example, Descartes' "clear and distinct perceptions" or

Hume's simple impressions. In this sense, early modern philosophy is based on "intuition" (intellectual or sensory). Note, however, that an "intuition" of an idea's adequacy does not, of itself, establish the independent existence of the object represented by the idea. As far as the early modern view is concerned, there may be no such objects; or, if there are, this needs to be established by some other means (e.g., an argument or some other sort of intuition).

We see, then, that for Foucault the key to Classical knowing is the idea, that is, mental representation. Classical thinkers might disagree about the actual ontological status of ideas (their formal reality); but they all agreed that as representations (epistemically, if not ontologically) they were "non-physical" and "non-historical"; that is, precisely as representing their objects, they could not be conceived as having any role in the causal networks of the natural or the human worlds. From this it further followed that language—precisely as a physical and/or historical reality—could have no fundamental role in knowledge. Language could be nothing more than a higher-order instrument of thought: a physical representation of ideas, having no meaning except in relation to them.

Foucault maintains that the great "turn" in modern philosophy occurs with Kant (though presumably he is merely an example of something much broader and deeper). Kant raises the question of whether ideas do in fact represent their objects and, if so, how (in virtue of what) they do so. In other words, ideas are no longer taken as the unproblematic vehicles of knowledge; it is now possible to think that knowledge might be (or have roots in) something other than representation. This did not mean that representation had nothing at all to do with knowledge. Perhaps some (or even all) knowledge still essentially involved ideas' representing objects. But, Foucault insists, the thought that was only now (with Kant) possible was that representation itself (and the ideas that represented) could have an origin in something other than representation.

This thought, according to Foucault, led to some important and distinctively modern possibilities. The first was developed by Kant himself, who thought that representations (thoughts or ideas) were themselves the product of ("constituted" by) the mind. Not, however, produced by the mind as a natural or historical reality, but as belonging to a special epistemic realm: transcendental subjectivity. Kant thus maintained the Classical view that knowledge cannot be understood as a physical or historical reality, but he located the grounds of knowledge in a domain (the transcendental) more fundamental than the ideas it subtended. We must add, of course, that Kant also did not think of this domain as possessing a reality beyond the historical and the physical; it was not metaphysical. But this metaphysical alternative was explored by the idealistic metaphysics that followed Kant. Another—and in some ways more typically modern—view was that ideas were themselves historical realities. This could be most plausibly developed, as Herder did, by tying ideas essentially to language, now regarded as the primary (and historicized) vehicle of knowledge. But such an approach was not viable in its pure form, since to make knowledge entirely historical would deprive it of any normative character and so destroy its character as knowledge. In other words, even when modern thought made knowledge essentially historical, it had to retain some functional equivalent of Kant's transcendental realm to guarantee the normative validity of knowledge.

At this point, *The Order of Things* introduces the two central features of thought after Kant: the return of language and the "birth of man". Our discussion above readily explains why Foucault talks of a return of language: it now has an independent and essential role that it did not have in the Classical view. But the return is not a monolithic phenomenon. Language is related to knowledge in diverse ways, each of which corresponds a distinctive sort of "return". So, for example, the history of natural languages has introduced confusions and distortions that we can try to eliminate through techniques of formalization. On the other hand, this same history may have deposited fundamental truths in our languages that we can unearth only by the methods of hermeneutic interpretation. (So these two apparently opposed approaches—underlying the division of analytic and continental philosophy—are in fact, according to Foucault, complementary projects of modern thought.) But there is yet another possibility: freed from its subordination to ideas, language can function (as in the Renaissance) as an autonomous reality—indeed as even more deeply autonomous than Renaissance language, since there is no system of resemblances binding it to the world. Even more, Foucault suggests, language is a truth unto itself, speaking nothing other than its own meaning. This is the realm of "pure literature", evoked by Mallarmé when he answered Nietzsche's (genealogical) question, "Who is speaking?" with, "Language itself". In contrast to the Renaissance, however, there is no divine Word underlying and giving unique truth to the words of language. Literature is literally nothing but language—or rather many languages, speaking for and of themselves.

Even more important than language is the figure of man. The most important point about "man" is that it is an epistemological concept. Man, Foucault says, did not exist during the Classical age (or before). This is not because there was no idea of human beings as a species or of human nature as a psychological, moral, or political reality. Rather, "there was no epistemological consciousness of man as such" (*The Order of Things*, [1973: 309]). But even "epistemological" needs construal. There is no doubt that even in the Classical age human beings were conceived as the locus of knowledge (since humans possess the ideas that represent the world). The notion of man, on the other hand, is epistemological in the Kantian sense of a transcendental subject that is also an empirical object. For the Classical age, human beings are the locus of representations but not, as for Kant, their source. There is, in Classical thought, no room for the modern notion of "constitution".

Foucault illustrates his point through a striking discussion of Descartes' cogito, showing why it is an indubitable certitude within the classical episteme, but not within the modern episteme. There are two ways of questioning the force of the cogito. One is to suggest that the subject (the thinking self, the I) that Descartes concludes necessarily exists in the act of thinking is something more than just the act of representing objects; so we can't go from representation to a thinker. But for the Classical Age this makes no sense, since thinking is representation. A second criticism would be that the self as representer may not be "really real" but merely the "product of" (constituted by) a mind that is real in a fuller sense. But this objection has weight only if we can think of this "more real" mind as having the self as an object in some sense other than representing it. (Otherwise, there is no basis for saying that the self as representer is "less real".)

But, once again, this is precisely what cannot be thought in Classical terms.

The Analytic of Finitude

At the very heart of man is his finitude: the fact that, as described by the modern empirical sciences, he is limited by the various historical forces (organic, economic, linguistic) operating on him. This finitude is a philosophical problem because man as a historically limited empirical being must somehow also be the source of the representations whereby we know the empirical world, including ourselves as empirical beings. I (my consciousness) must, as Kant put it, be both an empirical object of representation and the transcendental source of representations. How is this possible? Foucault's view is that, in the end, it isn't—and that the impossibility (historically realized) means the collapse of the modern episteme. What Foucault calls the "analytic of finitude" sketches the historical case for this conclusion, examining the major efforts (together making up the heart of modern philosophy) to understand man as "empirico-transcendental".

The question—and the basic strategy for answering it—go back, of course, to Kant, who put forward the following crucial idea: that the very factors that make us finite (our subjection to space, time, causality, etc.) are also conditions necessary for the possibility of empirical knowledge. Our finitude is, therefore, simultaneously founded and founding (positive and fundamental, as Foucault puts it). The project of modern (Kantian and post-Kantian) philosophy—the analytic of finitude—is to show how this is possible.

Some modern philosophy tries to resolve the problem of man by, in effect, reducing the transcendental to the empirical. For example, naturalism attempts to explain knowledge in terms of natural science (physics, biology), while Marxism appeals to historical social sciences. (The difference is that the first grounds knowledge in the past—e.g., an evolutionary history—whereas the second grounds it in a revolutionary future that will transcend the limitations of ideology.) Either approach simply ignores the terms of the problem: that man must be regarded as irreducibly both empirical and transcendental.

It might seem that Husserl's phenomenology has carried out the Kantian project of synthesizing man as object and man as subject by radicalizing the Cartesian project; that is, by grounding our knowledge of empirical truths in the transcendental subject. The problem, however, is that, as Foucault sees it, the modern notion of man excludes Descartes' idea of the cogito as a "sovereign transparency" of pure consciousness. Thought is no longer pure representation and therefore cannot be separated from an "unthought" (i.e., the given empirical and historical truths about who we are). I can no longer go from "I think" to "I am" because the content of my reality (what I am) is always more than the content of any merely thinking self (I am, e.g., living, working, and speaking—and all these take me beyond the realm of mere thought). Or, conversely, if we use "I" to denote me simply as a conscious being, then I "am not" much of what I (as a self in the world) am. As a result, to the extent that Husserl has grounded everything in the transcendental subject, this is not the subject (cogito) of Descartes but the modern cogito, which includes the (empirical) unthought. Phenomenology, like all modern thought, must accept the unthought as the ineliminable "other" of man. Nor are the existential phenomenologists (Sartre and Merleau-Ponty) able to solve the problem. Unlike Husserl, they avoid positing a transcendental ego and instead focus on the concrete reality of man-in-the world. But this, Foucault claims, is just a more subtle way of reducing the transcendental to the empirical.

Finally, some philosophers (Hegel and Marx in one way, Nietzsche and Heidegger in another) have tried to resolve the problem of man's dual status by treating him as a historical reality. But this move encounters the difficulty that man has to be both a product of historical processes and the origin of history. If we treat man as a product, we find ourselves reducing his reality to something non-human (this is what Foucault calls the "retreat" from man's origin). But if we insist on a "return" to man as his own proper origin, then we can no longer make sense of his place in the empirical world. This paradox may explain the endless modern obsession with origins, but there is never any way out of the contradiction between man as originator and man as originated. Nonetheless, Foucault thinks that the modern pursuit of the question of origins has provided us with a deeper sense of the ontological significance of time, particularly in the thought of Nietzsche and Heidegger, who reject Hegel's and Marx's view of the return to our origin as a redemptive fullness of being, and instead see it as a confrontation with the nothingness of our existence.

From Archaeology to Genealogy

Foucault explicitly presents *The Order of Things* as an "archaeological" approach to the history of thought. Three years later, in 1969, he published *The Archaeology of Knowledge*, a methodological treatise that explicitly formulates what he took to be the archaeological method that he used not only in *The Order of Things* but also (at least implicitly) in *History of Madness* and *The Birth of the Clinic*. The key idea of the archaeological method is that systems of thought and knowledge (epistemes or discursive formations, in Foucault's terminology) are governed by rules, beyond those of grammar and logic, that operate beneath the consciousness of individual subjects and define a system of conceptual possibilities that determines the boundaries of thought in a given domain and period. So, for example, *History of Madness* should, Foucault maintained, be read as an intellectual excavation of the radically different discursive formations that governed talk and thought about madness from the seventeenth through the nineteenth centuries.

Archaeology was an essential method for Foucault because it supported a historiography that did not rest on the primacy of the consciousness of individual subjects; it allowed the historian of thought to operate at an unconscious level that displaced the primacy of the subject found in both phenomenology and in traditional historiography. However, archaeology's critical force was restricted to the comparison of the discursive formations of different periods. Such comparisons could suggest the contingency of a given way of thinking by showing that the people living in previous ages had thought very differently (and, apparently, just as effectively). But mere archaeological analysis could say nothing about the causes of the transition from one way of thinking to another and so had to ignore perhaps the most forceful case for the contingency of entrenched contemporary positions. Genealogy, the new method first deployed in *Discipline and Punish*, was intended to remedy this deficiency.

Foucault intended the term "genealogy" to evoke Nietzsche's genealogy of morals, particularly with its suggestion of complex, mundane, inglorious origins—in no way part of any grand scheme of progressive history. The point of a genealogical analysis is to show that a given system of thought (itself uncovered in its essential structures by archaeology, which therefore remains part of Foucault's historiography) was the result of contingent turns of history, not the outcome of rationally inevitable trends.

History of the Prison

Discipline and Punish, published in 1975, is a genealogical study of the development of the "gentler" modern way of imprisoning criminals rather than torturing or killing them. While recognizing the element of genuinely enlightened reform, Foucault particularly emphasizes how such reform also becomes a vehicle of more effective control: "to punish less, perhaps; but certainly to punish better". He further argues that the new mode of punishment becomes the model for control of an entire society, with factories, hospitals, and schools modeled on the modern prison. We should not, however, think that the deployment of this model was due to the explicit decisions of some central controlling agency. Foucault's analysis shows how techniques and institutions, developed for different and often quite innocuous purposes, converged to create the modern system of disciplinary power.

At the core of Foucault's picture of modern disciplinary society are three primary techniques of control: hierarchical observation, normalizing judgment, and the examination. To a great extent, control over people (power) can be achieved merely by observing them. So, for example, the tiered rows of seats in a stadium not only makes it easy for spectators to see but also for guards or security cameras to scan the audience. A perfect system of observation would allow one "guard" to see everything (a situation approximated, as we shall see, in Jeremy Bentham's Panopticon). But since this is not usually possible, there is a need for "relays" of observers, hierarchically ordered, through whom observed data passes from lower to higher levels.

A distinctive feature of modern power (disciplinary control) is its concern with what people have not done (nonobservence), with, that is, a person's failure to reach required standards. This concern illustrates the primary function of modern disciplinary systems: to correct deviant behavior. The main goal is not revenge (as in the case of the tortures of premodern punishment) but reform, where reform means primarily coming to live by society's standards or norms. Discipline through imposing precise and detailed norms ("normalization") is quite different from the older system of judicial punishment, which merely judges each action as allowed by the law or not allowed by the law and does not say that those judged are "normal" or "abnormal". This idea of normalization is pervasive in our society: e.g., national standards for educational programs, for medical practice, for industrial processes and products.

The examination (for example, of students in schools, of patients in hospitals) is a method of control that combines hierarchical observation with normalizing judgment. It is a prime example of what Foucault calls power/knowledge, since it combines into a unified whole "the deployment of force and the establishment of truth" (1975 [1977: 184]).

It both elicits the truth about those who undergo the examination (tells what they know or what is the state of their health) and controls their behavior (by forcing them to study or directing them to a course of treatment).

On Foucault's account, the relation of power and knowledge is far closer than in the familiar Baconian engineering model, for which "knowledge is power" means that knowledge is an instrument of power, although the two exist quite independently. Foucault's point is rather that, at least for the study of human beings, the goals of power and the goals of knowledge cannot be separated: in knowing we control and in controlling we know.

The examination also situates individuals in a "field of documentation". The results of exams are recorded in documents that provide detailed information about the individuals examined and allow power systems to control them (e.g., absentee records for schools, patients' charts in hospitals). On the basis of these records, those in control can formulate categories, averages, and norms that are in turn a basis for knowledge. The examination turns the individual into a "case"—in both senses of the term: a scientific example and an object of care. Caring is always also an opportunity for control.

Bentham's Panopticon is, for Foucault, a paradigmatic architectural model of modern disciplinary power. It is a design for a prison, built so that each inmate is separated from and invisible to all the others (in separate "cells") and each inmate is always visible to a monitor situated in a central tower. Monitors do not in fact always see each inmate; the point is that they *could* at any time. Since inmates never know whether they are being observed, they must behave as if they are always seen and observed. As a result, control is achieved more by the possibility of internal monitoring of those controlled than by actual supervision or heavy physical constraints.

The principle of the Panopticon can be applied not only to prisons but also to any system of disciplinary power (a factory, a hospital, a school). And, in fact, although Bentham himself was never able to build it, its principle has come to pervade aspects of modern society. It is the instrument through which modern discipline has been able to replace pre-modern sovereignty (kings, judges) as the fundamental power relation.

Foucault's genealogy follows Nietzsche as well as existential phenomenology in that it aims to bring the body into the focus of history. Rather than histories of mentalities or ideas, genealogies are "histories of the body". They examine the historical practices through which the body becomes an object of techniques and deployments of power. In *Discipline and Punish*, Foucault shows how disciplinary techniques produce "docile bodies": bodies of prisoners, soldiers, workers and schoolchildren were subjected to disciplinary power in order to make them more useful and at the same time easier to control. The human body became a machine the functioning of which could be optimized, calculated, and improved. Its functions, movements and capabilities were broken down into narrow segments, analyzed in detail and recomposed in a maximally effective way.

By historicizing the body, Foucault's genealogies also have distinctive philosophical implications. They question the naturalistic explanatory framework that understands human nature—uncovered by science—as the basis for such complex areas of behavior as sexuality, insanity or criminality. A key idea in Foucault's historical analysis of the modern penal institutions is that they operate with markedly different rationality than those that are aimed solely at retribution through pain. He effectively reveals the double role of the present system: it aims at both punishing and correcting, and therefore it mixes juridical and scientific practices. Foucault argued that the intervention of criminal psychiatry in the field of law that occurred at the beginning of the nineteenth century, for example, was part of the gradual shift in penal practice from a focus on the crime to a focus on the criminal, from the action to agency and personality. The new idea of the "dangerous individual" referred to the danger potentially inherent in the criminal person. The new rationality could not function in an effective way in the existing system without the emergence of new forms of scientific knowledge such as criminal psychiatry that enabled the characterization of criminals in themselves, beneath their acts. Foucault suggests that this shift resulted in the emergence of new, insidious forms of domination and violence. The critical impact of *Discipline and Punish* thus lies in its ability to reveal the processes of subject formation that operate in modern penal institutions. The modern prison does not just punish by depriving its inmates of liberty, it categorizes them as delinquent subjects, types of people with a dangerous, criminal nature.

History of Modern Sexuality

Foucault's history of sexuality was originally projected as a fairly straightforward extension of the genealogical approach of *Discipline and Punish* to the topic of sexuality. Foucault's idea is that the various modern fields of knowledge about sexuality (various "sciences of sexuality", including psychoanalysis) have an intimate association with the power structures of modern society and so are prime candidates for genealogical analysis. The first volume of this project, published in 1976, was intended as the introduction to a series of studies on particular aspects of modern sexuality (children, women, "perverts", population, etc.). It outlined the project of the overall history, explaining the basic viewpoint and the methods to be used.

On Foucault's account, modern control of sexuality parallels modern control of criminality by making sex (like crime) an object of allegedly scientific disciplines, which simultaneously offer knowledge and domination of their objects. However, it becomes apparent that there is a further dimension in the power associated with the sciences of sexuality. Not only is there control exercised via other people's knowledge of individuals such as doctors' knowledge, for example; there is also control via individuals' knowledge of themselves. Individuals internalize the norms laid down by the sciences of sexuality and monitor themselves in an effort to conform to these norms. Thus, they are controlled not only as *objects* of disciplines but also as self-scrutinizing and self-forming *subjects.*

Foucault shows how sexuality becomes an essential construct in determining not only moral worth, but also health, desire, and identity. Subjects are further obligated to tell the truth about themselves by confessing the details of their sexuality. Foucault argued that modern sexuality was characterized by the secularization of religious techniques of confession: one no longer confesses the details of one's sexual desire to a priest; one goes to a doctor, a therapist, a psychologist, or a psychiatrist.

The book begins with a repudiation of the "repressive hypothesis", the idea that sexuality in the Victorian era was repressed and discourse on it silenced. Foucault claims that it was not repression that characterized the primary attitude of modern society towards sex; rather, sexuality became the object of new kinds of discourse—medical, juridical and psychological – and that discourse on it actually increased. Sexuality was inextricably linked to truth: these new discourses were able to tell us the scientific truth about ourselves through our sexuality.

Although the book is a historical study of the emergence of modern sexuality in the nineteenth century, Foucault's targets were also contemporary ideas and practices. The prevalent views on sexuality in the 1960s and 1970s held that there was a natural and healthy sexuality that all human beings shared simply in virtue of being human, and this sexuality was presently repressed by cultural prohibitions and conventions such as bourgeois morality and capitalist socio-economic structures. Repressed sexuality was the cause of various neuroses and it was important to have an active and free sexuality. The popular discourse on sexuality thus fervently argued for sexual liberation: we had to liberate our true sexuality from the repressive mechanisms of power.

Foucault challenged this view by showing how our conceptions and experiences of sexuality are in fact always the result of specific cultural conventions and mechanisms of power and could not exist independently of them. The mission to liberate our repressed sexuality was thus fundamentally misguided because there was no authentic or natural sexuality to liberate. To free oneself from one set of norms only meant adopting different norms in their stead, and that could turn out to be just as controlling and normalizing. He wrote mockingly that the irony of our endless preoccupation with sexuality was that we believed that it had something to do with our liberation.

In order to challenge the dominant view of the relationship between sexuality and repressive power, Foucault had to re-conceive the nature of power. His major claim is that power is not essentially repressive but productive. It does not operate by repressing and prohibiting the true and authentic expressions of a natural sexuality. Instead it produces, through cultural normative practices and scientific discourses, the ways in which we experience and conceive of our sexuality. Power relations are "the internal conditions" of our sexual identities.

Foucault outlined what became one of the most influential contemporary understandings of power in a series of short propositions over three pages of *The History of Sexuality, Volume 1*. He elucidated and developed this understanding of power in a number of essays, lectures and interviews throughout the rest of his life, but the basic idea was already present in these pages. We should not try to look for the center of power, or for the individuals, institutions or classes that rule, but should rather construct a "microphysics of power" that focuses on the multitude of loci of power spread throughout a society: families, workplaces, everyday practices, and marginal institutions. One has to analyze power relations from the bottom up and not from the top down, and to study the myriad ways in which the subjects themselves are constituted in these diverse but intersecting networks.

Although dispersed among various interlacing networks throughout society, power nevertheless has a rationality, a series of aims and objectives, and the means of attaining them. This does not imply that any individual has consciously formulated them. As the example of the Panopticon shows, power often functions according to a clear rationality irrespective of the intentions and motives of the individual who guards the prison from the tower. Despite the centrality of the Panopticon as a model for power, Foucault does not hold that power forms a deterministic system of overbearing constraints. Power should rather be understood and analyzed as an unstable network of practices implying that where there is power, there is always resistance too. Just as there is no center of power, there is no center of resistance somewhere outside of it. Resistance is rather inherent in power relations and their dynamics, it is "the odd term in the relations of power" (1976 [1978: 96]). While power relations permeate the whole body of society, they may be denser in some regions and less dense in others.

Foucault's short but influential discussion of biopower also first appears at the end of *The History of Sexuality, Vol. 1*. Foucault contrasts it to what he calls sovereign power: a form of power that was historically founded on violence—the right to kill. It was exercised mainly by "deduction" (taking something away): it consisted of the right to appropriate a portion of the nation's wealth, for example by imposing a tax on products, goods and services, or by demanding a portion of the subjects' time, strength, and ultimately life itself. The obligation to wage war on behalf of the sovereign and the imposition of death penalty for going against his will were the clearest forms of such power. But Foucault claims that the West has undergone a profound transformation in its mechanisms of power since the seventeenth century. Deductive and violent sovereign power has been gradually complemented and partly replaced by biopower, a form of power that exerts a positive influence on life, "that endeavors to administer, optimize, and multiply it, subjecting it to precise controls and comprehensive regulations" (1976 [1978: 137]). This era of biopower is marked by the explosion of numerous and diverse techniques for achieving the control of populations: techniques that, for example, coordinate medical care, normalize behavior, rationalize mechanisms of insurance, and rethink urban planning. The aim is the effective administration of bodies and the calculated management of life through means that are scientific and continuous. Mechanisms of power and knowledge have assumed responsibility for the life process in order to optimize, control, and modify it. The exercise of power over living beings no longer carries the threat of death, but instead takes charge of their lives.

The rationality of biopower is markedly different from that of sovereign power in terms not just of its objectives, but also of its instruments. A major consequence of its development is the growing importance of norms at the expense of the juridical system of the law. Foucault claims that the dominance of biopower as the paradigmatic form of power means that we live in a society in which the power of the law has subsided in favor of regulative and corrective mechanisms based on scientific knowledge. Biopower penetrates traditional forms of political power, but it is essentially the power of experts and administrators.

The genealogical attempt to historicize the body is prominent also in *The History of Sexuality, Vol. 1*, but now Foucault's target is the naturalist explanations of sex and sexuality. At the end of the book Foucault takes up the question of whether we can find a scientific truth about sex. He makes clear that his genealogical investigation of sexuality implies a challenge to a certain kind of explanatory framework of sexuality and gender: the idea of sex as a natural foundation or an unobserved cause, which supports the visible effects of gender and sexuality. He critically appraises the idea of a natural, scientifically defined true sex by revealing the historical development of this form of thought. He does not claim that sex, understood as the categories of maleness and femaleness, was invented in a particular historical period. He rather analyses the ways in which these categories were founded and explained in discourses claiming the status of scientific truth, and how this allegedly "pure" explanation in fact constituted these categories so that they were understood as "natural". This idea has had enormous influence on feminist philosophers and queer theorists. Judith Butler has appropriated this idea in her influential book *Gender Trouble* to argue that allegedly scientific ideas of sex as a natural and necessary ground for sexual and gendered identities in fact have a normative function: they constitute our conceptions of "normal" men and women and their "natural" sexual desire for each other.

Sex in the Ancient World

Foucault's final engagement with traditional philosophy arises from the turn toward the ancient world he took in the last few years of his life. *The History of Sexuality* had been planned as a multi-volume work on various themes in a study of modern sexuality. The first volume, discussed above, was a general introduction. Foucault wrote a second volume (*Les aveux de la chair*) that dealt with the origins of the modern notion of the subject in the practices of Christian confession, but he never published it. (It was published posthumously in 2018.) His concern was that a proper understanding of the Christian development required a comparison with ancient conceptions of the ethical self, something he undertook in his last two books (1984) on Greek and Roman sexuality: *The Use of Pleasure* and *The Care of the Self*.

These treatments of ancient sexuality moved Foucault into ethical issues that had been implicit but seldom explicitly thematized in his earlier writings. What emerges out of his historical studies of ancient sexuality is a particular conception of ethics that he traces to antiquity. In the ancient conception, ethics referred to the practice through which one forms oneself as an ethical subject following the prescriptive elements of morality. It concerns the way in which moral rules can be adopted and problematized by the subjects themselves.

The importance of a study of ethics becomes apparent when we try to make visible the difference between the morality of antiquity and that of Christianity. Foucault's specific goal was to compare ancient pagan and Christian ethics through the test-case of sexuality and to trace the development of Christian ideas about sex from the very different ideas of the ancients. He argues that, contrary to what is often believed, on the level of moral codes of behavior, there are in fact striking similarities between antiquity and Christianity. Both shared, for example, a concern that sexual expenditure could harm an individual's health, and they both valued conjugal fidelity and sexual abstinence. But there was a strong contrast in the ways these two cultures understood and practiced these ideals and demands.

In the Christian view sexual acts were, on the whole, evil in themselves and most forms of sexual activity were simply forbidden. A main emphasis in Christian morality is therefore on the moral code, its systematicity, its richness, and its capacity to adjust to every possible case and to embrace every area of behavior. The rules in Christian monasteries, for example, were not only very severe, but also extremely detailed. The morality of antiquity, on the other hand, is one in which the code and rules of behavior are rudimentary. The ancient Greeks' view was that sexual acts were natural and necessary, but subject to abuse. They emphasized the proper use (*chresis*) of pleasures, where this involved engaging in a range of sexual activities (heterosexual, homosexual, in marriage, out of marriage), but with proper moderation. Their texts discussing morality therefore lay down very few explicit rules or guidelines on the kinds of sexual acts that one should engage in. More important than the moral rules was the relationship that one had with oneself, the choice of the "style of existence" made by the individual. Sexual austerity, for example, was not practiced as a result of prohibitions, but because of a personal choice to live a beautiful life and to leave to others memories of a beautiful existence. Sex for the Greeks was a major part of what Foucault called an "aesthetics of existence": the self's creation of a beautiful and enjoyable existence.

Foucault's last two books are an attempt to make a contribution to the task of rethinking ethics, but they are also a continuation of his attempt to rethink the subject. Now the focus is on the forms of understanding that subjects create about themselves and the practices by which they transform their mode of being. In his study of ancient Greek ethics, Foucault continued to pursue his idea that there was no true self that could be deciphered and emancipated, but that the self was something that had been—and must be—created. There is, however, a whole new axis of analysis present in his late studies of the subject. While his earlier genealogical studies investigated the ways in which power/knowledge networks constituted the subject, his late work emphasizes the subject's own role in this process. It therefore offers a more complex understanding of the subject. Subjects are not simply constructed by power; they themselves partake in that construction and modify themselves through practices of the self. They are not just docile bodies, but actively refuse, adopt and alter forms of being a subject. One way of contesting normalizing power is by shaping oneself and one's lifestyle creatively: by exploring opportunities for new ways of being, new fields of experience, pleasures, relationships, modes of living and thinking.

Foucault after Foucault

Foucault left instructions that there should be no posthumous publication of his writings that he had not published in his lifetime. But Foucault had allowed taping of his lectures, and his estate decided that this amounted to permission to publish edited versions of his public lectures based on his notes and tape recordings. This decision has allowed print editions of the annual courses of lectures that he delivered at the Collège de France from 1970–71 through 1983–84 (except for a sabbatical year in 1976–77) as well as other lectures he gave in different universities around the world. This has made an enormous body of important material available. Some of it covers work later published, but some presents ideas that appear nowhere else.

The lecture series *Security, Territory, Population* (1977–1978) and *The Birth of*

Biopolitics (1978–1979) have been especially influential and introduce Foucault's ideas on *government* and *governmentality*. "Government" becomes Foucault's preferred term for power, while "governmentality" functions as his main theoretical tool for analyzing its rationality, techniques, and procedures in the modern world.

Foucault shows that while government historically referred to a wide range of practices, from religious guidance of the soul to ruling over a territory and its inhabitants, in the context of the modern state it has come to mean governing a population. Population as the object of modern forms of government both required and encouraged the development of specific forms of knowledge such as statistical analysis as well as macro-economic and bio-scientific knowledge. The modern state had to take care of the life and the wellbeing of its population, and Foucault therefore calls the politics of the modern state *biopolitics*.

In Foucault's original formulation, the term "governmentality" referred to the specific historical development of the essentially modern, complex techniques of power that focused on the population. Later Foucault also gave the term a more general meaning as "the way in which one conducts the conduct of men". His key claim was that to understand the practice of government in this broad sense of controlling people's conduct, one had to study the specific technologies of power, but also the rationality underpinning them. The practices and institutions of government are always enabled, regulated, and justified by a specific form of reasoning or rationality that defines their ends and the suitable means of achieving them. To understand power as a set of relations, as Foucault repeatedly suggested, means understanding how such relations are rationalized. It means examining how forms of rationality inscribe themselves in practices and systems of practices, and what role they play within them.

The exposition and analysis of the historically changing governmental rationalities was a pivotal goal of Foucault's lectures. His analysis makes clear that modern governmental rationality has two major features. On the one hand, the development of the modern state is characterized by the centralization of political power: a centralized state with highly organized administration and bureaucracy has emerged. While this feature is commonly analyzed and also criticized in political thought, Foucault also identifies the evolution of a second feature that appears to be antagonistic to this development. He claims that the modern state is also characterized by individualizing power—or "pastoral power" as he also calls it. This is power that relies on individualizing knowledge about a person' life. The modern state required the development of power technologies oriented towards individuals in an attempt to govern their conduct in a continuous and permanent way. The result is the intervention of the state in the everyday life of individuals for example, their diet, mental health, and sexual practices.

The analysis of governmentality does not replace Foucault's earlier understanding of power. His method of analysis is similar to the one he used to study the techniques and practices of power in the context of particular, local institutions such as the prison. What had to be analyzed, but also questioned, were the historically specific rationalities intrinsic to practices. At the same time, Foucault's analysis of governmentality adds new and important dimensions to his understanding of power.

While his studies of disciplinary power were restricted to specialized institutional contexts, with the notion of government he was able to study larger, strategic developments beyond the scope of his "microphysics of power". He was able to transfer his understanding of power to domains such as the state that were traditionally regarded as objects of political theory. With the idea of power as government, Foucault was also able to clarify his understanding of resistance. Because government refers to strategic, regulated and rationalized modes of power that have to be legitimized through forms of knowledge, the idea of critique as a form of resistance now becomes crucial. To govern is not to physically determine the conduct of passive objects. Government involves offering reasons why those governed should do what they are told, and this implies that they can also question these reasons. Foucault claims that this is why governmentality has historically developed in tandem with the practice of political critique. The practice of critique must question the reasons for governing *like that*: the legitimate principles, procedures and means of governing.

In the lecture series *The Birth of Biopolitics*, Foucault also engages in a lengthy examination of neoliberal governmentality. This analysis has become seminal for contemporary political theory. Many political commentators now see the year 1979, when Foucault delivered his lectures, as the inauguration of the dominance of neoliberal economic policy in Europe and the United States. Almost forty years after its expanding application, Foucault's topic and his insights appear farsighted. His analysis of neoliberalism is distinctive in at least two significant ways. First, he analyzes neoliberalism as a historically novel form of governmentality—a rationality of governing connected with specific technologies of power. On Foucault's account neoliberalism is not understood just as an economic doctrine, but as a governmental form that is directed toward specific objectives, regulates itself through continuous reflection, and, essentially, aims to ensure that capitalism works. It comprises a coherent political ontology, a set of philosophical background beliefs about the nature of society, markets, and human beings. However, it is not an ideology in the sense of consisting only of ideas or false beliefs. Its political ontology necessitates and rationalizes a specific technology of power—specific practices of governing, as well as a particular way of reflecting on and problematizing these practices.

Foucault also emphasizes that neoliberal governmentality should be viewed as a particular way of producing subjects: it produces an economic subject structured by specific tendencies, preferences, and motivations. It aims to create social conditions that not only encourage and necessitate competitiveness and self-interest, but also produce them. Foucault discusses the work of the American neoliberal economists, in particular Gary Becker and his theory of human capital, in order to show how neoliberal subjects are understood as navigating the social realm by constantly making rational choices based on economic knowledge and the strict calculation of the necessary costs and desired benefits. Such subjects must make long-term and short-term investments in different aspects of their lives and acquire sufficient economic knowledge to be able to calculate costs, risks, and possible returns on the capital invested.

Foucault never published any of the material developed in these two lecture series, and in the lectures in the 1980s he turned to examine texts from ancient philosophy. Many of the ideas developed there were later published as *The Use of Pleasure* and *Care of the Self*. His studies of ancient sexuality, and, particularly, the idea of an aesthetics of existence also led him to the ancient idea of philosophy as a way of life rather than a search for theoretical truth. Although *The Use of Pleasure* has some discussion of Plato's conception of philosophy, Foucault's treatments of the topic are primarily in lectures that he had no time to develop for publication. Some of these lectures discuss Socrates (in the *Apology* and in *Alcibiades I*) as both a model and an exponent of a philosophical life focused on "care of the self" and follow the subsequent ancient discussions of this topic in, for example, Epictetus, Seneca, and Plutarch. Other lectures deal with the ancient ideal of "truthful speaking" (*parrhesia*), regarded as a central political and moral virtue. Here Foucault discusses earlier formulations of the notion, in Euripides and Socrates, as well as its later transformations by the Epicureans, Stoics, and Cynics. This research project might have been the most fruitful of all Foucault's engagements with traditional philosophy. But his early death in 1984 prevented him from completing it.

Resources

Chapter One:

- Volume I (1986), *Persons and Places: Fragments of Autobiography*, edited by William G. Holzberger and Herman J. Saatkamp, Jr., Introduction by Richard C. Lyon.
- Volume II (1988), *The Sense of Beauty: Being the Outlines of Aesthetic Theory*, edited by William G. Holzberger and Herman J. Saatkamp, Jr., Introduction by Arthur Danto.
- Volume III (1989), *Interpretations of Poetry and Religion*, edited by William G. Holzberger and Herman J. Saatkamp, Jr., Introduction by Joel Porte.
- Volume IV (1994), *The Last Puritan: A Memoir in the Form of a Novel*, edited by William G. Holzberger and Herman J. Saatkamp, Jr. Introduction by Irving Singer.
- Volume V (2001–2008), *The Letters of George Santayana*, edited by William G. Holzberger and Herman J. Saatkamp, Jr.

    - *Book One: [1868]–1909*, published 2001.
    - *Book Two: 1910–1920*, published 2002.
    - *Book Three: 1921–1927*, published 2002.
    - *Book Four: 1928–1932*, published 2003.
    - *Book Five: 1933–1936*, published 2003.
    - *Book Six: 1937–1940*, published 2004.
    - *Book Seven: 1941–1947*, published 2006.
    - *Book Eight: 1948–1952*, published 2008.

- Volume VI (2011), *George Santayana's Marginalia: A Critical Selection*, edited by John McCormick and Kris Walters Frost. Introduction by John McCormick.
  - *Book One: Abell–Lucretius*
  - *Book Two: McCord–Zeller*
- Volume VII (2011–2016), *The Life of Reason*, edited by Marianne W. Wokeck and Martin A. Coleman. Introduction by James Gouinlock.
  - *Book One: Reason in Common Sense*, 2011
  - *Book Two: Reason in Society*, 2013.
  - *Book Three: Reason in Religion*, 2014.
  - *Book Four: Reason in Art*, 2015.
  - *Book Five: Reason in Science*, 2016.
- Volume VIII (2019), *Three Philosophical Poets: Lucretius, Dante, and Goethe*, edited by Kellie Dawson and David Spiech. Introduction by James Seaton.

Chapter Two:

- The abbreviations used to cite Camus's work (P, R, MS, RRD, N, and LCE) are defined in the section 'Works in English' below.
- Collected Works in French
- Théâtre, Récits, Nouvelles, R. Quilliot (ed.), Paris: Gallimard, 1962.
- Essais, R. Quillot and L. Fauçon (eds.), Paris: Gallimard, 1965.
- Œuvres Complètes, Vols. I–IV, R. Gay-Crosier (ed.) Paris: Gallimard, 2006–09.

- Works in English
- Reference marks are given for cited English translations.
- The Plague, New York: Alfred A. Knopf, 1948 [P].
- The Plague, New York: Alfred A. Knopf, 2021 [P 2021].
- The Rebel: An Essay on Man in Revolt, New York: Alfred A. Knopf, 1954 [R].
- The Myth of Sisyphus and Other Essays, New York: Alred A. Knopf, 1955 [MS].
- The Fall, New York: Alfred A. Knopf, 1957.
- Caligula, and Three Other Plays, New York: Alred A. Knopf, 1958.
- Resistance, Rebellion, and Death, New York: Alfred A. Knopf, 1961 [RRD].
- "Nuptials at Tipasa", in Lyrical and Critical Essays, 1968 [N].
- Lyrical and Critical Essays, New York: Alfred A. Knopf, 1968 [LCE].
- The Stranger, New York: Vintage, 1988.
- Between Hell and Reason, Hanover, NH: Wesleyan University Press, 1991 [Camus' Between Hell and Reason available online].
- "Christian Metaphysics and Neoplatonism", in J. McBride, Albert Camus: Philosopher and Littérateur, New York: St. Martin's Press, 1992, pp. 93–165.
- Notebooks 1942–1951, New York: Marlowe, 1995.
- Notebooks 1935–1942, New York: Marlowe, 1996.
- Camus at Combat: Writing 1944–47, J. Lévi-Vatensi (ed.), Princeton: Princeton University Press, 2006.
- Camus and Sartre
- Sartre, J.P., "Camus's The Outsider," in Literary and Philosophical Essays, New York: Collier Books, 1962.
- Sprintzen, D.A., and A. van den Hoven (eds.), Sartre and Camus: A Historic Confrontation, Amherst, NY:

Humanity Books, 2004.

Chapter Three:

- 1936a, La Transcendance de l'ego: Esquisse d'une description phénomenologique, Paris: J. Vrin. Translated as
- 1957, The Transcendence of the Ego: An Existentialist Theory of Consciousness, Forrest Williams and Robert Kirkpatrick (trans.), New York: Noonday Press.
- 2004, The Transcendence of the Ego: A Sketch for a Phenomenological Description, Andrew Brown (trans.), London: Routledge. doi:10.4324/9780203694367
- 1936b [2012], L'imagination, Paris: F. Alcan. Translated as The Imagination, Kenneth Williford and David Rudrauf (trans.), London: Routledge, 2012. doi:10.4324/9780203723692
- 1938 [1965], La Nausée: Roman, Paris: Gallimard. Translated as Nausea, Robert Baldick (trans.), Harmondsworth: Penguin, 1965.
- 1939a [1970], "Une idée fondamentale de la phénoménologie de Husserl: l'intentionnalit", La Nouvelle Revue française, 304: 129–132. Reprinted in Situations 1. Translated as "Intentionality: A Fundamental Idea of Husserl's Phenomenology", Joseph P. Fell (trans.), Journal of the British Society for Phenomenology, 1(2): 4–5, 1970. doi:10.1080/00071773.1970.11006118
- 1939b [1948], Esquisse d'une théorie des émotions, Paris: Hermann. Translated as The Emotions: Outline of a Theory, Bernard Frechtman (trans.), New York: Philosophical Library, 1948.
- 1940 [2004], L'Imaginaire: Psychologie

Phénoménologique de l'imagination, Paris: Gallimard. Translated as The Imaginary: A Phenomenological Psychology of the Imagination, Arlette Elkaïm-Sartre (ed.), Jonathan Webber (trans.), London: Routledge, 2004.

- 1943 [1956, 2018], L'être et le néant: Essai d'ontologie phénoménologique, Paris: Gallimard. Translated as
- 1956, Being and Nothingness: An Essay on Phenomenological Ontology, Hazel E. Barnes (trans.), New York: Philosophical Library.
- 2018, Being and Nothingness: An Essay in Phenomenological Ontology, Sarah Richmond (trans.), London: Routledge.
- 1945–49, Les Chemins de la liberté (The roads to freedom), Paris: Gallimard. Series of novels L'âge de raison (The age of reason, 1945), Le sursis (The reprieve, 1945), and La mort dans l'âme (Troubled sleep, 1949).
- 1946a [2007], L'existentialisme est un humanisme, (Collection Pensées), Paris: Nagel. Translated as Existentialism is a Humanism, John Kulka (ed.), Carol Macomber (trans.), New Haven, CT: Yale University Press, 2007.
- 1946b [1948/1995], Réflexions sur la question juive, Paris: P. Morihien. Translated as Anti-semite and Jew, George J. Becker (trans.), New York: Schocken Books, 1948 (reprinted with preface by Michael Walzer, 1995).
- 1946c [1955], "Matérialisme et Révolution I", Les Temps Modernes, 9: 37–63 and 10: 1–32. Reprinted in Situations III, Paris: Gallimard, 1949. Translated as , "Materialism and Revolution", in Literary and Philosophical Essays, Annette Michelson (trans.), New York: Criterion Books, 1955.

- 1947a [1967], Baudelaire, Paris: Gallimard. Translated as Baudelaire, Martin Turnell (trans.), London: H. Hamilton, 1949. Reprinted, Norfolk, CT: New Directions, 1967
- 1947b [1949], Huis-Clos, Paris: Gallimard. First produced 1944. Translated as No Exit, in No Exit, and Three Other Plays, New York: Vintage Books, 1949.
- 1947c [1949], Les Mouches, Paris: Gallimard. First produced 1943. Translated as The Flies, in No Exit, and Three Other Plays, New York: Vintage Books, 1949.
- 1948a [1988], "Qu'est-ce que la littérature?", Les Temps modernes. Collected in Situations II. Translated in "What Is Literature?" and Other Essays, Bernard Frechtman (trans.), Cambridge, MA: Harvard University Press, 1988.
- 1948b [1967], "Conscience de soi et connaissance de soi", Bulletin de la Société française de Philosophie, n° 3, avril-juin 1948. Translated as "Consciousness of Self and Knowledge of Self", in Readings in Existential Phenomenology, Nathaniel Lawrence and Daniel O'Connor (eds), Englewood Cliffs, NJ: Prentice Hall, 1967.
- 1948c [1949], Les mains sales: pièce en sept tableaux, Paris: Gallimard. First produced 1948. Translated as Dirty Hands, in No Exit, and Three Other Plays, New York: Vintage Books, 1949.
- 1952a [1963], Saint-Genêt, Comédien et martyr, Paris: Gallimard. Translated as Saint Genet: Actor and Martyr, Bernard Frechtman (trans.), New York: George Braziller, 1963.
- 1952b [1968]. "Les communistes et la paix", published in Situations VI. Translated as "The Communists and Peace", in The Communists and Peace, with A Reply to

Claude Lefort, Martha H. Fletcher and Philip R. Berk (trans.), New York: George Braziller, 1968.

- 1957 [1963/1968], Questions de méthode, Paris: Gallimard. Later to be a foreword for Sartre 1960. Translated as Search for a Method, Hazel E. Barnes (trans.), New York: Knopf, 1963. Reprinted New York: Random House, 1968.
- 1960a [1976], Critique de la Raison dialectique, tome 1, Théorie des ensembles pratiques, Paris, Gallimard. Translated as Critique of Dialectical Reason, volume 1: Theory of Practical Ensembles, Alan Sheridan-Smith (trans.), London: New Left Books, 1976. Reprinted in 2004 with a forward by Fredric Jameson, London: Verso. The second unfinished volume was published posthumously in 1985.
- 1960b, Les Séquestrés d'Altona (The condemned of Altona), Paris: Gallimard. First produced 1959.

Chapter Four:

- 1954, "Introduction" to Le Rêve et l'existence, Paris: Desclée de Brouwer. This is an introduction to the French translation, by Jacqueline Verdeaux, of Ludwig Binswanger, Traum und Existenz, 1930.
- 1954, Maladie mentale et personnalité, Paris: Presses universitaires de France.
- 1962, Maladie mentale et psychologie, Paris: Presses universitaires de France; translated as Mental Illness and Psychology, Alan Sheridan (trans.), New York: Harper and Row, 1976. Significantly revised version of the 1954 book.
- 1972, L'histoire de la folie à l'âge classique, Paris: Gallimard (first published as Folie et déraison, Paris:

Plon, 1961). Translated as History of Madness, Jean Khalfa (ed.), Jonathan Murphy and Jean Khalfa (trans.), New York: Routledge, 2006.

- 1963, Raymond Roussel, Paris: Gallimard. Translated as Death and the Labyrinth: The World of Raymond Roussel, Charles Ruas (trans.), Garden City, NY: Doubleday, 1986.
- 1963, Naissance de la clinique, Paris: Presses universitaires de France. Translated as The Birth of the Clinic, Allan Sheridan (trans.), New York: Pantheon, 1973.
- 1966, Les mots et les choses, Paris: Gallimard. Translated as The Order of Things, Alan Sheridan (trans.), New York: Vintage, 1973.
- 1969, L'archéologie du savoir, Paris: Gallimard. Translated as The Archaeology of Knowledge, Allan Sheridan (trans.), New York: Harper and Row, 1972.

Chapter Five:

- 1947, Situations I: Critiques littéraires, Paris: Gallimard. Partially translated in Literary and Philosophical Essays, Annette Michelson (trans.), London: Rider, 1955. Reprinted New York: Collier Books, 1962.
- 1948, Situations II, Paris: Gallimard.
- 1949, Situations III: Lendemains de guerre, Paris: Gallimard.
- 1964b, Situations IV: Portraits, Paris: Gallimard.
- 1964c, Situations V: Colonialisme et néo-colonialisme, Paris: Gallimard. Translated as Colonialism and Neocolonialism, Azzdedine Haddour, Steve Brewer, and Terry McWilliams (trans), London: Routledge, 2001. doi:10.4324/9780203991848

- 1964d, Situations VI: Problèmes du marxisme 1, Paris: Gallimard.
- 1965, Situations VII: Problèmes du marxisme 2, Paris:, Gallimard.
- 1971, Situations VIII: Autour de 68, Paris: Gallimard.
- 1972, Situations IX: Mélanges, Paris: Gallimard. Material from Situations VIII et IX translated as Between Existentialism and Marxism, John Mathews (trans.), London: New Left Books, 1974.
- 1976, Situations X: Politique et autobiographie, Paris: Gallimard. Translated as Life/Situations: Essays Written and Spoken, Paul Auster and Lydia Davis (trans), New York: Pantheon, 1977.
- 1981, Œuvres romanesques, Michel Contat, Michel Rybalka, G. Idt and G. H. Bauer (eds), Paris: Gallimard, Bibliothèque de la Pléiade.
- 1988, "What is Literature?" and Other Essays, [including Black Orpheus] tr. Bernard Frechtman et al., intro. Steven Ungar, Cambridge, Mass.: Harvard University Press.
- 2005, Théâtre complet, Paris: Gallimard, Bibliothèque de la Pléiade.
- A.1.3 Posthumous works by Sartre
- 1983a, Cahiers pour une morale, Paris: Gallimard. Translated as Notebook for an Ethics, David Pellauer (trans.), Chicago, IL: University of Chicago Press, 1992.
- 1983b [1984], Carnets de la drôle de guerre, septembre 1939 - mars 1940, Paris: Gallimard. Reprinted in 1995 with an addendum. Translated as The War Diaries: Notebooks from a Phoney War, Quinton Hoare (trans.), New York: Pantheon, 1984.
- 1983c, Lettres au Castor et à quelques autres, Simone de Beauvoir (ed.), Paris: Gallimard

- Tome 1: 1926–1939
- Tome 2: 1940–1963
- Some translated in Quiet Moments in a War. The Letters of Jean-Paul Sartre to Simone de Beauvoir, 1940–1963, Simone de Beauvoir (ed.) and Lee Fahnestock and Norman MacAfee (tr. and intro.), New York: Charles Scribner's Sons, 1993.
- 1984, Le Scenario Freud, Paris: Gallimard. Translated as The Freud Scenario, Quinton Hoare (trans.), Chicago, IL: University of Chicago Press, 1986.
- 1985, Critique de la raison dialectique, tome 2, L'intelligibilité de l'histoire, Paris: Gallimard. Translated as Critique of Dialectical Reason, Volume 2: The Intelligibility of History, Quintin Hoare (trans.), London: Verso, 1991. Reprinted 2006, foreword by Frederic Jameson, London: Verso. [unfinished].
- 1989, Vérité et existence, Paris: Gallimard [written in 1948]. Translated as Truth and Existence, Adrian van den Hoven (trans.), Ronald Aronson (intro.), Chicago, IL: University of Chicago Press, 1992.
- 1990, Écrits de jeunesse, Michel Contat and Michel Rybalka (eds), Paris: Gallimard.

Chapter Six:

- 1954, "Introduction" to Le Rêve et l'existence, Paris: Desclée de Brouwer. This is an introduction to the French translation, by Jacqueline Verdeaux, of Ludwig Binswanger, Traum und Existenz, 1930.
- 1954, Maladie mentale et personnalité, Paris: Presses universitaires de France.
- 1962, Maladie mentale et psychologie, Paris: Presses universitaires de France; translated as Mental Illness and

Psychology, Alan Sheridan (trans.), New York: Harper and Row, 1976. Significantly revised version of the 1954 book.

- 1972, L'histoire de la folie à l'âge classique, Paris: Gallimard (first published as Folie et déraison, Paris: Plon, 1961). Translated as History of Madness, Jean Khalfa (ed.), Jonathan Murphy and Jean Khalfa (trans.), New York: Routledge, 2006.
- 1963, Raymond Roussel, Paris: Gallimard. Translated as Death and the Labyrinth: The World of Raymond Roussel, Charles Ruas (trans.), Garden City, NY: Doubleday, 1986.
- 1963, Naissance de la clinique, Paris: Presses universitaires de France. Translated as The Birth of the Clinic, Allan Sheridan (trans.), New York: Pantheon, 1973.
- 1966, Les mots et les choses, Paris: Gallimard. Translated as The Order of Things, Alan Sheridan (trans.), New York: Vintage, 1973.
- 1969, L'archéologie du savoir, Paris: Gallimard. Translated as The Archaeology of Knowledge, Allan Sheridan (trans.), New York: Harper and Row, 1972.
- 1971, L'ordre du discours, Paris: Gallimard. An English translation was published in Robert Young (ed.), Untying the Text: A Post-Structuralist Reader, Routledge & Kegan Paul, 1981, pp. 51–78.
- 1975, Surveiller et punir, Paris: Gallimard. Translated as Discipline and Punish, Alan Sheridan (trans.), New York: Pantheon, 1977.
- Histoire de la sexualité, 3 volumes, Paris: Gallimard. Translated as History of Sexuality, 3 volumes, Robert Hurley (trans.), New York: Pantheon Books.
- 1976, La volonté de savoir. Translated as Introduction,

1978.

- 1984, L'usage des plaisirs. Translated as The Uses of Pleasure, 1985.
- 1984, Le souci de soi. Translated as Care of the Self, 1986.
- Dits et écrits vol I–IV, 1980–1988, Paris: Gallimard, 1994, édités par D. Defert & F. Ewald. These include virtually all Foucault's previously published shorter writings and interviews. Some of the more important items are translated in Essential Works of Foucault, 1954–1984, 3 volumes, edited by Paul Rabinow, New York: The New Press, 1997–1999.
- Cours au Collège de France, 1970–1984, François Ewald and Alessandro Fontana (eds), Paris: Gallimard, 1997–2015. Translated as Lectures at the Collège de France, Arnold Davidson (ed.), Graham Burchell (trans.), 2003ff.
- 2011, Le beau danger, Philippe Artières (ed.), Paris: EHESS.
- 2012, Mal faire, dire vrai: Fonction de l'aveu en justice, Fabienne Brion and Bernard H. Harcourt (eds), Louvain-la-Neuve: Presses universitaires de Louvain. Translated as Wrong-Doing, Truth-Telling: The Function of Avowal in Justice, Stephen W. Sawyer (trans.), Chicago: The University of Chicago Press, 2014.
- 2013, La grande étrangère: A propos de littérature, Philippe Artières, Jean-François Bert, Mathieu Potte-Bonneville and Judith Revel (eds), Paris: EHESS.
- 2013, L'origine de l'herméneutique de soi, Henri-Paul Fruchaud and Daniele Lorenzini (eds), Paris: Vrin. Translated as About the Beginning of the Hermeneutics of the Self, Graham Burchell (trans.), Chicago: The

University of Chicago Press, 2015.

- 2015, «Qu'est-ce que la critique?» suivi de «La culture de soi», Henri-Paul Fruchaud and Daniele Lorenzini (eds), Paris: Vrin. English translation forthcoming, The University of Chicago Press.
- 2016, «Discours et vérité» précédé de «La parrêsia», Henri-Paul Fruchaud and Daniele Lorenzini (eds), Paris: Vrin. English translation forthcoming, The University of Chicago Press.
- 2017, Dire vrai sur soi-même, Henri-Paul Fruchaud and Daniele Lorenzini (eds), Paris: Vrin.
- 2018, Les aveux de la chair (Histoire de la sexualité IV), ed. Frédéric Gros, Paris: Gallimard.

Also By Thrinadh Sai

EMBLEM: Poetry and Prose

EMBLEM is a collection of poetry and prose. And also an experience of love, pain, death, birth, nature, and human life. This book is divided into five chapters, and each chapter serves a different purpose. Every page of this book gives you pleasure and becomes a symbol of your life. It shows the light in the darkness. It gives hope in hopelessness. The emblem is not just a book of poetry, but it is a collection of experiences, feelings, and emotions of individual human beings.

ALSO BY THRINADH SAI

Death Ceremony: The Journey from Birth to Death

This is a philosophy and psychology book that will help you comprehend human behavior and the emotional journey that leads to life and existence. We spoke about a variety of real-life scenarios to better understand how our emotions influence our conduct.

Soul and Soil: Collection of Poetry & Prose

Soul and Soil is a collection of poetry and prose about love, life, mankind, the earth, nature, women, men, souls, soil, and many other topics. It is divided into seven parts, each of which serves a distinct purpose, deals with different suffering, and cures a particular heartbreak. Soul and Soil takes readers on a trip through life's most painful experiences, finding sweetness in them because there is sweetness everywhere if you are ready to search.

Hunger, Humor, Humanity: And Other Stories

I feel that the short story is as distinct from the novel as poetry is and that the finest tales are closer in spirit to poetry than to novels. Short fiction appears to be more focused - hand grenades of ideas, if you will. They hit, they erupt, and you never forget them when they work. Long fiction has a different vibe than short fiction: it's a lot smokier and less defined. A short narrative is a splinter, a sliver, a vignette. It's a biopsy of the human condition, but it lacks the ability to think for itself. A short story is a love affair; a novel is a marriage. A short story is a photograph; a novel is a film.

About The Author

THRINADH SAI

Thrinadh Sai is an author from India. In his poetry and prose, he discusses love, life, mankind, the earth, nature, women, men, souls, soil, and many other topics. He is now venturing into the area of short stories. He makes his works available to the public in order to promote progressive healing and onward growth. He enjoys exploring nature and hopes to be a full-time writer when he is not writing poems or publishing books

Printed by Libri Plureos GmbH in Hamburg,
Germany